I0763137

The Four Georges

WONDERS WONDERS WONDERS &
WONDERS
DEDICATED to the Wonderfull Wonderfull Wonderer

The Four Georges

AN AWFULLY BRITISH KIND OF MONARCHY, 1714-1830

JEREMY BLACK

For Linda Colley

Page 2: 'Wonders wonders wonders & wonders – dedicated to the wonderfull wonderfull wonderer' (1782). The print shows Britannia and America, several British ministers, and George III. Some appear as couples shaking hands. John Wilkes is shaking hands with George III. Lord Shelburne shakes hands with Charles James Fox. Britannia is shaking hands with a Native woman, representing America, wearing a feathered headdress and holding a staff topped with a liberty cap. 'Come, come, shake hands, and let's be friends,' to which America replies, 'With all my heart, I've gained my ends.' (Library of Congress)

First published 2025

Amberley Publishing
The Hill, Stroud
Gloucestershire, GL5 4EP

www.amberley-books.com

ISBN 978 1 3981 2317 5 (hardback)
ISBN 978 1 3981 2318 2 (ebook)

British Library Cataloguing in Publication Data.
A catalogue record for this book is available from the British Library.

1 2 3 4 5 6 7 8 9 10

Typesetting by SJmagic DESIGN SERVICES, India.
Printed in the UK.

Appointed GPSR EU Representative: Easy Access System Europe Oü, 16879218
Address: Mustamäe tee 50, 10621, Tallinn, Estonia
Contact Details: gpsr.requests@easproject.com, +358 40 500 3575

CONTENTS

Preface 7

Acknowledgements 15

Abbreviations 16

1 'Church, and King, and the Royal Family': An Era of Change 18

2 The Inheritance of Monarchy 36

3 George I 60

4 George II 94

5 Interlude: Frederick I 127

6 George III, A Monarch in Contention 143

7 George III, Father of the Nation 169

8 George IV 188

9 British Monarchs and the Others 208

10 The Georges and Political Development 224

11 Postscripts to the Present 243

Selected Further Reading 252

Endnotes 254

Index 280

PREFACE

'One of the dancing bears was at the Horse Guards Gate, and as the coach passed by, got upon his hind legs, and held a long staff between his forefeet; at which his Majesty laughed very heavily.'

Old England, 10 March 1753,
George II going to Parliament.

'I don't communicate it to any soul but the King, nor send any copy of it to England.'

Charles, 2nd Viscount Townshend, Secretary of State
for the Northern Department, in 1725 with George I in
Hanover, on secret diplomacy with Sweden.[1]

From Peril to Greatness is the theme for the history of Britain 1714-1830. This is the age of the first four Georges. They were not some inconsequential backdrop to Britain's development in this period but central figures in its politics. This book puts them in their age and illuminates the latter through them. It draws on my earlier work, notably full-length biographies of George II and George III, but is based on a re-examination, founded on extensive archival work and a rethinking of the period, its continuities and its changes, but, above all, the role of the rulers.

As such, this is a book about people as well as institutions and symbols. Yet, these people can be difficult to fathom. They had no obligation to write confessional letters or diaries about their motivations, feelings, and awareness of contexts and contingencies. Nor were they supposed to depart from majesty. Sources vary greatly, being most plentiful for George III and least for the taciturn[2] George I, but, whether plentiful or not, it is mistaken to assume that what survives is necessarily 'accurate' in the sense of revelatory, which is very much a modern view.

As a result, the historian has to resort to more caution and hesitation than is preferable for most readers. Moreover, for the first two Georges and Frederick, Prince of Wales, who predeceased his father, George II, it is very much a case of comments *about* the monarch and not *by* him.[3] That inherently does not mean error, but it is necessary to understand that those comments by others reflect biases of their own. Thus, in 1719, William, 1st Earl Cadogan, the Master of the Robes, a general who had made his name as a protégé of John, 1st Duke of Marlborough and in command against the Jacobites in Scotland in 1716, wrote, probably to Sir Francis Dashwood of a Court appointment and informing him that the Peerage Bill was to be presented to Parliament, adding:

> The King [George I] has the matter so very much at heart, and believes it so highly important for his service, that His Majesty cannot doubt of the concurrence and assistance of all those who are his real friends, and who either have received, or expect to receive any mark of his favour. I can assure you these are the King's own thoughts, and not the insinuations of his ministers for particular views as has been suggested. I beg you to communicate this where you think proper.[4]

In the event, George, instead, moved to a settlement that entailed dropping this legislation. George might have saved the 'Duke of S' (Shrewsbury) from impeachment when the recent Tory ministry was attacked in 1715, but evidence for that sign of favour to Charles,

1st Duke of Shrewsbury, a prominent member of that ministry, is unclear.[5] Shrewsbury continued to be Lord Chamberlain until July 1715, though he had ceased to be Lord Lieutenant of Ireland in September 1714 and Lord Treasurer the following month.

In 1726, Thomas, Duke of Newcastle, Secretary of State of the Southern Department, sent Horatio Walpole, envoy in Paris, a private letter on international relations including the information that George I was very pleased at the tone of firmness of the Foreign Minister of France, Britain's ally. Maybe so. George had asked France to move troops into Germany in order to reassure Prussia.[6] In 1738, the French envoy reported that as far as he could judge George II would be very angry if the Jülich-Berg succession dispute in Germany was regulated without him playing a role, whereas the ministers were indifferent.[7] Again, possibly so, but the evidence is scanty.

Indeed, too often, it is a case of problematic claims made on the basis of little or no evidence. For example, in 1746 the French Foreign Minister said it would be best for George II to drop Austria in return for France agreeing not to support the Jacobites, but that as George, as he claimed, thought it best to follow the advice of John, Lord Carteret in preference to the advice of his ministers, he would not do so.[8] Again, maybe, but this judgement denied George the agency of making his own decisions.

The kings worked, as most monarchs did, through conversation and the resulting correspondence and discussion of others, the latter usually formal bureaucratic instructions. Frequent reference to the Closet indicated such conversation, as it referred to the room where the King saw his ministers and diplomats[9] for confidential discussions, and thus brought them into royal confidence. The well-accepted significance of the Closet underlined the continued role of the monarch, and also of personal links as opposed to institutional practice, and of conversation rather than correspondence. As a result of its formulaic style and institutional character, official correspondence did not always make the distinctive role of the king apparent.

That role is, however, revealed in diplomatic reports and the private correspondence of ministers. In January 1757, Joseph, Count Haslang, the experienced Bavarian envoy, reported on a one-to-one conversation of over half an hour in George II's 'Cabinet' or 'Closet,' in which the King pressed his views on German politics with clarity, arguing in particular for the need for peace and the preservation of a balance of power.[10] Diplomatic and non-British primary sources are particularly significant for George I and George II, not least as they would often express themselves in German in such correspondence and conversations, unlike their relations with their British ministers. These sources are among the original features of this book and support interpretations different from secondary works that rely overmuch on British primary sources.

In searching for the reports from foreign envoys, it is important to note that rulers could be closest to envoys from second-rank powers, such as General Ernst Diemar, the envoy from Hesse-Cassel, for much of the reign of George II, and these therefore have to be scrutinised. It is also necessary to supplement diplomatic reports with private correspondence, and with British postal interceptions (which are not all in the particular series in the National Archives), to remember that the relevant reports are not only in the Britain series but also in those of envoys to Hanover, as in 1755, when conversations with George II are recorded.[11] (Though these can appear in the Britain series.)[12]

The responses from foreign ministers are pertinent: in 1784 Charles, Count of Vergennes, the experienced French Foreign Minister, commented on the satisfactory dispositions shown by George III in a discussion with the French envoy over Turkish-Russian relations, but added that George's stance was not always that of his ministry and that he was obliged to follow the latter.[13]

As an instance of the relevant private correspondence of ministers, in 1759 Thomas, Duke of Newcastle, then First Lord of the Treasury, wrote to his closest ally, Philip, Lord Chancellor

Hardwicke: 'The King said, he was in possession of Osnabrück and part of the Elector of Cologne's country, etc. Must he give them up?'[14] The remark expressed his wish to make acquisitions for Hanover. The papers of Thomas, 2nd Lord Grantham, the Foreign Secretary in 1782-3, an experienced envoy who had been close to the King as Vice-Chamberlain of the Household in 1770-1, recorded an instructive Closet discussion with George III about the forming of a new ministry: 'The King said Lord Shelburne had constantly expressed that Pitt (the Younger) was cold, reserved etc, even threw gloom into society. He betrayed great symptoms of jealousy of Pitt.'[15]

For George I and George II, but not for George III, there is the value of official and private correspondence arising from visits to Hanover. This not only led to official correspondence arising from the regency in Britain, but also the private letters designed to make the system flow and which commented on apparent trends. Thus, in 1752, Newcastle wrote from Hanover to his brother Henry Pelham, the First Lord of the Treasury: 'I gave the King a general account of your letters. He is in extremely good and reasonable humour; and willing to hear, and disposed to do, what is right.'[16]

In an 'entre nous' from Hanover in 1755 that shows how sources can be half- hidden, Robert, 4th Earl of Holdernesse, a Secretary of State, wrote to Newcastle concerning

> ... the accounts of the fleets contained in Sir Thomas Robinson's last private letter to me; the King seemed overjoyed at the probable success of his measures in America... His Majesty read over and approved the Office letter to your Grace, and talked of your zeal and ability to serve in the strongest terms and in the kindest manner; The King entered much into conversation upon Parliament and party matters and said you had promised to write me word at a proper time, how *some people* stood affected to his measures.[17]

There could be reluctance to reveal royal opinions and correspondence, not least for reasons of propriety.[18] Questions of safety could also play a role for commentators, the *Weekly Miscellany* noting on 27 October 1733:

> The actions of sovereign princes are of so high and uncontrollable a nature, that they claim an exemption from open censures, at least during their lives, or while they are in professed amity with the princes or states under which a writer lives; so that it is often indiscreet if not dangerous to intermeddle on so captious a subject.

Politicians were mindful of the need to be careful if they sent a letter 'by the common post'.[19]

In 1728, a report in the *Kopenhagischer Post-Reuter* of 30 April about a Hanoverian-backed project for an Altona company that would be detrimental to British trade led to diplomatic complaints and correspondence in which George II's role was emphasised: 'The King took notice with great surprise... His Majesty wonders the more... His Majesty's sense as to that company must be very well understood at Copenhagen... His Majesty thinks it proper'[20]

The extent to which a King was engaged, however, clearly varied. In 1733, the Secretary of State for the Northern Department wrote to the envoy in Denmark rather blandly: 'His Majesty is of opinion that the conduct of Denmark is very right in this conjuncture, and makes no question but that the Danish court will continue in the same prudent way.'[21] The tone was very different in 1755 when the Secretary of State underlined to the newly-appointed envoy to St Petersburg George's determination to win Russian support: 'I am particularly commanded by the King to press your departure, as every day may be of the utmost consequence in the present critical state of Europe.'[22]

Biography always has to struggle with significance and emphasis. The respective length of the reigns ensures that the emphasis should be on George II and George III. There are also more specific reasons for this, as in some respects the short British reign of George I, 1714-27,[23] can be seen in a sequence starting with William III and Anne. Correspondingly, the reign of George IV can be aligned with that of William IV (r. 1830-7).

Given the degree of attention devoted to George III, it is necessary to redress the implicit bias by considering George II at greater length than is usually the case. This approach also serves to draw attention to a wealth of material hitherto neglected. This tendency has been exacerbated by the recent focus on the digitalisation of George III's correspondence. There is no comparable project for George I or George II, because they were episodic correspondents. As a result, it is necessary to turn to a systematic trawl of diplomatic and political correspondence in order to capture these kings' reported comments. As a consequence, George I and George II can appear far more remote characters than George III and George IV, other than through the pens of mordant critics, notably John, Lord Hervey and Horace Walpole for George II. This then becomes a cumulative process, with attention further focused on George III due to his importance for those interested in American history.

At any rate, the monarch was at the centre of the swirl of information, rumour and opinion that was part of the process of politics. Thus, in 1745, Newcastle's confidant, Andrew Stone, described a conversation with Pelham about a meeting with George II in which foreign affairs played a role, irrespective of Pelham's very different ministerial responsibilities as First Lord of the Treasury:

> His Majesty talked warmly of the project of attacking the King of Prussia which Mr Pelham no otherwise argued against than by saying that it would be impracticable to enter into new engagements for conquests to be made, of that kind. But he did not think what he said made any impression.[24]

The monarchs could be the recipient of sharp rejoinders, as described in a letter by Benjamin Kennicott, an Oxford academic:

> The King was asking at Court today, what was become of Lord Paulet's notion?[25] And being answered, 'Dropped for want of a second,' he asked the Duke of Newcastle, why *he* had not agreed to second it, as he frequently expressed his wishes for his (the King's) staying at home. The King lately asking the Lord Chancellor[26] whether he did love now and then to visit his seat in Cambridgeshire; the Chancellor answered 'Yes, but not in Term time.'[27]

The last was a reference to George II going to Hanover during the parliamentary session. Notwithstanding the problems, the Georges are more open to us than their predecessors; and that makes this a particularly exciting book to write.

ACKNOWLEDGEMENTS

I have a number of debts that I am happy to acknowledge without which this book would not have been possible. The Universities of Durham and Exeter, British Academy, the Beinecke and Huntington Libraries, the Yale Center for British Art, the German Academic Exchange Scheme, and the Leverhulme and Wolfson Foundations provided valuable support on archival research trips. Material from the Royal Archives is cited by permission of His Majesty the King. I would like to thank the Duke of Bedford, the Marquess of Bute, Earl Fitzwilliam and the Wentworth Woodhouse Trustees, the late Earl of Harrowby and the Trustees of the Harrowby MS Trust, the Earl of Elgin, the Earl of Malmesbury, the late Earl Waldegrave, Lady Lucas and John Weston-Underwood for permission to consult their collections of manuscripts, and the History of Parliament Trust for permission to consult its transcripts. I am most grateful to Nigel Aston, Jonathan Barry, Marl Danley, Grayson Ditchfield, Perry Gauci, Bill Gibson, Crawford Gribben, Will Hay, Philip Mansel, and Richard Wendorf for their comments on an earlier draft.

This work is dedicated in friendship to Linda Colley, whose article, 'The Apotheosis of George III: Loyalty, Royalty and the British Nation', *Past and Present*, 102 (Feb. 1984), pp. 94-129, remains a key work on the subject.

ABBREVIATIONS

Add.	Additional Manuscripts
AE.	Paris, Ministère des Affaires Etrangères
AM.	Archives de la Marine
AN	Paris, Archives Nationale
Ang.	Angleterre
AST. LM. Ing.	Turin, Archivio di Stato, Lettere Ministri, Inghilterra
Beinecke	New Haven, Connecticut, Yale University Library, Beinecke Library
BL.	London, British Library
Chewton	Chewton Mendip, Chewton House, papers of James, 1st Earl Waldegrave
Copenhagen	Copenhagen, Danske Rigsarkivet, Dept. of Foreign Affairs, reports from London
CP.	Correspondance Politique
CRO.	County Record Office
Cumb. P.	Cumberland Papers
Darmstadt	Darmstadt, Staatsarchiv, Gräflich Görtzisches Archiv, F23
Dresden	Dresden, Hauptstaatsarchiv
Eg.	Egerton Manuscripts
EK	Englische Korrespondenz

Exeter	Exeter, Devon Record Office, Addington (Sidmouth) papers, 152M
Farmington	Farmington, Connecticut, Lewis Walpole Library
FO.	Foreign Office Papers
Hanover	Hanover, Niedersachsisches Hauptstaatsarchiv
HL	San Marino, California, Huntington Library
HHStA	Vienna, Haus-, Hof-, und Staatsarchiv, Staatskanzlei
HMC	Historical Manuscripts Commission
LO	Loudoun papers
MD	Mémoires et Documents
Munich	Munich, Bayerischer Hauptstaatsarchiv, Geheimes Staatsarchiv, Gesandtschaften
NA	London, National Archives
NAS	Edinburgh, National Archives of Scotland
NeC	Clumber Papers
NLS	Edinburgh, National Library of Scotland
NUL	Nottingham, University Library
RA	Windsor Castle, Royal Archives
SP	State Papers
Stuart P	Stuart Papers

'CHURCH, AND KING, AND THE ROYAL FAMILY': AN ERA OF CHANGE

> The first quadrille was in the act of forming, and the Prince was walking to the dais on which his seat was placed,[1] when I saw every one without the slightest sense of decorum rushing to the windows, which had been left wide open because of the extreme sultriness of the weather. The music ceased and the dance stopped; for we heard nothing but the vociferous shouts of an enormous mob who had just entered the square, and were running by the side of a post-chaise and four, out of whose windows were hanging three [in fact two] nasty French eagles. In a second the door of the carriage was flung open and, without waiting for the steps to be let down, out sprang Henry Percy – such a dusty figure – with a flag in each hand – pushing aside everyone who happened to be in his way, darting upstairs, into the ballroom, stepping hastily up to the Regent, dropping on one knee, laying the flags at his feet, and pronouncing the words "Victory, Sir! Victory!'[2]

Major Henry Percy, one of Wellington's aides-de-camp, brings the news of victory at Waterloo to a society ball at Mrs Boehm's house in St James's Square, London. Percy was immediately promoted to brevet Lieutenant-Colonel by the Prince Regent, a classic instance and setting for royal favour.

In 1830, when George IV died, bringing his last years of illness to a close, Britain was the world power, its navies policing the oceans and its prestige strong as a result of the total defeat of Napoleonic France in 1815. That was not the situation just over a century earlier in 1714, when the very succession of the new Hanoverian dynasty was contested by 'James III and VIII', the 'warming pan baby' of 1688 and the Stuart claimant from 1701 to 1766. Indeed, there was to be rebellion, in effect civil war, in 1715-16, and British ministers anxiously watched to see if France would intervene. In the event, it did not in 1715-16, unlike its unsuccessful efforts to invade England in 1744, 1745-6, 1779, and, in Ireland, in 1796 and 1798. However, the French did intervene successfully in Britain's American colonies in 1778-83.

The transition in national fortune was astonishing. At the close of 1759, 'the Year of Victories', in which the bells were repeatedly rung with the triumphs of victory, Robert, 4th Earl of Holdernesse, one of the two Secretaries of State, observed:

> Though many and great have been the victories obtained by former Kings of England over their enemies in divers countries, yet Providence had reserved for His Majesty to be first whose arms should triumph victorious in the four parts of the World within the course of the same year. This is as unparalleled in History as the magnanimous moderation His Majesty has shown amidst successes.[3]

In effect, Britain had been a failed state in the seventeenth century, indeed repeatedly a state that had failed, the 'mid-seventeenth century crisis' being just more serious than other reverses, and then, in addition, there was revolution and civil war (in Scotland and Ireland) in 1688-91. Yet, by 1830, the monarchy was part of a distinctive and successful British nation. The monarchical political system that had spectacularly failed in 1642, 1649, and 1688 could now cope without crisis or violence with the idiosyncrasies and weakness of George IV, and with pressures for reform. In comparison, in France, between 1815 and 1870 four dynasties (two from branches of the usurping Bonaparte family) occupied the French throne.

The comparative context is instructive. France, Spain, Sweden, Portugal, the Holy Roman Empire, Poland, and the House of Orange that ruled the Netherlands all faced fundamental political crises between 1790 and 1810. In contrast, George III had confronted a serious and successful imperial revolution in 1775-83 and a difficult war with Revolutionary and then Napoleonic France from 1793 to 1815, but he had avoided an existential challenge at home, the rebellion in Ireland in 1798 being short-lived and totally unsuccessful.

That was not the case for the family Electorate of Hanover, conquered by the French in 1803, and having already been occupied by the Prussians in 1801. The Anglo-Hanoverian link slackened after 1755, the last visit by George II to Hanover. Although George III was definitely strongly interested in Hanover, and more so than was understood by historians prior to the 1970s, he still did not visit the Electorate once during his very long reign, and there was not the immediacy of concern consistently shown by his two predecessors. When he became King of Hanover (having earlier dropped the title King of France) in 1814, he knew nothing about it due to his ill-health, and the gain was essentially for his heir, George IV.

Overall, there was a move by Britain towards imperial destiny and maritime identity, rather than the Continental links (and army-based monarchy in some cases) emphasised from Charles II to George II, links that had repeatedly caused tension. The accession of the Hanoverians led to a revival of these links and this army monarchy after an anglicisation (to a degree, 'Britishisation') of monarchy under Queen Anne, an anglicisation not successfully revived until the reign of George III. Thus, in February 1745, at Vintner's Hall, London, with George Dodington in the chair, a meeting with a strong Tory/Opposition Whig complexion, included among the toasts:

> 'Church, and King, and the Royal Family.'
> 'Great Britain UnGermanized.'
> 'That German measures may never get the better of English Liberties.'[4]

Drawing on traditional and still potent assumptions that had not been shattered by the disruptions of the seventeenth century, not least the understanding of the country and nation as a kingdom, monarchs centred on themselves issues of changing identity and interest, obviously so for their dynasties but also for their countries. Thus, in 1756, George II received a series of Addresses blaming the Newcastle ministry for failures in North America and for the loss of Minorca to French invasion, a loss made inevitable by a humiliating naval failure to relieve the garrison. James Wallace, one of the four Under Secretaries, presented the first Address in a positive light, as, indeed, he needed to do to relieve popular pressure. Whatever the gloss, the central role of the Court was clear:

> This day, the City of London has begun the dance of Addresses for an Enquiry etc, by waiting upon the King with theirs. It is very dutiful towards His Majesty, and no less hearty as to granting of subsidies; and the whole drawn with decency; so that it may possibly do more good than hurt; as the rest of the corporations are all gaping after the effect of it at court.[5]

In 1755, a pamphleteer in support of the government warned about the danger of criticism of Crown and ministry, criticism that was to be focused on George III in the 1760s:

> How necessary is it, for good government, that the monarch on the throne, and his ministry in their cabinet, be sheltered as

> it were from the poisonous arrows of scandal and detraction? Their characters should be sacred as their persons. But if every half-starved impertinent scribbler be permitted to tell the *one*, that he is taking gigantic strides to subvert the religion and the laws of the country ... it would be very dangerous.[6]

The monarch was a patron of culture, with political consequences. With George III, there was a successful national style linked to the monarch and self-consciously opposed to foreign exemplars. In place of the earlier shared international styles of the Baroque and then the Rococo, there was the foundation of the Royal Academy, the history paintings of Benjamin West, and George's patronage of Handel's music and of the explorations of James Cook and discoveries by William Herschel. Subsequently, as Prince Regent, the future George IV was in conscious rivalry with Napoleon. He, however, was to find it very difficult to strike a sure note, and this contrasted with the ability to formulate a consistent and successful 'style' shown by George III and by the other British 'monarch' of the period, George Washington, America's first President.

The monarch's person was an embodiment of power. John Clavering reported from Hanover in December 1716 when George I was there for his first visit as King-Elector: 'Here are a vast number of foreign ministers which makes the Court very splendid, besides a prodigious quantity of strangers from all parts.'[7]

The physicality of the monarch was both literal and metaphorical and was perceived accordingly. James, 2nd Earl of Fife, wrote in March 1783: 'The Duke of Portland's arrangement, after being in the King's pocket till Sunday from Friday, was entirely given up yesterday and I suppose Mr Pitt will be declared Minister.'[8] This assessment of ministerial changes was mistaken, as William Pitt the Younger did not then wish to play ball. The legacy of this period was monarchy of a certain type that was to be part of the character of the modern British world, a situation matched for America by the particular monarchy of the Presidency, an elective monarchy that is especially effective because it is not seen as such a monarchy.

The emphasis was always on the ruler, and understandably so as George I and George II remained able to fulfil their royal duties until death, while George III was duly replaced by a Prince Regent. Throughout these reigns, in an echo of established royal style (for example that of Louis XIV of France) whom the King spoke to, for how long, and in whose presence were subjects of attention,[9] as was the case in his choice of hunting companions. In 1717, George I did not eat with Walpole in Newmarket,[10] in 1752, George II would not talk to the French envoy at Hanover,[11] and in 1772, at a time of tension over the adultery of George III's sister, the Queen of Denmark, George, angry at the Danish reaction to the crisis, did not talk to the Danish envoy, while George II rumped, or showed his back to, those he disliked.[12] In 1725, false rumours that the President of the Austrian War Council, Prince Eugene, was to go to Hanover to see George I during the growing international crisis attracted press attention.[13] Six years earlier, a Secretary of State expressed the hope that George would stay two or three days at The Hague on his return to London from Hanover:

> I hope his presence will remove all the doubts and difficulties that might remain on the part of the States [States General, Dutch federal assembly], establish an entire good correspondence between us and them, and be very popular in that country.[14]

Similarly, that year a meeting between George and Frederick William I of Prussia was described by Charles, 3rd Earl of Sunderland, the First Lord of the Treasury: 'This visit and interview must and will have the best effects all over Europe.'[15] As personal presence was a key element, the fitness until death of George I and George II was very valuable.

Courtiers and members of the royal family had their lives in part set by the occasions and locations of court life. In 1716, Benjamin Hoadly, a royal chaplain who had lately become Bishop of Bangor, noted when the Prince of Wales was regent for the King, who was in

Hanover: 'I go twice a week to Hampton Court, first to the Prince's Levee then to the Drawing Room.'[16] Indeed, due to proximity to the monarch, Court appointments, both lay and ecclesiastical, were seen as very important in themselves and with more general reference to political and ministerial favour. Hill Mussenden wrote from London soon after the accession of George II:

> It is not yet known what the fate of our great minister [Walpole] will be, but his son-in-law Lord Malpas having lost his place of Master of the Robes is reckoned a bad omen.[17]

George II fully understood the significance of personal contact:

> The King entirely approves the several steps you have taken with the Bavarian Ministers, in order to induce them to assist in placing such persons about the Elector of Cologne as would endeavour to persuade him to adopt the system, which His Majesty has ever steadily pursued and supported.[18]

Nevertheless, there were other individuals that had to be considered, notably heirs and spouses. Thus, in 1716, when Townshend lost his Secretaryship of State, a change that the Prince was reported angered by,[19] Edmund Gibson, Bishop of Lincoln, wrote to William Nicolson, Bishop of Carlisle: 'The chief thing laid to the charge of Lord Townshend and others of the Ministry is an endeavour to make the Prince more popular than the King: and in effect to set up the Prince against the King.'[20]

Philip Yorke added: 'It is the opinion of some that the smoothness with which all matters have been transacted with the Regent during the King's absence has been an umbrage of objection against the ministry.'[21]

Who was invited to dine by a Prince of Wales was worthy of note, as in 1732 when at a time of Anglo-Prussian differences the Prussian envoy, Count Degenfeld, was not invited to a birthday dinner.[22]

Wives were part of the story for George II and George III, whereas those of George I and George IV had separated before their accession, which affected the range, content and tone of Court ceremonial. Sophia Dorothea was formally separated from George I by a legal act, whereas the future George IV and Caroline of Brunswick simply lived apart. Queen Caroline, George II's spouse until her death in 1737, was central to Court life, and indeed, in the absence of a Queen, played a major role when she was Princess of Wales. Her choices had political significance, as in 1716 when she had a German midwife and a stillborn child, refusing, despite ministerial pressure, the help of Sir David Hamilton, a leading practitioner in midwifery who had been doctor to Queen Anne.[23] In its issue of 8 March 1735 describing Caroline's birthday, the *London Journal*, a pro-government paper, noted:

> The appearance of persons of quality of both sexes on Saturday at St James's was so numerous, that several of the prime nobility could not get beyond the first or second rooms. Their habits, particularly those of the ladies, were extremely rich, and most beautifully fancied. Her Grace the Duchess of Bedford was esteemed the finest, having a gold stuff most curiously embroidered and valued at 200 guineas. The Duchess of Portland appeared in jewels of an immense value. The gentlemen wore for the most part cut velvets of flowered silks; and it is assured that there was hardly a suit worn either by the ladies or gentlemen but was of our own manufacture.

The articulate Caroline was frequently able to express her well-informed views, including to foreign envoys,[24] but was of particular significance when her husband went to Hanover in 1729, 1732, 1735 and 1736, which pushed her role to the fore, not least because the young Frederick, Prince of Wales was not seen as an alternative. The ministers in London were in correspondence with those accompanying the King, but they were also at the Queen's command, as in 1735, when Thomas, Duke of Newcastle, the Secretary of State left in London, wrote to the envoy in The Hague concerning a Dutch complaint about press reporting: 'The Queen has been pleased in a very particular manner, to order me to prosecute this affair.'[25] The Queen's interest in foreign news was captured in an account from Kensington from the Countess of Bristol to her husband in July 1735:

> The Queen received many letters yesterday, all which brought good news, as Her Majesty was pleased to inform us last night in the Gallery. The Persians having had a vast victory over the Turks is reckoned of great consequence. Her Majesty was pleased to say also that now the Russians had joined the Emperor's army, he had 140,000 men in the field, very good troops.[26]

Caroline was also influential over Church patronage, while her openness to philosophical approaches to religion struck some critics as radical.

After her death, her successor as female confidante and much else, Amalie Sophie Marianne von Wallmoden, Countess of Yarmouth, the last royal mistress to be honoured with a peerage, also took an interest in politics, domestic and international, including discussing matters with ministers, MPs and diplomats.[27]

As the representative of the country, as well as that of the Anglo-Hanoverian link, the king was the person with whom foreign diplomats sought personal meetings, official and social. A French report of 1784 that described Britain as a democracy under the form of monarchy, as well as a republic tending to monarchy, indicated the sense of fluidity surrounding monarchy and argued correctly that foreign policy was a key dimension, with the monarch representing the nation and negotiating for it, but with the nation requiring that he did so in accordance with its interests.[28] Thus, a Whig (opponent) pamphlet of 1793 noted: 'To declare war is, by the constitution, the prerogative of the King; but to grant or withhold the means of carrying it on, is (by the same constitution) the privilege of the people, through their representatives.'[29]

Letters would be presented to the king by diplomats on behalf of foreign rulers,[30] while diplomats, both British and foreign, could be instructed to speak to the king in order to convey what could not be written down.[31] The kings used audiences to establish not only the platitudes of good relations, as today, but also views on policy, both governmental and individual.[32] Diplomats were the personal representatives of the sovereign and difficulties could be created if, as with George II in 1747, there was a refusal to sign the relevant credentials.[33] George II had a reputation of being willing to choose envoys without consulting the ministry.[34] This was far rarer with George III or George IV. The readiness of diplomats for office was seen as a product of their social position. This was often closely related to the diplomatic rank of the official appointed. Selection was an expression of regard, respect and reciprocity. To show his friendship and regard for Charles Emmanuel III of Savoy-Piedmont, King of Sardinia, George II sent Algernon, 3rd Earl of Essex to Turin in 1732. Essex was the first British envoy to that Court with the rank of Ambassador, and had been a contemporary of Charles Emmanuel at Turin Academy.[35] In 1749, the French were upset that they had been sent an Earl (Albemarle) and not a Duke (Richmond, who also held a French title);[36] the latter was concerned about inadequate allowances,[37] although the failure of France to offer an envoy of equivalent rank was also cited as a reason.[38] Albemarle was a friend of the King.

The same year, Arthur Villettes, the long-serving and effective Resident in Turin, was replaced by an Envoy Extraordinary and Plenipotentiary: 'the King judging it proper, in the present circumstances of affairs, to send a person of rank and quality to the court of Turin (as a mark of his great regard for his Sardinian Majesty) has made choice of William, 4th Earl of Rochford.' In 1740, ministers were divided about sending William, Lord Harrington, a Secretary of State, to Berlin: 'The Chancellor said if no person of distinction went from England any future miscarriage would be attributed to that...' When Simon, 1st Earl Harcourt was appointed Ambassador to Paris in 1768, the Secretary of State reflected, 'there cannot be the smallest doubt but that his most Christian Majesty [Louis XV] will look upon the nomination of a person of his Lordship's high rank, distinguished abilities, and amiable disposition, as a fresh proof of the King's constant desire to preserve a good understanding between the two courts.'[39] Harcourt had been Governor to George as Prince of Wales and, later, the special ambassador to negotiate George's marriage to Charlotte of Mecklenburg-Strelitz.

Poor relations with his nephew, Frederick the Great of Prussia (r. 1740-86), were reflected by the representation of George II at Berlin by a mere Secretary in 1745 and 1747, and by nobody from May 1747 until the following April, again from November 1748 until 1750, and from 1751 until May 1756. Similarly, John Burnaby was sent to Stockholm in 1739 as a Secretary, Harrington noting: 'In the situation we at present stand with your court, the King did not think fit to appoint a minister of a higher rank.'

Diplomats were regarded as in a different bracket from career bureaucrats, as gentlemen, not players, privileged servants of the Crown whose period of diplomatic service could alternate with other posts that today would be seen as in different career patterns. Diplomatic service could enhance the chance of holding a great office of state, one of the Secretaryships of State. A number of diplomats were thus promoted, including Methuen, Craggs, Carteret, Townshend, William Stanhope, Robinson, Chesterfield, Holdernesse, Rochford and Grantham.[40]

Major household posts were often filled with former diplomats. Stephen Poyntz became Governor to the Duke of Cumberland, and Sir Everard Fawkener the Duke's secretary. Thomas Robinson returned from Vienna in 1748 as 'a great favourite with the King',[41] to be a Lord of Trade (1748-9) and then Master of the Great Wardrobe (1749-54), rather than the embassy to Spain that was mentioned,[42] until he became a Secretary of State in 1754, a step George encouraged.[43] John, 3rd Duke of Dorset found the household more congenial on his return from Paris in 1789; he became Lord Steward and held that post until shortly before his death in 1799. Thus, just as the royal Court was the best training place for diplomatic life, service abroad in foreign Courts as the king's personal representative suited one for Court office at home. In 1755, George II was reported as wanting Rochford to move from being envoy in Turin either to Paris or to become First Gentleman of the Bedchamber.[44]

Such appointments are a reminder of the extent to which diplomats were royal servants, rather than officials of an impersonal state. If they fell foul of the monarch, as Henry Legge did in 1748 for example, when he was sent to Berlin, then they were in a dire position. The inexperienced Legge, a good parliamentarian, was criticised by George II for being 'dazzled' by Frederick II and thus supporting an Anglo-Prussian alignment, a policy that displeased George. In turn, George III was unimpressed with William Eden's conduct in France: 'I cannot say I am pleased with the tone of Mr. Eden's letters and think it highly advisable that one who had admitted a French minister to hold every sort of sore language should be got from thence, when I am confident it will of itself cease.'[45]

Conversely, royal favour was of course important. In 1724, George I turned down the proposal from his Secretaries of State that William Finch, then in Sweden, go to Florence:

> His Majesty being entirely satisfied with the services you have done him at Stockholm, and convinced by your dispatches of your being so thoroughly acquainted with the affairs of the North that it would be difficult to supply your place there with one equally versed in that part of his business, we found him very averse to the removing you from thence, but as an encouragement to your continuing there His Majesty chose rather to add to your present allowance that of Plenipotentiary.[46]

The role of the king and the need to manage him was captured in a letter of 1750 to Sir Charles Hanbury Williams from his friend and ministerial ally Henry Fox:

> The Duke of Newcastle, Mr. Pelham, the Duke of Bedford, have all agreed that you should go to Turin, Sir James Gray to Poland, and Mr. Villettes to Venice; The Duke of Newcastle proposed it to the King who approved of it, but added that the Czarina having desired it, it was necessary a minister from him should go to Warsaw *now*, and unfortunately you are the only one who can ... when you are at Hanover you must, if you would act discreetly, behave as one who is trying to be well with, and agreeable to His Majesty rather than as one who may presume he is already so, which last I fear is not your case.

In order to help, Fox had 'begged' George's partner (a modern term but one that better describes their relationship than the sexual emphasis of mistress), the Countess of Yarmouth, to assist the envoy. Newcastle saw her as responsible for royal views on embassies.[47] Dorset was very much George III's choice for Paris in 1784, while Sir Robert Murray Keith, the previous year, was assured that George had spoken in his favour.[48]

Royal favour was important not only for who was chosen, but also for the rank at which they entered. Appointed Envoy Extraordinary to The Hague in September 1739, Robert Trevor wanted the additional appointment as Plenipotentiary, which would have given him more money and status, but found George II resistant. Horatio Walpole was able to write in December 1740 that the King 'began to relent on your account, but complained of the great sums employed, in support of his foreign ministers'. George was always reputed to be concerned about money. It was not until the following July that Trevor gained the promotion he coveted.[49] Equally, royal favour was affected by, and usually mediated through, the ministerial politics of the period.

The monarchs were principally interested in foreign policy[50] and could draw, accordingly, on information and advice from the Hanoverian government as well as that of Britain.[51] It was expected by both British and foreign diplomats that the king would be kept informed, and British diplomats returning home or meeting George I and George II in, or travelling to or from, Hanover, were instructed to analyse the situation in order to report to the King in person.[52] The kings saw and commented on important despatches,[53] and decided which the Council was to discuss.[54] They read intercepted correspondence from or to foreign diplomats, whether intercepted in London or in Hanover.[55] Audiences with foreign envoys were not restricted to pleasantries, but covered policy, often in detail.[56] Visits to Hanover provided more opportunities for negotiations, as the French Foreign Minister noted in 1755.[57]

The constitutional significance of the king was both a cause and symbol but not necessarily a guide to political consequence, even if the two biggest shifts in political fortune – the ushering in of one-party Whig rule in 1714 and its destruction in the early 1760s – owed much to George I and George III respectively. As George II discovered in 1744-6 (and George III in the early 1800s), popularity did not always coincide with unchallenged authority. In the former case, the Jacobite threat led to a significant rallying to the dynasty, which was seen as the exemplary defender and representative of Protestantism. This provided a strong rebuff to critical earlier discussion about Hanoverianism. Similarly, in the 1800s, the French threat led to a rallying around the King. Yet, in neither case, was there comparable success for the King in the choice and sustaining of first minister.

Providence appeared to be working in favour of the sovereign in surviving and then triumphing during the 1745-6 crisis. It must never be forgotten that the ruler was Supreme Governor of the Church, and that this was a religious age, even if the description in 1792 by François Noël, a diplomat and journalist, of a country 'où la superstition du Royalisme est fondée sur le fanaticisme religieux'[58] was going too far. However, in 1746, the revived reputation of the dynasty, which focused on victory at Culloden, did not match the political success of the monarchy. Already poor, George's relations with his ministers got worse when he faced pressure to take William Pitt into office, a course which Newcastle urged in order to broaden the ministry and to diminish opposition attacks in the Commons. George treated the pressure as an insult, one that underlined why he disliked the Pelhams, who, he felt, limited his options and failed to show due respect. George also continued to take advice from John, Lord Carteret, now Earl Granville, and was believed by Newcastle to do so.

Such a policy was similar to that of Continental rulers who could focus all the initiative on their own choice of advisor. In Britain, however, parliamentary management rested on policy and political consequences that affected, indeed could limit, royal choice, as ministerial cohesion prevailed or failed to do so. So also in Ireland, where until the Act of Union under George III, they were kings, but without their position being of particular policy note.

In February 1746, with the Jacobites still undefeated, the political crisis in Britain was brought to a head when the Pelhams and their supporters resigned their posts. George's attempt to form a new ministry round Carteret was thwarted by a lack of backing in the Commons or among major financiers. As a result, George had to turn to the Pelhams and accepted that he was led by parliamentary men. The weakness of the Court had been clearly demonstrated. This process was also shown in the royal household, then and on other occasions. Horace Walpole reported in 1747:

> Lord [William, 2nd Earl] Cowper has resigned [a Lordship of] the Bedchamber on the Beefeaters [Captain of the Yeomen of the Guard] being given to Lord [Hugh, 2nd Viscount] Falmouth: the latter, who is powerful in elections insisted on having it; the other had nothing but a promise from the King, which the ministry had already twice forced him to break.[59]

Ministers were wary if the king stood off and did not provide support, waiting to see what would happen,[60] but royal commitment, in turn, could lead to problems. This issue was intertwined with that of tensions within the political élite. As metioned, the king enjoyed a degree of initiative in deciding not only with whom to speak but also which issues should be referred to the Council.[61] In 1747, the two Secretaries of State, Newcastle and Philip, 4th Earl of Chesterfield, disagreed over peace negotiations with France. 'The King called for the Paper, and altered it himself, as you now have it,'[62] which thus gave further authority to the instruction. Yet, soon after, Chesterfield felt able to write: 'The King is convinced that [Henry] Pelham and I were the true prophets and is come over sincerely to our opinions.'[63] Earlier that year, Newcastle had pressed George II on Anglo-Dutch secret links and George angered the Duke by only discussing a peace feeler with France via his fellow Secretary of State, Chesterfield.[64]

Britain was not a parliamentary monarchy in which the monarch was subsumed within established conventions of Parliament's role and the attendant parliamentary politics. Nor was the extent to which these conventions would constrain the monarch fixed or obvious to contemporaries, although they were far more set than those affecting the Princes of Orange in the United Provinces (the Netherlands).

The consolidation and subsequent reinforcement of the 'Glorious Revolution' of 1688-9 can look as if a Providential 'hidden hand' was somehow working. Less positively, the compromise was contentious and difficult, not least due to royal views over ministerial appointments. George III was to be seen (in some quarters) as anti-ministerial in this respect, but George II's stance, notably, but not only, in 1744, 1746 and 1754-7, had scarcely been easy for his ministers or indeed himself.

The politeness of advice could not conceal the tensions at play, as in 1745, when George I, absent in Hanover, was given suggestions in apparently deferential terms that were anything but.

The Secretary of State in London, Newcastle, delivered the views of the Regency Council, noted that the suggestions came from

> ... a sense of our duty to His Majesty, and a just concern for his service, and that of our country ... with the utmost submission ... we lay our thoughts ... before His Majesty, in a manner, which nothing but our duty to the King could have engaged us to have done; that we might not reproach ourselves, or be reproached by others, with the ill consequences of neglecting this opportunity of detaching the King of Prussia from France,[65]

At a time when George did not wish to do this. Yet, ministers also needed the king, to conserve their position and to deploy the patronage which was a constant feature of the economy of politics, especially during the 200 days a year when Parliament was not in session.

The progressivist account of monarchy in the long eighteenth century, that from 1688 to 1832, one in which it adapts to change and circumstances, is both attractive and problematic. It is attractive, in that it accords with similar discussion of other developments, notably economic and financial, but also for example religious; in doing so, it deflects attention from the Victorian tendency to see the pre-1832 situation as one of corruption, if not failure and reaction. Instead, the emphasis should be on both pre-1832 developments and on long-term trends.

Less positively, this approach can lead to an underplaying of issues and problems in the pre-1832 period in particular contingencies, as in 1783 when 'the most dreadful of all calamities, a civil war'[66] was feared. Linked to this problem, there is the danger that a 'Whiggish' impression may be created. This choice of word is heavily ironic, as the idea of gradual development in a positive direction, that which is generally seen as Whiggish, is in this case to a degree the antithesis of the view of the Whigs of the late eighteenth and early nineteenth century, with their criticism of

George III and George IV as dangerous constitutional innovators. Yet, as a reminder that even 'Whiggery' were a moveable feast, the cohesion of Crown and ministry that was opposed by the Whig opposition under George III and George IV was in practice that seen with the governing 'Old Corps Whigs' under George I and George II. This serves as a reminder of the need to employ terms such as Whig with care, attentive to their changing meaning and applicability. This is certainly true for the evaluation of the monarchy.

The sense of contingencies, and the need to unpick supposed long-term trends or at least longer-term situations, can be taken further by realising that within units, such as reigns, each was itself diverse, not least as a consequence of learned experience. Furthermore, the stage of a reign could also appear significant, as in the argument that toward the end of a reign there would be a wish for a more placid and stable situation. Yet, this view was taken by the French envoy with respect to George II in 1755[67] but proved in the event to be totally mistaken. The King supported the use of force against the French in North America, which led to the outbreak of a major conflict. This created a set of contingencies that created a vortex of crisis the following year, one that broke the ministry and took Britain into a dangerous war.

THE INHERITANCE OF MONARCHY

> A rude mob were gathered around some ballad-singers, one of whom carried a figure seated in a chair, and which was intended to represent the person of the French king. It was dressed in all the fantastic modes which could be contrived to make it ridiculous, and excite the laughter of the populace ... a song, which was a vulgar kind of burlesque, adapted to ridicule the meagre emaciated figure which they bore aloft ... this low kind of mummery applauded by several whose appearance seemed to denote that they were of more than middling station in life... To make a crowned head the subject of mockery is an insult on royalty in general.
> *Centinel*, 13 September 1757

Monarchy scarcely began anew in 1714. But nor was it a timeless feature of a British constitution that could be traced back for many centuries. Instead, although some elements were continued and Charles II stressed his continuity with his fathers, monarchy had literally started anew in 1660. Moreover, there had also been a violent change of monarch in 1688-9, one that changed the dynasty, as that line continued to be denied the throne until it died out in 1807. These changes could be justified and harmonised with the past publicly by political and constitutional formulations, but they were abrupt demonstrations of a more general process of constitutional change that moved from the battlefields and murder sites of the late fifteenth century to the ecclesiastical, religious, and related judicial and political changes of the protracted crisis of the Reformation. The changes in 1688-9 and 1714 showed that religion was more important than heredity.

To posterity, there may appear to be calm and harmony, but that was not the background to the world of the Hanoverian rulers. That world can be dated accurately to the accession of George I in 1714, but 1660 is also worthy of attention. It was the year of George's birth and of the return of monarchy in the person of Charles II. Charles was a close relative of the Hanoverians, for the Hanoverian claim was a result of the Stuart antecedents of George's mother. Heir to the throne until her death in 1714, she was a granddaughter of James I and a self-consciously Stuart princess.

A focus on 1660 is also pertinent because kings rule and are assessed in the context of their subjects. Most of those who were adult in 1714 had been born after 1660, which was a key date in collective memory, both individual and communal. Lastly, the significance of 1660 is found in the events it reversed and the rifts it sought to end – concerning peace and punishment. Looming over our period was the execution in 1649 of Charles I, the closest to a saint in the Anglican world, and the brooding figure of Oliver Cromwell, a militarist who had grasped power and created a new form of monarchy with the Protectorate established in 1653, thc second constitution of the republic offering him the Crown.

Indeed, the aftermath of defeats, total defeats, conditioned the monarchy that George I inherited in 1714. Charles I had risked all, not so much in 1642 by leaving London and beginning what became a bitter civil war, but rather in 1648 by helping start another one in which the Royalists and their newfound Scottish allies were rapidly and completely defeated. This second disaster precipitated the declaration of a republic and the trial and execution of the

King, outcomes that would not have seemed probable when the first Civil War ended in 1646.

Kings had been killed before in England, – William II, Edward II, Richard II, Henry VI, and Edward V – and dynasties had been overthrown with the king killed, notably Harold in 1066 and Richard III in 1485. In 1649, royal coats of arms were removed, statues toppled, and monarchy, both substance and paraphernalia, consigned to the past, rather as Papal authority, monasteries and the Catholic church had been under the Tudors. Charles I was not brought down by a dynastic challenge, and nor would Louis XVI be.

There was a revival of a monarchical form in the person of Oliver Cromwell's Protectorate. Moreover, unlike with George Washington and the American presidency, there was an attempt at a hereditary status in that his son, Richard, succeeded him when he died in 1658. However, this attempt to provide continuity for what might have been a pseudo-monarchical pseudo-elective situation comparable to that of the House of Orange in the United Provinces (modern Netherlands) was ended by Richard's weakness and lack of drive. Instead, the unexpected play of events led to the accession in 1660 of Charles I's eldest son, Charles II (r. 1660-85).

It proved difficult to restore the assumptions and trust on which the practice of monarchy rested. Religious suspicion was a key element. Distrust of both Charles II and James II (r. 1685-8) focused on their Catholic sympathies and, in James's case, an overt conversion to Catholic doctrine. Religion was fundamental to monarchy as both institution and concept. Monarchy had the key root and route of continuity, but these drew heavily on religious and Classical elements and on warrior roles. Charles II was unable to meet these expectations other than primarily as relief from Interregnum chaos.

Nevertheless, considerably more astute than his father and helped by an absence of any equivalent to the earlier crises of 1638-41, Charles skilfully (at least in comparison with father and brother) rode out the crisis of the Popish Plot and the subsequent Exclusion

Crisis of 1679-81, an attempt to determine the succession by excluding James, one that anticipated the eventual failure of James when he became King. Republicanism was no real option. It had been discredited by the execution of Charles I and its aftermath. Royalist writers sought to damn Charles' opponents as republicans, for example Robert Brady linked Presbyterians and sectarians as opponents of the monarchy in his *An Introduction to Old English History* (1684). In turn, Whig opponents of the Crown sought to deny any link with or sympathy towards republicanism. But there were still republican arguments which drew on Classical sources and political and religious stances, as in Henry Neville's highly controversial book *Plato Redivius* (1681). Nevertheless, the crisis remained in a monarchical context, and outmanoeuvring his parliamentary rivals Charles regained control and strongly built up the royal position in his last years.

James II

James II and VII in Scotland was able to succeed in 1685 and to suppress risings in England and Scotland with little difficulty, less than George I was to face in 1715-16 and far less than George II in 1745-6. As part of another War of the Succession, James, Duke of Monmouth, an illegitimate son of Charles II, claimed the throne. Invading, Monmouth was heavily defeated at Sedgemoor. He escaped, but unlike Charles after his total defeat by Cromwell at Worcester in 1651, was captured and executed. The contrast between the fate of the two men was generally instructive of the role of chance.

Born in St James's Palace in 1633, baptised by William Laud, Archbishop of Canterbury, and named after James I (and VI), James II (and VII) looked back to a world before the Civil War. Convinced of divine approval, James moved toward Catholicisation of England after his victory at Sedgemoor on 6 July 1685. In his speech opening the parliamentary session that November, James made it clear that he wanted both a large permanent army and, in violation of the Test Act, no limitation on his right to employ Catholic officers, declaring: 'There is nothing but a good force of well-disciplined troops in constant pay that can defend us from such as, either at home or abroad, are disposed to disturb us.' Parliament was opposed, whereupon James prorogued it. Parliament never met again in his reign, and he pressed ahead with his policies, encountering printed and other criticism that he greatly resented.[1]

James's stance was challenged by the succession. He had two daughters, Mary and Anne, from his Protestant first marriage to Anne Hyde, with Mary married to James's nephew, William III of Orange, who was the leading Dutch political figure and a Protestant. James's fifteen-year-long second, Catholic, marriage to Mary of Modena, an Italian princess, had produced no surviving children. As a result, the birth of a Prince of Wales in June 1688, the future 'James III and VIII', was a major upset because it would ensure another Catholic monarchy. Critics spread the inaccurate rumour that a baby had been smuggled into the Queen's bed in a warming pan.

The more volatile situation combined with a move toward war in Western Europe. Keen to keep Britain out of the camp of his rival, Louis XIV of France, who was James's cousin, William of Orange, invited by the seven 'Immortals' of later Whig legend, invaded England that November. William brought with him a substantial army as he expected a difficult campaign, but benefited from a collapse of will on the part of James, who had an army twice the size of William's. James had been a brave (mainly naval) commander earlier in his life, but, in 1688, he suffered from a waning of resolve and a series of debilitating nose-bleeds, and he failed to lead his army into battle. Nor did George I and George II in response to the later Jacobite risings, but each had loyal and competent commanders, John, 2nd Duke of Argyll and William, Duke of Cumberland respectively. There was also a haemorrhage of support, culminating in the flight of Lieutenant-General John Churchill from James's camp at Salisbury to William's side, and that of Princess Anne from London.

William refused to halt his march on London in order to allow negotiations to proceed, as the Tory leaders, who were less unfavourable to James than were the Whigs, would have preferred. James fled the capital, throwing the Great Seal of England into the Thames. Fear of the London mob and of anarchy led to the Archbishop of Canterbury and leading peers taking control of the city. Captured and returned to London, where his presence obstructed the creation of a new political and constitutional order, James was finally driven abroad by Dutch pressure.

Had James prevailed as he had against Monmouth in 1685, then he would have been able to remould the political system, using the force he controlled and ensuring that it was better funded. This would have matched comparable governmental developments on the Continent and led to a British version of the system described as absolutism, one very different from rule by Hanoverians. Whereas the Hanoverians did not try to rule without Parliament and preferred to discuss abdication and/or a return to Hanover, as with George III in 1782-3, in response to crisis, victory for James in 1688 would have cemented the successful reaction against Parliament in Charles's last years after the Exclusion Crisis. Abroad, James would probably have allied with Louis XIV, whereas William declared war on him in May 1689.

After a few months that year in France, James returned, not to England, but to his kingdom of Ireland: a Catholic King ruling over a Catholic nation until the Williamite invasion of 1690. That year saw the two Kings fight a battle at the River Boyne, which in some ways was a contest between monarchy by hereditary claim and monarchy by appointment. William's victory led to James returning to France, while further Jacobite defeat led to the Treaty of Limerick in 1691. The subsequent reaffirmation and strengthening of the Protestant Ascendancy saw no religious toleration for Catholics in Ireland, which helped ensure a difficult position there for the Hanoverians.

In exile, James took part in plots for his restoration, but they were doomed by English naval power (ironically, given James's commitment to the navy), and notably so in 1692 when a French fleet intended to cover invasion was crushed at Barfleur. James saw these failures as signs of a lack of divine support and spent much time in devotion. In 1697, as a condition of peace, Louis recognised William III, and in 1701 James died of a brain haemorrhage at the age of 67, a good age for the period. Buried in the Church of the English Benedictines in Paris, his tomb was looted during the French Revolution, being rebuilt from 1828 in accordance with a commission by George IV, who was keen on dynastic reconciliation.

By then, the main line of the Stuarts had come to an end. James II had had one son, 'James III', James Francis Edward Stuart, who claimed the throne until his death in 1766. He had two sons, Charles Edward Stuart, or Bonnie Prince Charlie, who claimed the throne until he died in 1788, and then his younger brother, Henry, or Henry IX, a Cardinal, who as a Catholic priest could not marry, did not leave the priesthood, and died in 1807 without children.

William III

A power vacuum had been created in the winter of 1688-9 within the context of a successful invasion and conspiracy, culminating in a Dutch occupation that drew on significant English support. Most people did not want any breach in the hereditary succession, not only because of the example of 1649 but also due to a belief that civil power came from God. Indeed, William had initially (and falsely) claimed that he had no designs on the Crown. However, as the situation developed favourably for him, especially when James had been driven into exile, William made it clear that he sought the throne. This was achieved in 1689 by declaring it vacant, a legal fiction based on James's flight from London being depicted as an abdication, and by inviting William and Mary to occupy it as joint monarchs. All Catholics were debarred from the succession. In short, however much government derived its authority from God, the exercise of this authority and the type of government were left to humans, although divine (ie Protestant) sanction was claimed, and thus denied to the exiled Stuarts, not least through the 'warming pan' story. Yet, in 1660 and 1689, the action was very clearly human, and, in effect, a rump of Parliament acted as kingmaker. The situation would have been different had the Jacobites succeeded in 1715-16 or 1745-6, because they would have ruled by virtue of the Stuart claim.

1689 saw an innovation redolent of medieval solutions, joint monarchy. William III became King with his wife co-ruler as Mary II. That solution could have led to a new Anglo-Dutch ruling family, an outcome encouraged by William's role as royal warrior in 1688-90. In 1690, he was in command when James was defeated at the battle of the Boyne, which was swiftly followed by the conquest of Ireland. Thereafter, William returned to his earlier focus on resisting the French advance in the Low Countries, now with the benefit of assistance from British forces. He won additional prestige by regaining the fortress of Namur in 1695. In Nicholas Rowe's play *Tamerlane* (1701), the protagonist of Christopher Marlowe's 1587 play was reworked to appear as William III, with his eventually defeated Ottoman (Turkish) rival Bajazet as Louis XIV. In 1732, Philip Yorke (later 1st Earl of Hardwicke), as Attorney-General, was unsure of bringing libels to the attention of the Commons, but he suggested that an attack on William and the motives of the 'Glorious Revolution' would be 'an occasion wherein you would carry every Whig in the House along with you.'[2]

However, there was to be no dynastic continuity as William and Mary had no children. This might be related to a degree of bisexuality or homosexuality on William's part, but neither prevented other monarchs from having children. The problem, as with Anne, whose husband Prince George of Denmark was no homosexual (or later William IV), was rather that of an inability to have an heir who would survive childhood, although in William III's case, unlike those of Anne and William IV, there were no children. This underlines the significance of George I, II and III and Prince Frederick all having children who grew to adulthood and all having male children. In that respect, they fulfilled the ultimate requirement for monarchy, as George IV did not; although George III's fecundity ensured that the last did not lead to crisis, and Victoria was born to his fourth son, Edward, Duke of Kent.

Anne's rights in the succession had been subordinated to those of William. This was more easily done because Anne was younger than Mary. So that, when Mary died of smallpox in 1694, the joint monarchy was succeeded by William ruling alone, and Anne did not come to the throne until 1702 when William died childless. The compensatory provision in the Bill of Rights, that Anne and her issue should come before any issue of William from a second marriage, was not necessary. This provision was a major qualification of the hereditary principle, one necessary due to the circumstances of 1689, and one not required subsequently. It was consistent, however, with divine right theory, via the divine right of Providence.

There was also a major shift in the nature of monarchy in Scotland, where the Convention of the Estates declared the throne forfeit with the departure of James VII (James II of England). The contractual nature of the Revolution Settlement, the extent to which the Crown had been obtained by William and Mary on conditions, was far more apparent in Scotland than in England. The offer of the Crown to William and Mary was made conditional on their acceptance of the Claim of Right issued by the Scottish Convention, which stated that James VII had forfeited the Crown by his policies and that no Catholic could become ruler of Scotland, nor hold public office. The Scottish Parliament also gained greater independence from William than from his predecessors. The degree of radicalism in the Scottish constitutional settlement, which included the disestablishment of the Scottish Episcopalian Church, reflected fundamentally different political circumstances from those in England, including the far greater impact of William's wishes in the latter.

Both short and long-term circumstances were significant in the Scottish case. The pattern of restrictions on the Crown was far more entrenched in the Scottish case, in part due to the reaction against Mary, Queen of Scots but, more consistently, as a result of the lack of automatic aristocratic support for monarchy, a situation that reflected longstanding contentious factional domestic politics. This was not to be a problem for the Hanoverians due to the removal of the separate Scottish political culture with the Union of 1707.

The financial settlement for the Crown in England left William with an ordinary revenue that was small for his peacetime needs, obliging him to turn to Parliament for support. This continued to be a particular issue in wartime. On 13 May 1748, George II thanked MPs for 'the ample provision you have made for the service of the current year. Nothing could have contributed so much to the putting an end to the calamities of war, and reducing our future expenses, as those well-judged supplies.' The Civil List in effect made rulers employees of the state. Moreover, a standing (permanent) army was prohibited unless permitted by Parliament. This was a key limitation on royal power that reflected anger with James's policies. William had to accept the discipline of parliamentary monarchy: regular meetings of Parliament, which ended the royal right to call and dismiss Parliament at will; frequent elections; and reliance on ministers who could manage Parliament and state finances. The last was a longstanding requirement but now one that was more urgent because Parliament was often in session. There were ten general elections between 1695 and 1715.

However, the extent to which William was still able to impose his views indicated his political importance as the arbitrator of both Court factionalism and the ministerial struggle for influence. This role was not really compromised by the emergence of political parties, because they lacked the structure and ethos necessary to provide clear leadership and agreed policy, and certainly did so until the 1700s, when such groups became more coherent and therefore effective, albeit still in search of royal favour.

The public presentation of William drew on established themes, notably those of royal warrior and Protestant hero. Thus, Antonio Verrio's murals on the King's Staircase at Hampton Court glorified William as Alexander the Great, a potent figure for verification by comparison. Yet there was also a change in the assessment of monarchy, one that looked toward the present situation. From the late seventeenth century, there was a move away from the Baroque sensibilities and themes that had characterised the presentation of rulers and rulership, past as well as present, fictional as well as factual. These sensibilities and themes had looked back to the presentation of rulers by Classical as well as Christian writers, a process brought together anew by Renaissance Humanists as they sought to extol past and present Western rulers with reference to Classical forbears. From the Reformation and Counter-Reformation, this approach had come with an older, stronger sense of the monarch as defender of the Church. It brought with it the idea of the monarch as the embodiment of the national religion.

However, from the late seventeenth century, in part as a reaction to Absolutism, both British and Continental, and in part as a product of a more utilitarian approach to rulership, there was more of an emphasis on specific factors in the assessment of particular rulers. A focus on factual analysis, on observation rather than traditional authority, a focus in line with the intellectual prospectus offered in the seventeenth century by Francis Bacon and René Descartes, was intended to provide a more realistic account. Linked to this, the understanding and presentation of truth moved from moral precepts to the search for specific facts, and a concern with origins and development led to an interest in change. The idea of constant attributes, very much related to the 'humours' of the individual, was replaced by one that provided opportunities to understand change in terms of success and failure, and, linked to this, of an interplay of circumstances and character.

In a reaction against what he saw as irrational, the Calvinist William refused to touch for the King's Evil (scrofula); although Anne was to do so later. Alongside his undoubted interest in display and in warrior kingship, his was a monarchy that had some links with the self-conscious rationality termed 'political arithmetic', as well as with the Scientific Revolution, which encouraged a sense that predictable rules or laws existed in the natural world. The understanding of monarchy in the century after the 'Glorious Revolution' reflected the growing impact of the ideas of balance linked to the Newtonian exposition of mechanistic physics. Understanding the state in these terms meant an approach to monarchy as part of a well-ordered system rather than as a sacral intermediary with God. The religious dimension continued but in this new context.

The new style of perception was also related to reportage by an expanding press, with in England the end of pre-publication censorship in 1695 followed in 1701 by the foundation in London of the *Daily Courant*, the first daily newspaper. Moreover, the interplay between the Crown and adversarial parliamentary politics invited a changed view of the monarch as an individual who could be readily compared with predecessors and potential successors.

In 1702 (accession of Anne), as in 899 (Edward the Elder), 1100 (Henry I), 1199 (John), 1307 (Edward II), 1399 (Henry IV), 1603 (James I) and 1901 (Edward VII), there was the coincidence of a change of monarch at the turn of the century. That can be helpful, even if, or especially because, there is not necessarily a major shift, still less a change in dynasty. The death of William III in 1702 was important because it brought to an end the prospect of an Anglo-Dutch ruling house. There was to be the marriage in 1734 of George II's eldest daughter, Anne, with William IV of Orange, and the Orange interest was strongly backed by the British in key moments in Dutch factional politics in 1747 and, even more, in 1787. However, William IV of Orange (not William IV of Britain) was a cousin of William III with no claim on the British succession. His son, William V (1748-1806), driven out by French Revolutionary forces in 1795 and who spent his last years in exile at Kew, was in effect a cadet British prince, a grandson of

George II, but due to the large number of George's successors, including Frederick Prince of Wales's four sons, William V was of scant dynastic significance.

In part the peaceful accession of George III brought the 'Glorious Revolution' to fruition, but George I had brought about a very different foreign link from that of William III, that with the German Electorate of Hanover, a principality totally without the republican tendencies and federal constitution of the United Provinces. The Whig allegiance to the 'Glorious Revolution' followed by the 'Old Corps' Whig support for the Hanoverians tended to encourage the rejection or downplaying of earlier political arguments. John Locke was marginalised in public discourse along with the radical Commonwealth arguments that had some traction until the 1720s.[3] In contrast, American colonists under George III operated along those earlier assumptions that had lost relevance in Britain, where monarchy for Whigs was now the solution and not the problem.[4]

As with William III, the Hanoverian link could be presented in terms of a national continuity guaranteed by Parliament. Indeed, Classical references appeared most appropriate for monarchy after 1688, not in a republican context, but, rather with reference to a new monarchical destiny, first with William and later with George. Each could be considered as a new Augustus, a figure who would bring peace and stability after division, conflict and chaos, a description both of the late Roman Republic and of seventeenth-century British instability. It was correctly pointed out that William and George were not Cromwells, and they benefited from the comparison with Augustus who was presented as a peacemaker and creator.

Given the significance of the 'Glorious Revolution', William's reputation was exploited by Whig writers such as John Toland[5] and drawn into subsequent political disputes. On 1 January 1732, the *Weekly Register*, a London Whig paper, published 'An answer to the infamous libel on the memory of the late King William, printed in *Fog's Journal*, a Jacobite newspaper, of Saturday last', an answer that included the justified claim that he 'set a bound to the conquests of Lewis the Great' (Louis XIV). There was also controversy in Bristol in the 1730s as to whether to erect a statue to William. It was proposed in 1731, cast in 1733 and finally put up in 1736. The one erected in Hull in 1734 declared him 'our Great Deliverer'.

Although repeated praise in England for Arthur, Alfred and Elizabeth I reflected a determination to find a native structure to monarchy, the incorporation of foreigners from 1603 on had been a successful one, and notably so from 1689. Anglicisation might not be enough to please critics, some of them well-informed, but as the Stuarts had repeatedly been forced to understand, a foreign dynasty, initially of foreign-born monarchs, now had to accept the principles and exigencies of parliamentary monarchy. This was the very basis of the right to the throne enjoyed by the monarchs from 1689, and, more particularly, with the Hanoverian dynasty from 1714.

Anne

Born in 1665, Anne died aged 49. Poor health greatly reduced her vigour, which was far less than that of, say, Christina of Sweden (r. 1632-54). No cipher and a devout Anglican, Anne had no domestic programme of change. She was a relatively uncontroversial figure, and political criticism in her reign centred on ministers, not monarch. Her options were also constrained by the degree to which her reign was lived in the shadow of war, the War of the Spanish Succession in which Britain was involved from 1702 to 1713. If, in 1708, she was the last British ruler to veto an Act of Parliament, this did not produce a crisis. The notion of mixed monarchy and government by king-in-Parliament was long-established, and it worked.

Comparing monarchs was a habitual practice, and, in Anne's case, the comparison was with Elizabeth I. This might now seem implausible, but it did not at the time, and the comparison was made in publications and in correspondence. Sir John Chardin, a prominent merchant, wrote in 1703:

> The reign of the Queen proves as successful, glorious, and beloved as that of the renowned Elizabeth and England saw nothing like since her in point of reciprocal confidence and love between the sovereign and the people, and her Majesty's reign is like to be as fatal to the King of France [Louis XIV] as the other to the King of Spain [Philip II].

Supporters of intervention in Continental politics, as under Anne, cited Elizabeth's backing for the Dutch Revolt from 1585. More fancifully, the play *Zelmane: or The Corinthian Queen* (1705) made a direct comparison between the protagonist, an able war leader, and Anne. The glories of her reign, notably in war, were contrasted with George I and George II by those keen to criticise the government.[6]

Anne was able and not as dependent on her favourites, notably Sarah Churchill, Duchess of Marlborough, as was believed by some contemporaries. Her political part was to be unduly minimized, for the continued role of the monarch as arbitrator was amply demonstrated by Anne's central importance in the struggle for primacy at Court and among her ministers. Anne, moreover, enjoyed personal popularity with churchmen in particular, but also the wider population.

An instructive change arose from the re-placing of the monarchy in London. Whitehall had been the centre of power over the previous two centuries, at once royal palace and the seat of government. However, in 1698, fire destroyed the palace and only the Banqueting Hall remained. Despite proposals to do so, Whitehall was not rebuilt as a palace. Instead, on a pattern that was to be continued by the Hanoverians, the monarchs focused Court life on smaller palaces: St James's, Kensington, Hampton Court, and Buckingham House.

These, however, were not appropriate as locales of a governing process that was growing in scale. Instead of remaining with the Court, administration was rehoused in new buildings on the Whitehall site, which linked civil servants to ministers and kept both physically close to Parliament. Ministers came to see the king or wrote to him, but there was a distance. The perception and reality of royal power was affected, as at times the Crown could appear tangential to this new nexus, or at least part of a more multi-faceted governmental process. This was indeed the case, but separating government out made the situation more apparent.

The role of Parliament was also enhanced by the union of the Edinburgh and Westminster parliaments in 1707, the sequel to the personal union achieved in 1603 when James VI of Scotland became James I of England. The 1707 Union reflected anxiety that England and Scotland would choose different options when Anne died and, linked to this, tensions over the possibility of a different Scottish foreign policy, notably being closer to France. The Act of Security of 1704 had underlined the threat that the Scottish Parliament would select a monarch without consulting England and so break the 1603 personal union. However, Anne's ministers, rather than Anne herself, were the key players in the Union.

Legacies

A sense of change from earlier Stuart policy was captured in a parliamentary speech of 1710 by Robert Walpole, the prominent Whig MP and from 1721 to 1742 first minister, a speech supporting the impeachment of the Tory High-Churchman Henry Sacheverell. Walpole drew a clear contrast between what he saw as the pre-1688 authoritarian Stuart doctrine of monarchy and the post-'Glorious Revolution' situation. This contrast helps explain how Whigs responded to what they subsequently perceived as unwelcome royal initiatives:

> The doctrine of unlimited, unconditional passive obedience [to a monarch] was first invented to support arbitrary and despotic power... What then can be the designs of preaching this doctrine now, unasked, unsought for, in her Majesty's

> reign, where the law is the only rule and measure of the power of the Crown, and of the obedience of the people.

Walpole was soon after sent to the Tower, but that was due to Anne's Tory ministers, not the Queen.

Anne had seventeen pregnancies from her marriage to Prince George of Denmark (who predeceased her), but none survived to adulthood, an appalling tragedy and a very different reason for discontinuity than Charles II's failure (and that of his brother Henry, Duke of Gloucester) to have legitimate children, James II's Catholicism, and William and Mary's childlessness. James's sister Henrietta who had married Philip of Orléans, brother of Louis XIV, had four children, one of whom, Anne Marie, was alive in 1714. Married to Victor Amadeus II of Savoy-Piedmont, she had two children who were more closely related to Anne than George I. As a result, he was sensitive about that line, in 1719 writing to the Emperor Charles VI that he was opposed to a plan by Victor Amadeus that his heir, Charles Emmanuel, marry an Archduchess, which, in the absence of Charles having sons, would have linked Charles Emmanual very closely to the Habsburgs and made him a candidate for Emperor. George complained that Victor Amadeus' ministers acted as supporters of a Catholic claimant to the British Crown.[7] In the event, Charles Emmanuel married Anna Christine of Sulzbach in 1722. The death in 1701 of the most long-lived of Anne's children, William, Duke of Gloucester, meant clarification of the succession was required, which resulted in the Act of Settlement.

This provided for the succession of the Electoral house of Hanover, the claim of which derived from the daughter of James VI and I, Elizabeth. In 1613, she had married Frederick V, Elector Palatine, the short-lived King of Bohemia and Protestant hero in the early stages of the Thirty Years' War (1618-48) – as a result Elizabeth was known as the 'Winter Queen'. Six of James VI and I's children died young or without issue, only Charles I and Elizabeth had children. She had 13, of whom only two had legitimate issue:

Edward, a Catholic, who had two daughters, and her youngest daughter Sophia (1630-1714), who married Ernst August of the north German Protestant princely house of Brunswick-Luneburg. The future George I was the eldest of their large family of six boys and one girl. Moreover, the joint inheritance of Ernst August and his brothers shaped the Duchy of Hanover, which in 1692 became one of the now nine electorates of the Holy Roman Empire. This was the background to the new dynasty that came to the throne of Britain.

That was not a background about which much was known in Britain, except that it was Protestant. Instead, the vivid examples of the past were to the fore and kept there in family recollection and the world of print. Resolution was a key lesson that was praised, as in 1729 with the publication of *The Conduct of Queen Elizabeth, towards the neighbouring nations; and particularly Spain; compared with that of James* (I). There were also references in the press to monarchs who were displaced, Prince Kantemir, the Russian envoy, reporting on 17 April 1733 during the Excise Crisis, on one to Richard II.

The legacy of the recent past was very much seen in the role of monarchy in contrasting approaches to politics, from the Jacobite to the Whig. For the latter, it is instructive to turn to a key instance of discussion about monarchy, for such discussion provided a background for the response to individual monarchs. 'Britannicus', a Classical-style pseudonym suggestive of national identity, wrote in the pro-government *Weekly Journal: or British Gazetteer* of 9 February 1733:

> How great soever my veneration is for Crown'd heads, yet I can never give my assent to this High-Church or Romish doctrine, vis that kings whether good or bad, are accountable for their actions to none but God. At this rate let kings tyrannise, murder innocent subjects, ravish wives and daughters, raise heavy taxes by his own command, oblige them to embrace false religions, and what else is insupportable

for them, the Papists, and nonjurors, swear we are not to resist any such tyrants, but passively obey them, although their transactions are against the law of God and common justice... I am sure those persons they call Whigs have too great souls than to live under tyranny, popery, and arbitrary power, and will for ever bless the happy revolution which the immortal King William [III] brought about to make us and posterity enjoy our religious and civil rights and liberties ... the Papists and Nonjurors are for an absolute Empire... In an absolute Empire, the rule of the people's obedience is only the Sovereign's will, as it is in Muscovy, Turkey, and all such Princes as retain entire the right of conquest ... a Supreme Empire we Whigs take to be when a King has a supremacy and sovereignty over all, but his absolute power is limited and restrained by reciprocal pacts, laws and stipulating betwixt Prince and People ... and to these pacts the King and people are also equally bound before God and man.

The attitudes of parliamentarians revealed considerable respect for the royal position, although this did not prevent opposition. In August 1717, General Thomas Erle, long-standing Whig MP for Wareham, explained his views to James Craggs:

The King is certainly master of choosing who he thinks fit to employ. Those who would force others upon him, would think it hard usage to be treated so themselves in their particular concerns.I am under no apprehension but that both him and the public will be well served by those who are now in the administration. No one doubts their capacity. But there are so many who will be judges of their own, that the contention here, who shall have the power and the profit, will never be at an end. It is always happy for England when the people are possessed, that the King governs them himself. They have always had, and always will have submission for the Crown which they never will have for one another, whilst we are divided into parties as

> we are. No honest man will come into measures to compel the King to employ anyone, let his capacity be what it will, nor to distress those employed, out of peevishness to the person. But if the Public is apparently in danger by evil counsels the cry will then be general; and there are many instances how fatal it has been to our Kings when they have been tenacious of a favourite, who has justly incurred the odium of his subjects. God be thanked that cannot be the case now. We are governed by a wise and experienced Prince who knows how to choose and when to dismiss, according as he is served.[8]

Erle's support for Walpole, then in opposition during the Whig Split of 1717-20, led to his being forced to resign all his posts in March 1718.

The overhang of seventeenth-century politics very much affected collective and individual memory, as well as the presentation of monarchy, in the eighteenth. In 1723, the invalid Josiah Hort, Bishop of Ferns, wrote from London about the 26 January issue of the *Weekly Journal or British Gazetteer*, which he felt used radical Whig language about the monarchy for Jacobite ends, a linkage that was widely noted:

> You will find in it an affected, panegyric on those who put King Charles the 1st to death. The author introduces his poem with a letter wherein he professes his zeal for his present Majesty [George I], and for the memory of King William. This is only to obtrude himself upon the world for a Whig, the better to work mischief under that character. But the father of it is plainly some Jacobite who begot this bastard in rancour, with a design to lay it at the door of the Whigs. It is evidently calculated to inflame people's minds against the administration, and will captivate the multitude if no remedy be applied.[9]

On 2 September 1749, the *Remembrancer*, a London newspaper, its title itself a reference to the value of the past, noted: 'On the ruins of King James the Second's government a new one was established, which undertook not only to perpetuate the liberty of this country, but to restore the liberty of Europe.' The contrasting understanding of the constitution was not only a product of political division in the present, but also a legacy of the past. Joseph Yorke, an MP and diplomat, observed in 1753:

> I am convinced that the constitution of no country is so little known as that of England. Half the world imagine that all government is confusion with us; and the other that our kings are as arbitrary as any other, and that all they do in a view to satisfy the nation is pure grimace.[10]

The kings certainly did not see themselves as arbitrary. Instead, as with the freedom of the press, they could become frustrated by the legal freedoms of the people which were differently expressed from the situation which applied in Hanover. Thus, in 1748, it was reported that George II was angry with wartime grain exports to France. The contrast between king and people was not the prime one in political rhetoric; instead, it was between ministers and people. Yet, Hanoverian issues, in the shape of issues to the benefit of the Electorate, allowed opponents, both international and domestic, to seek to contrast king and nation, as Frederick II did in 1749.[11] Frederick II was believed to be trying to use Hanoverian issues to exploit this contrast: 'His view seems evidently to provoke the King, and to alienate as far as in him lies, the affections of the English from their sovereign, by mixing the affections of the Electorate with those of England.'[12] In the background was the issue of the separation of Hanover from Britain.

The Stuarts left another legacy in a strong belief in Court conspiracies, as in David Jones's *The Secret History of White Hall from the Restoration of Charles II down to the Abdication of the late King James* (1697).[13] Whig writers associated such conspiracies with Catholicising interests and authoritarianism. Mention was made repeatedly in print of the historical experience of Catholic monarchs, notably Mary (r. 1553-8).[14] The significance of the religious issue led to the circulation of rumours that the future George I was a secret Catholic.[15] Amidst this febrile atmosphere prominent figures such as Marlborough warned that the Tory government planned a Jacobite succession,[16] and there were suggestions of moving Hanoverian troops secretly into London.[17] The possibility of French help on behalf of the Jacobites was mentioned.[18]

Under George I and George II, conspiracies could be attributed by opposition to the government, as with accusations in 1720-1 about the fraudulent South Sea Company in which George I was heavily compromised financially as a result of having received free shares as Director.[19] Secret histories involving monarchy included the belief that John, 3rd Earl of Bute, from his resignation from office in 1763 on, was secretly directing Court policies, which was not the case. The Crown was less central and less a cause of suspicion, and reports of conspiracies tended not to focus on the Court. Indeed, the most prominent was that in the 1790s about support for radical movements in Britain.[20]

In 1726, seeking Austrian support for the Jacobite cause, the envoy in Vienna of 'James III and VIII' told Prince Eugene that he himself was Protestant and that 'whatever he might have heard of the apprehensions of the nation concerning Popery and slavery, it was nothing else than a malicious cant, industriously spread about by the Whigs.'[21]

In contrast to the emphasis under the Stuarts on conspiracies by the Crown in favour of Catholicisation, the Hanoverians remained true to the religious stipulations of the Revolution Settlement, which ensured that the monarch would be a Protestant. Thus, in Scotland, the Crown was represented at the General Assembly of the Church of Scotland by the Royal Commissioner and from the 1720s the Crown gave the annual Royal Bounty to the General Assembly in order to support catechists and missionary ministers against Catholicism. Alongside clerical tension toward colleagues who allegedly 'would have given Christian burial even to Pontius

Pilate himself, provided he had but in his lifetime used to cry "King George [I] forever,"'[22] the accommodation of the Whigs and the Church of England helped ensure stability in England. From 1722, as a reward for loyalty, a small *regium donum* (king's gift) was given annually to trustees from the Baptist, Independent and Presbyterian churches, the funds used to supplement the incomes of their indigent clerics.

It proved possible to install two Lutheran monarchs, George I and George II, in succession without damage to the Church. Both conformed to the Church of England, as the Jacobites were unwilling to do. The potential strains posed by their Lutheranism were further relaxed due to an emphasis, in response to Jacobitism, on a broad Protestant patriotism that could include Dissenters.[23] The royal family contributed to this, whether Cumberland at Culloden, or his mother, Caroline of Ansbach, having in 1704 refused marriage (at the price of conversion to Catholicism) to the future Emperor Charles VI before she married the future George II in 1705. This made reports that their daughter Amelia might marry Duke Charles of Lorraine[24] implausible. None of the Georges married a Catholic.

The religious dimension was widely treated as integral to politics and rulership. Thus, in 1716, Timothy Awbrey published his *Advice to the Clergy. A Sermon Preached at the primary visitation of John, Lord Bishop of Oxford.* He used the oft-cited text 'Render therefore unto Caesar the things which are Caesar's, and unto God the things that are God's,' and emphasised the need to obey the ruler. Richard Hurd, later one of George III's favourite bishops, and whom he visited in 1788 at Hartlebury Castle, referred in 1754 to a sermon preached by Dr John Brown in Cambridge:

> ... it was to prove that tyranny was productive of superstition of tyranny; that debauchery was the cause of free-thinking and free-thinking of debauchery. His conclusion was that the only way of keeping us from being a French province was

> to preserve our constitutional liberties, and the purity of our manners.[25]

From this perspective, it was crucial that the monarchs did not convert to Catholicism or show Catholic tendencies. As such, they contrasted not only with the Stuarts but also with many of the other German ruling families including Saxony, Württemberg and Hesse-Cassel. Instead, the Hanoverians were more like the ruling Hohenzollern house of Prussia. As so often, it is the change that did not occur that is crucial. Unless the Act of Settlement was repealed, a move toward Catholicism would have rendered the Hanoverian in question definitely ineligible for the Crown, which would be a constitutional solution, but pose a major political strain. There would have been implications within the ruling house, in domestic politics and international relations.

This, however, was a path that was not pursued. Avoiding civil war and upheaval was an unstated premise in the eighteenth century, rather like the Wars of the Roses under the Tudors, a fate to avoid at all hazard. That helped make pivotal the Hanoverian accession and the Jacobite risings in 1715 and 1745.

3

GEORGE I

> I am sorry to own the civil spirit among the people is very little better than ever, and that the army is necessary to contain them. But France is in a miserable condition, and our King respected abroad... I think there is nothing to apprehend for the public of very bad consequence ... when I reflect that scarce any new line came to the throne without some uneasiness and disturbance at first which afterwards died away and the government more firmly fixed than before.
> John, Lord Perceval, 1716[1]

The new dynasty brought a British commitment to Hanover, one that raised uneasy echoes about the concerns over foreign interests, influences and favourites already seen with James I in 1603 and William III in 1689, but not in the case of Henry Tudor in 1485. His Electoral background was crucial for contemporaries, but George I's reign (1714-27) tends also to be defined now in terms of his personal ethos as a warrior, the strength of the Jacobite challenge, his conflict with his son, and his ability to set the scene for a lasting limited monarchy.

Of the four monarchs under discussion, George is the least known, and the most poorly understood and presented from a British perspective, as opposed to one that focuses more on his

Hanoverian role and international interests. There are obvious explanations, not least the relative brevity of his reign, the difficulty he had in communicating with his British subjects, and his limited concern with his public image.[2] Yet, other factors were also pertinent. In particular, born in 1660, George came from a different tradition of monarchical practice from that which was to be evident with George III in particular. George I can be discussed as a Baroque monarch, one for whom traditional themes of activity and display were more significant than was the case with the bureaucratic kings of the late eighteenth century. George was primarily a warrior, as William III had been, but unlike William, whose life (1650-1702) was much shorter, this was a matter solely of his years before he came to the throne. George was not a great writer, but nor were his contemporaries, and it is in that context that he should be assessed.

Both Britain and Hanover were at war during the reign, Hanover with Sweden and Britain with Spain, but George did not fight in person, and the future George II, who had also had a military career, was not permitted to do so. He was the sole son, not a 'spare', as William, Duke of Cumberland was to be under George II, while the progeny of Frederick and then George III ensured that there was no shortage of 'spares' from the 1740s, indeed quite the reverse, even if George IV had to look to his brothers. The war with Spain (1718-20) occurred during the Whig Split when Prince George was aligned with the Whig opposition. The Jacobite rising of 1715-16 represented an opportunity for the prince that was not taken.

The North German tradition of rulership was very much one of diligence, given an added urgency by the competitive nature of the international system and of the remembered experience of the bitter Thirty Years' War (1618-48), during which Catholic forces had overrun the area, and subsequent struggles. Such struggles were crucial to the consolidation of the Brunswick-Luneburg inheritance and the ability to supersede the Brunswick-Wolfenbüttel branch, despite its powerful foreign allies. There was nothing inevitable in this process, nor in gaining part of the Swedish empire in the Great Northern War of 1700-21. This was crucial to the period of continual consolidation and expansion that had begun in the 1680s, one that saw a degree of aggressiveness and bred an over-confidence that might not have been apparent to later commentators but that was seen not only by the British opposition but also by other German and non-German rulers.

Born in 1660 as Georg Ludwig, the eldest surviving child of Ernst August of Brunswick-Lüneburg and Sophia of the Palatinate, George was then a long way from the British throne and remained at a distance when he became Elector in 1698. However, the death in 1700 of Anne's son, William, Duke of Gloucester, brought the succession to the fore. Under the Act of Settlement of 1701, the Hanoverian rulers would have to take coronation oaths committing them to rule 'according to the statutes in Parliament agreed' and to maintain the Protestant religion as established by law.

The Hanoverians also claimed a distant hereditary right via Matilda (*c.* 1156-1189), daughter of Henry II and wife of Henry the Lion, Duke of Saxony. In 1701, a medal was struck at the request of Sophia to mark her being named heiress to the Crown of England. The reverse depicted 'Matilda, daughter of Henry II, King of England, wife of Henry the Lion ... mother of Emperor Otto IV ... Progenitor of the House of Brunswick'. This medal grounded the Hanoverian claim on the succession in primogeniture and the history of the House of Guelph, and not on the Act of Settlement passed by Parliament in 1701. Pro-Hanoverian British historians, such as Laurence Echard, also focused on this argument. It was a claim advanced by John Wesley in his *Concise History of England* in 1776, in which he traced the legitimacy of the Hanoverian succession back to Matilda. History, in the sense of the sanction of the past, thereby served to establish and strengthen the claim. Sophia had been naturalised by Act of Parliament in 1705, as were her heirs, including George.

Such dynastic locating was scarcely new, but it remained important. Indeed, dynastic history was not only a traditional theme in England, and one that was crucial to state formulation, but was also pushed to the fore by the challenge posed by Jacobite claims – or believed to be posed by them. Yet the hereditary argument on behalf of the Hanoverians, an argument that might have served to lessen the penalty for any conversion to Catholicism, had no weight in Britain. Instead, legislation of 1689 and 1701 ensured that there was a degree of elective character to British kingship, and also grounded the kingship in a parliamentary dispensation designed to ensure permanence.

Dynasticism meanwhile had pushed George in a different direction. In order to help consolidate the greatly fractured Brunswick inheritance, George married his first cousin Sophia Dorothea in 1682 and had two children by her, the future George II in 1683 and a daughter, another Sophia Dorothea, in 1687. The couple moved apart, in part due to George being active on campaign, and each took lovers. George had a long relationship with Ehrengard Melusine von der Schulenburg, later Duchess of Kendal, by whom he had three daughters, and Sophia Dorothea had a relationship with Philipp Christoph von Königsmarck, a colonel in the army. The latter were indiscreet and appeared ready to elope, whereupon in 1694 Königsmarck was murdered and Sophia Dorothea kept in a form of house arrest in her native Celle until her death in 1726. The marriage was dissolved in 1694, with the divorce a cause of bitterness between George and his son. George was to be mocked in Britain as a cuckold, as in *Trick for Trick; or, The Hasty Cuckold* (London, 1714),[3] although criticised more for avarice.[4]

Prince George of Hanover, the future George II, usually known as George Augustus, became a naturalised British subject in 1705 and Duke of Cambridge the following year. But Anne saw his presence as a challenge to her royal majesty and a reminder of her mortality. In April 1714, she responded angrily to Sophia's attempt to have George summoned to take his seat in the House of Lords as Duke of Cambridge, and he was not sent for. Meanwhile, in accordance with a suggestion from the leading general of the 1700s, John, 1st Duke of Marlborough, then in exile, the future

George I had entered into correspondence with Austria's leading general, Prince Eugene.[5] There were discussions and rumours about using foreign troops to pre-empt a Jacobite takeover.[6]

There was speculation that the Tories would try to ensure the succession for 'James III', who made preliminary moves, but, when Anne died in August 1714, having to her satisfaction outlived Sophia, all passed peacefully, largely as a result of inadequate Jacobite preparations and a lack of foreign support. Sophia had died, aged 84, that June; and Georg Ludwig succeeded peacefully as George I, arriving in September.

George has left scant recognisable legacy to modern times, but his main reach to posterity was the accession of the Hanoverians. In part, that was an accident in that Sophia did not survive Anne. Had she done so, George as Elector would have had to come to the aid of his mother. There would have been the discontinuity of a double succession, as Sophia would probably not have lasted for long.

The description of George by his most recent biographer as 'the lucky King'[7] is questionable. He gained a kingdom and held onto it despite repeated challenges, indeed with greater ease than Augustus II of Saxony held Poland, let alone Frederick V, Elector Palatine's failed efforts to hold Bohemia in 1619-20; but the challenges were serious while Hanover was repeatedly threatened with attack. George's wife had betrayed him, causing a public scandal, and he, as King, had a terrible and lasting row with his own heir, and another with his son-in-law, Frederick William I of Prussia.

George's accession had been preceded by fear and rumour, but in the event, there was no Jacobite rebellion and no supporting French invasion. Torcy, the French Foreign Minister, argued that any rebellion without French help would inevitably fail, and that Louis XIV had taken up contrary commitments to Britain in the recent peace treaty. Torcy suggested that James appeared to have little support in Britain and that George had been declared King with the consent of all the nation, but added that the English were very inconstant and easily took offence, and that for James, therefore, the chance of becoming king lay in the future.[8] The French envoy was totally wrong to report war necessary for George in order to establish his authority, shift onto the British Exchequer the cost of his German troops, and weaken the Tories.[9]

However, just as it proved difficult to reconcile Hanoverian and British interests, so George found it impossible to maintain both the mixed ministry he, on the pattern of what Sophia had wished,[10] sought at the start of his reign,[11] and the united Whig one to which he then shifted. Moreover, the Whig faction that he favoured after the Whig Split of 1717 collapsed in 1720-1 due to its failure to manage a difficult domestic and international situation. Thereafter, he could not keep in office the ministers he backed such as John, Lord Carteret, who lost a Secretaryship of State in 1724 to a minister George actively disliked, Thomas, Duke of Newcastle. George was only lucky if the assessment allows for these and other serious difficulties. The description is not one George himself would have recognised.

The Crown was constrained in its freedom of political manoeuvre by the consequences of the party conflict. This made it very difficult for William III and Anne to create mixed ministries of Whigs and Tories, for the growth of party loyalty led party leaders to resign from or refuse to accept office because the monarch employed men of another party. As a result, Clayton Roberts claimed that 'in later Stuart England the power of party overwhelmed the power of patronage,'[12] a thesis that is of considerable importance for the early Hanoverian period; although party and patronage were closely interlocked, not separate categories.

Although it has been argued that the Tories were keen to serve the Crown, as Archbishop Sharp of York indeed told George in 1714,[13] and that George I and George II were willing to turn to the Tories, there is little evidence after 1715 for the second contention and, while the first is certainly true for many Tories, it probably underrates the role of Jacobite sympathies. Both Kings detested the Tories as the party whose ministry had negotiated the Peace of Utrecht in 1713, ending the War of the Spanish Succession and abandoning Britain's allies, including Hanover. Indeed, George I sought information on the negotiations of the Tory ministry, both in correspondence and by means of audiences.[14] The Utrecht issue was used by the Whigs to great effect throughout the period 1713-40 to discredit the Tories. George I and George II suspected, and were urged to do so by the Whigs, that the Tories were inclined to support Jacobitism. Moreover, the monarchs were opposed to the 'little Englander' stance of the Tories: their opposition to Continental commitments, an isolationism that threatened Hanover, and their hostility to Continental Protestantism. In these areas, Tory opinions and ideology, as well as Tory policies, conflicted with royal interests, for George I in particular was committed to helping co-religionists (Protestant Dissenters), and British diplomats were instructed accordingly.[15]

There were reports that certain Whigs, such as Charles, 2nd Viscount Townshend, supported 'a mixed Ministry'.[16] He was described by the French envoy as part of a moderate Whig cabal opposed to the Whigs who had been part of the 'Junto' group under Anne.[17] Nevertheless, it is not surprising that George I, allegedly also influenced by the Dutch and Bothmer,[18] and George II had little time for the Tories. George I appointed George Smalridge, Bishop of Bristol and Dean of Christ Church, as Lord High Almoner, which was seen as a sign of favour to the Tories;[19] but his refusal to sign the declaration in 1715 against the Pretender, a refusal he defended in print, led to his removal from that post and replacement by William Wake, the Bishop of Lincoln. In 1714, the French envoy reported that George II, then Prince of Wales, would 'not suffer the sight of any Tories, regarding them all as Jacobites',[20] while in 1719 Newcastle referred to George I's 'steady adherence to the Whig interest'. In 1721, he wrote:

> The report of the Tories coming in, having reached the King's ears, he has been so good as to declare to me and many other of his servants the concern he has at the report, and has

> assured us that he neither has or ever had any such thoughts, and is determined to stand by the Whigs, and not take in any one single Tory. He is very sensible the Whig Party is the only security he has to depend on, in which he is most certainly right, for it is impossible for his Government ever to be supported by any other Party... Could I imagine there was any design to introduce the Tories I should be as much alarmed as anybody for I shall always think it destructive to the King and the Government.[21]

In 1723, commenting that Carteret, who was seeking to supplant Walpole, had broken off with the Tories, Newcastle noted that Carteret was 'thinking to carry his point with the Whigs, which he knows agreeable to the King'.[22] Carteret's knowledge of German was a particular advantage, while speaking French was important in dealing with a monarch who was at least initially not confident in English.[23] Thus, Wake, appointed Archbishop of Canterbury in 1716, had 'the benefit of speaking French fluently'.[24]

Prominent Tories could attack the King as an individual, as when William Shippen told the Commons in December 1717 that he was

> ... unacquainted with our language and constitution; and it is therefore the more incumbent on his British Ministers to inform him, that our Government does not stand on the same foundations with his German Dominions, which, by reason of their situation and the nature of their constitution are obliged to keep up armies in time of peace.[25]

At times of political tension, as in 1717 and the mid 1740s, when the monarchs risked the defeat of their favoured ministers, James, Viscount Stanhope and John, Lord Carteret respectively, they were prepared to threaten that they would turn to the Tories for support, but there was little substance to these threats. When George I and George II sought Tory help they did so only in order to serve

Whig ministries and measures, or rather particular factions within Whig ministries. The inability and unwillingness of Tory leaders to offer this help made discussion of such schemes abortive, as in 1716-18. For practical purposes, George I and George II were party monarchs, whose wish to have Whig ministries represented a constraint, one they understood, on their political freedom of manoeuvre.

This constraint did not, however, oblige them to have a particular set of Whigs, either ministers or courtiers. The divisions within the Whig party, accentuated from 1714 onwards by political success and the consequent struggle for office and dominance, gave the monarch considerable freedom in his choice of ministers. There were essentially two types of Whig internal dispute. First, disputes within the Whig élite, notably the ministry, were very significant, and usually involved disagreements over pre-eminence, policy and patronage, as with the ducal rivalry in the army in 1714-15 between Marlborough and Argyle, one that came to involve George I and the Prince of Wales. In 1722-4, the conflict between Walpole and the former Sunderland group, led by Carteret and William Cadogan, related to disagreements over foreign policy as much as to a struggle for pre-eminence. They were inextricably intertwined as both involved an attempt to win royal support. Walpole's success in this struggle was important to the consolidation of his power.

There were also rivalries between Hanoverian ministers, but without the parliamentary dimension and public resonance of their British counterparts. The British and Hanoverian ministerial disputes could be aligned, which contributed greatly to the Whig Split in 1717-20, ensuring that the divisions among the British politicians were not the sole issue. There was a further interaction with contrasting international priorities and related alliance preferences.[26] On the whole, in the late 1710s Hanoverian ministers were less enthusiastic about alliance with France and more keen on that with Austria than their British equivalents, with Bothmer having a confidential correspondence with the Austrian Chancellor, Count Sinzendorf.[27]

The second type of Whig internal dispute was usually a consequence of the first. It was a formal parliamentary opposition by Whigs to the Whig ministry, such as that mounted by Walpole in 1717-20 and by William Pulteney in 1726-42. These oppositions often looked to the Tories for parliamentary support, but they differed fundamentally from the Tory opposition, in that there was a good chance that the opponents would be taken back into office and that they were often linked to ministerial factions.

Thus, despite being restricted to Whig ministries, George I and George II possessed considerable freedom as a result of Whig disputes, with links to the opposition Whigs through Bothmer and others.[28] The Crown was the arbiter of these disputes and the Court the principal sphere in which they were conducted. At the same time, the constitutional and political customs of the period ensured that royal support for Whig measures and ministers did not necessarily lead to ministerial stability.

Ministers needed royal support, and as a result the Crown was able to obtain considerable benefits: an enhanced Civil List, which was important to a ruler used to being frugal,[29] significant backing in international crises,[30] a larger army than would probably have otherwise existed, and support for Hanoverian interests, such as the subsidy treaty with Hesser-Cassel, by which Hessian troops destined for the defence of Hanover were paid by Britain and not by Hanover, a controversial policy.[31] George was widely reported to be mean.[32]

Walpole was expected to find money for George I's female German connections.[33] His longstanding mistress, Ehrengard Melusine von der Schulenburg, an aristocrat who had been Maid of Honour to Sophia, was made Duchess of Munster in 1716 and Duchess of Kendal in 1719. Keen on money, Melusine, who was known as 'the Maypole', was involved in corrupt practices including selling the expectancies to offices, and pressed ministers accordingly.[34] Walpole also had to spend time as a courtier, attending on the royal family, as on 3 July 1724 when he was present at George's review of the Foot Guards in Hyde Park.

The monarchs did not always heed ministerial wishes concerning patronage. In one such matter, in 1738, Thomas, Earl of Malton was informed that although Walpole had pressed George II, 'He had the misfortune and concern to find that he could not prevail.'[35] In this kind of situation there was potential for a serious conflict between Crown and ministry.

Rivalries among the ministers and courtiers were an integral aspect of Court society, as the position of each of the king's advisors was mutually dependent. This process directed attention on the king, while the language of service to the monarch fostered such an ambience. Part of the political game, and an important element of its culture, was avoiding making it seem as if the king's hands were being forced. In 1723, Charles, 2nd Viscount Townshend, Secretary of State for the Northern Department, noted, 'Nothing would give His Majesty greater offence than our making any such affair (between ministers) a matter of triumph, and the less we boast the more we certainly shall have to boast of.'[36] Resigning office was seen as weakening the credit of government and angered George I.[37]

Walpole was not George's favourite minister, and his serious weakness at French,[38] let alone German, compounded the situation. In 1721, Carteret kept up his own spirits and sought to preserve Newcastle's support for Sunderland by informing him that 'The King is resolved that Walpole shall not govern, but it is hard to be prevented.'[39] Walpole's early ascendancy and George I's need for him, owed much to chance: the acute financial crisis of 1720 caused by the bursting of the South Sea Bubble, and the deaths of Stanhope and Sunderland in 1721 and 1722. His success in the session of 1721 in performing the difficult task of defending Whig involvement in the South Sea Company consolidated Walpole's position as the leading ministerial spokesman in the Commons. He was to maintain this position until 1742, thanks to his refusal to follow the usual course of successful politicians, such as (recently) Harley, Bolingbroke and Stanhope, and obtain promotion to the Lords. Instead, his eldest son was created a peer, Lord Walpole of

Walpole, in June 1723, as eventually in 1742 was Walpole and finally, in 1756, his brother.

As government manager and principal spokesman in the Commons and a skilled finance minister, Walpole was invaluable to George, though it is unclear whether the King would have supported him against Sunderland in the rift that was prevented only by the latter's sudden death from pleurisy. In July 1723, Townshend claimed that the recent successful parliamentary session and the revival of credit had helped Walpole (his brother-in-law) and himself into George's good graces. The following month, Walpole congratulated himself on accurately predicting financial movements for George and on the flourishing condition of public credit: 'I think 'tis plain we shall have the whole supply of next year at 3 per cent.'

In 1721, Bishop Gibson had claimed that 'as long as our great men go on to agree among themselves, all is like to go very well.' This was not to be.[40] Walpole had to struggle hard in 1724-5 to remove from power his opponents within the ministry, Cadogan, Carteret, Macclesfield and Roxburgh. In late 1723, Carteret had 'great hopes from Cadogan and Roxburgh's being able to form a party', but in practice, the removal of Walpole's ministerial rivals did not lead to problems in Parliament.[41]

Over time, Walpole appears to have earned the respect of George. Commenting in early 1724 on the political situation in London, John, 2nd Earl of Stair had no doubt that George's support for Walpole was crucial: 'The King's favour is entirely declared on the side of Robert Walpole ... his Majesty confides entirely in Mr. Walpole for the management of his affairs. There is not the least struggle in that matter ... it looks as if before the end of the session of Parliament everything was to be modelled to be of a piece as far as Mr. Walpole cares to have it so.'[42]

Walpole cannot be described accurately as the prime minister in George I's last years, however: he never enjoyed sufficient influence with George, and Townshend's authority in the field of foreign policy was clearly independent of Walpole. There is, nevertheless, no truth in the reports which circulated in 1727 that George had planned to disgrace Walpole shortly before his death.[43]

Whereas George had a long-established relationship with his Hanoverian advisors and was able to choose and part with them as he wished, his earlier British ministers were largely unknown quantities to him and his choices were greatly constrained by party factors, an unwelcome necessity for any ruler. In addition, even accepting the role of party, the mutual tensions among ministers and would-be ministers – and their prominence and strength as politicians – were difficult to fathom. Those ministers who were most like courtiers were easier for George to appreciate, and notably if, as with James Stanhope, they had a military background, although that did not extend to his son, the future George II. In contrast, ministers and diplomats with a grounding in the House of Commons were harder to evaluate, most obviously Robert and Horatio Walpole.

A taciturn and reserved figure, George has been positively re-evaluated in recent decades, notably by Ragnhild Hatton,[44] who produced the only substantial biography of the King, a reminder of how an individual historian can play a major role in establishing the reputation of an individual monarch. Ragnhild Hatton was perhaps stronger on German than British sources, apt to neglect the dimensions of British politics. I believe she underplayed the extent to which George bears responsibility for a terrible breakdown in relations with his son in 1717, as well as for committing Britain to a risky and expensive international posture that led to war with Spain in 1718-20, and in 1720, as a result of pursuing Hanoverian interests, nearly resulted in conflict with Peter the Great of Russia.

George tried to adjust to his new royal role while continuing to follow his established interests in the army and hunting. Indeed, when George was at Göhrde, his hunting lodge in the Electorate, it was possible to talk to him for longer and more easily than anywhere else.[45] The 1725 painting of a royal hunting party in front of Göhrde depicts a splendid occasion. That year, the

Palatine envoy described George's court at Herrenhausen outside Hanover as very numerous and splendid.[46]

The nature of politics in Britain was very different from that in Hanover, and the conduct politicians thought appropriate in the former was not that understood by the King, who found it particularly difficult to appreciate the legitimacy of opposition. His failure to learn much English and his obvious preference for Hanover, such that in 1716 he was uneasy whenever his return to England was mentioned,[47] further contributed to this sense of alien rule, causing complaint among Whigs as well as Tories. British politicians found it necessary to travel to Hanover in order to advance their political interests.[48] This was not an easy journey. In 1719, George returned to London 'after an easy and speedy voyage'[49] but returning in 1726 his life was in danger and he was driven ashore near Rye. This added unpredictability, although Stair felt able to present the Anglo-Hanoverian relationship in a positive light, in that Hanoverian troops could be moved to Britain in response to any Swedish support for the Jacobite rising:

> There were 10,000 or 12,000 men on the Elbe in case the King of Sweden [Charles XII] or any other foreign power thought fit to support the rebellion, and ... Stade and Hamburg were at least as near Scotland as Carlskrona or any other port, from whence the rebels could be supported.[50]

Hanoverian motives frequently prevailed. Jacobite claims that George intended to replace British aristocrats executed for Jacobitism by 'German Barons'[51] were false, but it was certainly the case that British policy had to serve Hanoverian ends. In late 1716 the movement of Hanoverian and allied troops to the frontiers of Mecklenburg in order to deter Peter the Great led Stanhope to write from Göhrde to London:

> This situation of affairs here will, I am persuaded, incline all His Majesty's servants to be of opinion, that His Majesty hath

> judged very rightly, in sending order to his ministers at The Hague to sign the treaty with France without any delay.[52]

In 1718, Friedrich Bonet, the Prussian envoy, reported that George disliked Britain for its language, constitution, political parties and continual importunities for royal favour, whereas he was master of all of those in Hanover. It also brought him a diplomatic system which provided information he could not accrue from the British apparatus.[53] Bonet also noted that the Prince and Princess of Wales, then linked to the opposition, conspicuously always spoke English, and in 1714 the Princess discarded her French hairstyle for an English one.[54] Public from 1717, the rift between George and his son began a series of them between Hanoverian kings and their heirs. These disputes were the basis for political manoeuvring, focusing existing disputes, and also for extensive speculation and groundless rumours.[55] They were seen as an unreasonable return to the supporters of the Protestant Succession.[56]

Concerns about George's goals were exacerbated by a sense that his preference for Hanover entailed an abandonment of British national interests, as resources were expended for the aggrandisement of Hanover and the entire direction of foreign policy was set accordingly. Jacobite propaganda made much of the Germanic nature of the Hanoverian regime, while foreign powers such as Sweden claimed that Hanoverian motives prevailed.[57] This criticism of George was to continue after he died and was not restricted to Jacobites or Tories, the *Monitor* noting on 1 October 1757:

> Had King George the First taken as much care to ascertain our undoubted right to North America, and to a free navigation, as he did to increase his German dominions and to secure them from usurpation and contention, his royal son would not have been reduced to the necessity of exposing his crown and life in a long and expensive war with France and Spain.

This was a reference to the warfare of 1739-48 that started as the War of Jenkins' Ear with Spain.

William III had been both son and husband to Stuart princesses and was careful not to proscribe the Tories, whereas George was easier to attack. If individual Tories were accommodated, it was only at the price of abandoning their colleagues and principles. After George came to the throne in 1714, Tories were dismissed from most posts, in large part because of the alleged sympathy of many with Jacobitism, while parliamentary business was also resolutely partisan. In his *Concise History of England*, John Wesley, who was an opponent of party government, was to criticise George for aligning with political factions, as well as for Hanoverianism.[58]

By turning against the Tories, George encouraged their support for Jacobitism, but the rebellion of 1715-16 in Scotland and northern England was suppressed (and not supported in Ireland), as was a smaller-scale Spanish-backed rising in Scotland in 1719 and subsequent conspiracies. The major Spanish invasion attempt of 1719, with extensive military and naval preparations,[59] was dispersed by storms.

When George died in 1727, there was still much excitement in Continental Europe about the prospect of a Jacobite move.[60] That nothing happened could be attributed to George's legacy in Britain but may have rested more on the Anglo-French alliance. Indeed, the end of that alliance in 1731 led immediately to a serious invasion panic in England, which was a comment on the situation left by George.

Rather than any wholesale Hanoverian takeover, the situation was more like the dual monarchy of nineteenth-century Austria-Hungary. George adapted to British institutions, conforming to the Church of England, despite his strong Lutheranism. Unlike James II and 'James III', George was a pragmatist who was sensible enough to adapt and survive. Lacking the decisiveness, charisma and wiliness of Louis XIV and Peter the Great of Russia, George did not have an impact or win a reputation comparable to either, but their ambitions, and notably the transformative plans of the latter, were out of keeping with his position as well as his temperament.

In 1716, George, Prince of Wales had played a role in the Regency when George I went to Hanover for his first time as King, his views being reported by Townshend, the Secretary of State left behind in London.[61] However, differences between king and heir over position and patronage led to a full-scale breakdown in in the following year, one linked to division within the government. Such quarrels were a classic feature of dynastic politics, the tension between ruler and heir, and between those who looked to one or the other. They were scarcely unique to the Hanoverians (for whom they were very important), as Frederick William I of Prussia, George's nephew and son-in-law, and Victor Amadeus II of Sardinia were later to discover with their own sons, the future Frederick II, the Great, and Charles Emmanuel III respectively. Part of the art of royal politics entailed the ability to handle these tensions. Despite reports to the contrary,[62] the dispute itself was limited, for the Prince of Wales had no intention of trying to turn his father out, as Charles Emmanuel successfully did. Peter the Great had his son Alexis killed, while Frederick William I imprisoned Frederick and made him watch the execution of his close friend. George did not use force of this kind, and it would have been unacceptable in Britain where the law was cited during the 1717 dispute. He failed to build a rapprochement with the Prince of Wales. Instead, George relied on control of patronage to bring his son into line.

Tensions between George and his son, commented upon in 1714,[63] gathered pace in 1716, when George ensured the dismissal of his son's Groom of the Stole and friend, John, 2nd Duke of Argyll, a rival in the army of William Cadogan who enjoyed the King's favour and, unlike Argyll, was close to the Marlborough interest. Thus, the pronounced military factionalism of the War of the Spanish Succession (1702-13) played a role in the post-war world. Quarrels over prominence and patronage in the army were an important strand in the politics of the reign. There was a relationship with foreign policy, not least in the experience of opposition to France in the last two wars. There had been co-operation with Austria, including direct links with Prince Eugene of Savoy, one of the most influential Austrian figures until his death in 1736. Cadogan, who remained a significant figure until replaced by Argyll in 1725, proved close to Austria and unwilling to respond positively to the French alliance.

During his first return to Hanover in 1716, George limited his son's rights as Regent, a conspicuous show of lack of favour or confidence. The Prince attended Cabinet meetings frequently, but Sunderland and the Hanoverian minister Bothmer sent critical reports about what they alleged was his ambition and self-assertion. Despite Argyll's dismissal, the Prince continued to show favour both to him and to his brother, the Earl of Ilay (later a key ally of Walpole and, later still, 3rd Duke of Argyll), angering the King by so doing, ensuring that the belief that George would stay in Hanover until the spring of 1717[64] proved misplaced. Although there was a very tense international situation due to the move of Russian troops into Germany, Sunderland wrote from Göhre about the King's return to England, 'which is of so vast importance to the being of the King's government that whether it be some weeks sooner or later is of small consideration to the main thing of his return.'[65]

Stanhope was clear on the need for George to be present in order for parliamentary government to work, writing back to his counterpart in London about the latter's letter affecting the King's resolution:

> Touching [relating to] his holding the session of Parliament in person or not, it hath given me an opportunity to show His Majesty that his servants in England do not think it possible to carry those things in Parliament which seem absolutely necessary unless countenanced and supported by his presence. I verily believe this will determine him to take the resolution

> we all wish and that his presence will enable us to deal with Mr Lechmere [an opposition Whig] and all his followers.[66]

On his return, George made his displeasure apparent, and the Prince blamed Stanhope and Sunderland for this anger. The Prince's profile had become much higher while his father was away, his friend Charles Cathcart, who was in his household and the army, reporting:

> My master has reaped this benefit from his administration, the impressions that prevailed upon people's minds to his disadvantage are sufficiently removed, he is honoured and loved by those who have been most with him, more than can be expressed. The concern he showed the other night at the fire has done him great service in the City.[67]

The Prince had helped encourage firefighting operations and had authorised £1000 to help those who had lost out during 'the late dreadful fire'.[68]

Efforts to effect a reconciliation between father and son after the 1717 parliamentary session failed. Instead, George I made efforts to improve his image. He did not immediately travel back to Hanover, as had been widely predicted, but stayed in Britain, dispensing hospitality at Hampton Court on a scale unprecedented in his reign, Handel's *Water Music* being a by-product of royal display and hospitality. Assisted by his ministers, George actively wooed prominent politicians during his trip to Cambridge and Newmarket that October.

Difficulties climaxed in November 1717, in a dispute over the christening of Prince George's second son, George William (1717-18): George I had wanted the baby named George, while the Princess, Caroline of Ansbach, who was worried by a prediction about the name being dangerous, favoured William, a name she thought would also be more agreeable to the British nation.[69] Despite St George, George was seen as a German name. Moreover, the Prince and Princess sought as a godfather the Prince's uncle, George I's youngest brother, Ernst August, Prince – Bishop of Osnabrück and, also, from 1716, Duke of York. The King insisted on the choice of Thomas, Duke of Newcastle, the Lord Chamberlain, whom the Prince detested.

After the christening on 28 November 1717, the easily flustered Newcastle was convinced that the Prince had threatened him, and the King took the matter in hand, in part for political reasons. The dispute rapidly led to the expulsion of the Prince from St James's, and his establishment of a rival court at Leicester House. George I took charge of his grandchildren, who, he insisted, must remain at St James's, an insistence for which he gained legal support, which helped entrench and publicise the disagreement. The dispute earned the King much criticism, especially when the young George William died, although, according to the Austrian diplomat Johann, Freiherr von Pentenrriedter, the nobility – unused to the treatment Newcastle had received – favoured the King.[70]

George insisted that no one could hold offices in his own or his son's households and be received in both. The King's commitment to his ministers was linked to that of the opposition Whigs and the Prince. John, Lord Perceval noted that 'the Walpolites' were increasingly seen as 'the Prince's party'.[71] In April 1718, James Craggs, one of the Secretaries of State, wrote to Stair drawing attention to a crisis wider than Jacobitism:

> I perceive you still harp on a string which I begin to think will never produce harmony, the reconciliation in the Royal family. You say very truly how necessary it is, I wish I do not say as truly how improbable? ... the people of one Court place all their happiness in the distress of another, and I fear that all our treaties being broke and all the ill consequences of such a rapture would not only be good news to the Jacobites.[72]

There had been no real equivalent to this situation in the reigns of William III or Anne, as the division between Courts did not then exist. Rumours swirled, James, Duke of Liria, a Spanish general, writing to his father, James, Marshal-Duke of Berwick, the illegitimate son of James II and VII:

> I am very glad of Mr George falling out with his son and wish it may last long, but I believe there is something more in that business than ill words to the Duke of Newcastle and that the Prince is very capable of making a party to turn George out and put himself in his place.[73]

Perceval observed:

> In a difference of this nature you may believe everybody takes part as their interest, inclination or obligations lead him. Those in places or in pursuit of them justify the King in all. The disappointed, hopeless, and all who apprehend themselves ill-used do the same by the Prince with whom the Tories generally range, and also many whose good nature has been stirred.

The last was an oblique reference to how the Prince and Princess had been forced to leave their children.[74]

Prior to the rift in the royal family, Sunderland had remarked, 'Upon the whole, I don't doubt, but the King's steadiness will carry it.'[75] This was to be seen as a key element in the 1716-20 crisis and contrasted with uncertainty over George's views about those vying for his favour in 1723 and, to a lesser degree, 1726-7. In 1718, George was engaged in politics, asking, for example, how legislation was received in Scotland.[76]

The rift made it more likely that the Prince would support the opposition openly in Parliament, so it was fortunate for the ministry that Parliament was not yet in session. Bonet, the Prussian envoy, attributed the crisis in Parliament to one at Court, reporting a serious division of opinion over the treatment of the Prince. According to Bonet, the Lord Chancellor, Lord Cowper, the Lord

Privy Seal, the Duke of Kingston, the Lord Steward, the Duke of Kent and possibly Stanhope also, fearing a government defeat in Parliament, attempted to restrict the Prince's control of the funds allocated for the upbringing of his children. At the same time, as a reminder of the variety of possible developments, they sought to bring about a reconciliation between the King and his son through the mediation of Spencer Compton, the Speaker of the House of Commons, who was also Treasurer to the Prince and his leading parliamentary advisor. This course was said to have been opposed by Sunderland, Cadogan and Bernstorff. Rejecting the report that George might oblige the Prince to go to Hanover, Bonet went on to write that there were tensions within the ministry and that Cowper might resign.[77] There was also speculation about the possibility of a reconstitution of the ministry to include some Tories, a course that might be forwarded via Bernstorff.[78]

The failure to effect a reconciliation in the royal family had serious consequences in Parliament. There the Prince's supporters continued to vote with the opposition while the Prince regularly attended the House of Lords.[79] Responding to ministerial pressure,[80] George, despite his hopes of a visit, did not go to Hanover[81] and instead, spent the summer at Hampton Court. His public socialising had been displayed earlier in the year at Court, as with the great ball held on Twelfth Night on 6 January, a widely reported occasion attended by many aristocrats at which George played cards.[82] Gambling was a feature of Court life, *The Weekly Journal* of 22 February 1718 reporting that on the 17th, 'the King played at ombre with the Duchess of Monmouth and the Countess of Lincoln, and lost 3000 guineas.' The dispute affected the ministry's confidence in pursuing legislative business and encouraged the distribution of benefits to ensure support. In 1719, however, against the wishes of his British ministers, George felt able to go to Hanover as 'nothing happens to prevent him.'[83]

The Whig Split played a role in the way in which George's reign became part of the collective memory, being used, subsequently, by critics to argue that Hanoverian influences were to the fore. The

Protester on 21 July 1753, considered 'the bias of the Court to be wholly German.'[84] At the time, experienced British diplomats, such as Charles Whitworth in Berlin, felt that the orders they received from George via the German Chancery contradicted those from British ministers.[85]

In 1720, however, there was an end to the rift between King and Prince, an outcome in which Walpole played a part through the offices of Princess Caroline,[86] promising to make the Prince act as his father thought appropriate. Meanwhile, Stanhope and Sunderland brought George round, in part through the Duchess of Kendal. This reconciliation related to the state of the Civil List, the parliamentary grant to the Crown, which had been overspent. Ending the Whig Split would help ensure that the accumulated debt was paid off by Parliament,[87] which would greatly assist George's finances. As a precursor to the reconciliation, George's leading Hanoverian minister, Baron Bernstorff, who had accompanied him from London to Hanover in 1719, did not return to London. In a reminder of the key role of George in the working of the Anglo-Hanoverian polity, James, Viscount Stanhope had written about Bernstorff from Hanover:

> I cannot promise that the old man will be left behind but I may safely assure your Grace that though he should come the King will do whatever shall be proposed to him [George] to make everybody sensible that he [Bernstorff] is not to meddle in English business.[88]

This was seen as a key development, one that reflected George's significance, Newcastle reporting that November that the King

> ... has told Mr Bernsdorff and all the rest of the Germans, that if ever they pretend in any manner whatsoever to meddle in English affairs, he will turn them out of his service, and have nothing more to do with them. This the King has ordered us to tell everybody, and the fact is, the Germans have no more

> interest with him than the subjects of any other nation... This surely must be reckoned a great and very honest point gained by a ministry, that has the whole Jacobite party against them joined by that of the P— [Prince]. The world will now be convinced how scandalous those reports were that the administration were supported by the Germans, when the fact always was that the Germans would have done whatever laid in their power to have destroyed it, and betrayed them to the P— and his party. In short, it is impossible to say how resolved he is to support his servants and the Whig Party.[89]

Berndorff was compensated in part with money from the Irish Exchequer. That year, Craggs objected to the repeated need to find money for 'the filling of a new purse'.[90] This element of corruption[91] has been underplayed in recent discussions of George. It was less obvious under George II and far less prominent under George III.

On 23 April 1720, the Prince made his submission to his father at Court, and, next day, the opposition Whigs followed. Walpole took a major role in arranging the parliamentary dimension. On 6 May, he steered the Bill for tackling the Civil List debt through the Commons. This success demonstrated both Walpole's place in the new political system and his value to the government. Walpole had not only been reconciled with the King and ministry, but also publicly broken with the Tories who, understandably, did not respond positively to the reconciliation. Indeed, party government now reigned supreme with the Whigs, and ideas of a mixed ministry were shunted aside. The Tories were now far less significant in Parliament. On 11 June 1720, Walpole was made Paymaster-General, a post he had already held in 1714-15, with the agreement that he should become First Lord of the Treasury at the earliest opportunity, as occurred in 1721. The return of Walpole brought in his allies, with places found if necessary in the Royal Household. Paul Methuen, who had resigned as a Secretary of State with Walpole in 1717, became Comptroller of the

Household in 1720, moving on in 1725, when he was also made a Knight of the Bath, to become the Treasurer of the Household.

So 1720 brought reconciliations of a sort, although there was still the need to overcome the financial scandal of the South Sea Company that year, and to thwart the Jacobite Atterbury Plot in 1722. George was Governor of the Company, and the crash of what had basically become a fraudulent financial conspiracy was widely seen, and presented, as a crisis that exposed the corruption of the governing order. George had not paid for the South Sea shares he held and, like other prominent people, had taken them as bribes to promote the Company. As part of a lager pattern,[92] the Duchess of Kendal and George's half-sister, Sophia Charlotte von Kielmansegg, later Countess of Darlington, received large amounts of stock.[93] Hanoverian ministers asked for South Sea shares, encouraged by the reports of the money made by compatriots.[94] With the crash, George lost his prospects of massive winnings from the rise in his shares, but still made a gain of £45,304 from the crisis, a very significant sum.

Furthermore, when George visited Hanover as in 1723, 1725 and 1727, his son was still not left as regent in Britain, his understandable anger at this public slight being reported by diplomats.[95] George also turned down his son's request for a military post in any European conflict that might involve Britain, a situation that seemed in prospect in 1725-7. This was a punitive step given his military experience prior to 1714, including, allegedly, in 1727 when he was refused both an army command and permission to go as a volunteer.[96] The two men had been reconciled but only to the extent of a mutual coldness. There was little sign of any difference of opinion over policy, but they were reported as not speaking to each other.[97]

In his last years, George showed both political skills and a sense of responsibility. He was no incompetent and unyielding monarch threatening the end of Hanoverian rule in Britain. George also remained active, indeed the most active in his last years of all the Hanoverian monarchs, although George II was also active to the end. The ministerial correspondence covering George's visit to Hanover in 1725 shows the King playing an active role in scrutinising documents and mediating governmental decisions, although his knowledge of English was limited, and translation and the use of French and German were important throughout the reign. George's visits to Hanover in 1723 and 1725 also saw bouts of diplomatic activity in which he played a major role.

Meanwhile, the degree to which there were divisions within the Whig élite gave George opportunities for manoeuvre, though he could be pressed to part with ministers and courtiers who aroused the concern of their colleagues. Thus, in 1726, George was successfully pressed to part with Cadogan, his leading military advisor.[98] The division of foreign policy between two Secretaries of State provided further opportunity for royal influence. In 1724, the political impact of this division was lessened when George replaced John, Lord Carteret by Newcastle, who was aligned with Walpole and Townshend. The previous year, Townshend had informed Walpole from Hanover that George's preferences were now thoroughly welcome. Thus, Bernstorff was

> ... waiting in vain for an invitation to come hither and not daring to come without. The King is determined to remove Lord Midleton whenever you think it for the service ... our campaign on this side of the water has been much more successful than I dared to promise myself.[99]

Alan, 1st Viscount Midleton, Lord Chancellor of Ireland, was involved in the contentious dispute over a patent for manufacturing copper coinage for Ireland, a patent sold for £10,000 by the Duchess of Kendal to William Wood, a Wolverhampton ironmaster. This led to a controversy that threw discredit on the British connection.

George expected to be kept informed about diplomatic dispatches. In 1718, Stair in Paris was instructed by the Secretary of State to send material 'by every post because His Majesty who gives the greatest attention to your dispatches never fails to express some uneasiness when a mail comes without anything from you.' George received French translations of the dispatches.[100] George also had physical possession of key diplomatic material, including that communicated by foreign envoys, such that he was in a position to give instructions.[101] In 1719, Craggs informed Stair 'The King having still under consideration your weighty dispatches. I should wait for His Majesty's resolutions thereupon.'[102] George could still be kept in the dark by private correspondences between ministers and diplomats, but this practice, of which he was doubtless aware, did not lead to any collapse of royal support for the ministry. Ministerial correspondence makes the King's views and reasoning apparent, and he comes through as a man of considerable intelligence, not least in distinguishing the practice from the rhetoric of diplomacy. He spoke fluent German and French, his Latin was good, and he knew some Italian and Dutch. In 1719, Craggs wrote to Stair:

> The King observes from your Excellency's letters a continual suspicion, that the French do not act openly and above-board ... therefore His Majesty will be very cautious how he puts all his affairs into their hands... However, the King would have Your Excellency give them very good words, assure them of his desire to take them along with him.[103]

George's interest in the army led in 1727 to a senior Dutch minister telling the British envoy that he wanted to see such an army in the Netherlands 'as might be worthy to be commanded by His Majesty',[104] which would help provide security for the Dutch. There were indeed rumours that year that George would command an army, while Horatio Walpole suggested that he use his trip to Hanover in 1727 to concert strategy with Continental figures.[105] In 1725, George Tilson, an experienced Under Secretary, remarked of the visit by a Prussian minister to see George at Göhrde, 'One conference is worth a hundred letters.'[106] George had a longstanding experience of international relations that Anne had lacked (and which most of his ministers lacked as well), not least through military service and by meeting prominent figures abroad. Anne never left southern England. Another contrast was provided by George's concern with the marriage of his descendants, his son's children. This pushed relations with the Houses of Hohenzollern and Orange to the fore.

A successful warrior against the French in the 1670s, 1690s and 1700s, and the Turks in 1683-5, George was an enthusiastic rider and eager hunter. Just as he had a preference for the aristocracy over commoners, so George appointed officers and former officers as diplomats, including Stair, William Stanhope, Charles De Bourgay and Richard Sutton, and favoured foreign diplomats of military background such as Count Broglie and General Diemar. He looked with favour on courtiers and ministers who had extensive military service, notably James, Viscount Stanhope, who found George 'extremely good to me'.[107] This preference was a tendency that was subsequently to wane, although still be apparent with his son. George I's awareness of strategy and operational factors was shown in the international crisis of 1726-7 when military moves were considered.[108]

George was far from being a militaristic dolt. He had cultural and intellectual interests, including an active engagement with the scientific research of the Royal Society. George was keen to understand developments in physics, a field made fashionable by Newton. He wanted his granddaughters inoculated against smallpox. George planned the University at Göttingen, something brought to fruition during the reign of his son, and in 1724 founded the Regius Professorships in Modern History at the Universities of Cambridge and Oxford, in part to help educate diplomats.

George's reputation as a supporter of toleration, seen in his attempt to ease the position of Dissenters, can be related to enlightened ideas as well as to prudential political considerations, since such 'outsiders' tended to vote Whig, and encouraged Voltaire to dedicate his *Henriade* to him in 1727. When Voltaire took refuge in Britain, he was helped by George.

The leading London Whig tri-weekly newspaper, *The Flying-Post: or The Postmaster*, in its issue of 9 October 1714, offered verses on George's recent Declaration in Council that made the King appear a rational thinker as well as an enlightened leader. After a comparison with Classical Greece, came this encomium:

So on King George, as through the streets he rode,
Almost adored by us as a God;
Our eager eyes with joyful hearts we place,
Liking the features of his royal face;
Yet curious still we waited till he spoke,
To know the soul in that majestic look:
This declaration shows complete the King,
And tells the blessings which his reign will bring.

Nineteen days later, in another instance of depicting George as people wanted him to be rather than as he was, there was a poem to celebrate the coronation:

Advance, great monarch, in majestic state,
An able head supports the glorious weight:
But underneath that stately towering prize,
A greater weight, all Europe's safety, lies.
We now the gold and jewels cease to view,
And find the truest jewel lodged in you;
The Crown no brightness to the monarch brings,
The Crown takes lustre from the best of kings.

The issue of 11 June 1715 included a poem on how the accession had banished the eclipse of national honour, religion and liberties associated with the Toryism of Anne's later years, ending: 'To give Britannia once more light and day, / And drive her former darkness quite away.'

The remorseless character of this poetry shows how verses were used to express political allegiance in a bridging of partisanship with established tunes and rhythms. The issue of 16 June 1715 included, as many other verses did, a helpful direction as to the tune. 'A lamentation for the Late Times. To the Tune of, To you fair Ladies now at hand', offered as its last verse:

> Then God preserve our brave King George,
> And all his royal race;
> And may all those who dare to forge
> A papist for his place,
> O, may all men who have such views,
> O, may they die in wooden shoes.

A keen supporter of the fashionable Italian opera in London, George was a lavish patron of George Frideric Handel, whom he had appointed *Kapellmeister* at Hanover in 1710, and who had been awarded £200 annually for life by Queen Anne as a reward for his birthday ode of 1713 and for his thanksgiving for the Peace of Utrecht of that year. There is a popular story that Handel had deserted Hanover for England, and that George only became reconciled to him because of the quality of the *Water Music*, but this is inaccurate: in the early years of the reign, Handel remained in royal favour. Once George had come to the throne, Handel taught his granddaughters, and in 1723 was appointed a composer to the Chapel Road.

An assiduous supporter of opera, George attended 22 performances out of a possible 45 at the King's Theatre Haymarket in the 1714-15 season, 17 out of 29 in that of 1715-16, and 13 or 14 out of 25 in 1716-17. His annual subscription to the Royal Academy of Music founded in 1719-20, which was intended to produce Italian operas, was £1,000, and in the 1725-6 season he went to the opera 28 times, and 1726-7, attended many performances of Handel's *Admeto* in its opening season. In *Admeto*, King Admetus of Thessaly is saved by a loving wife, which was scarcely the case with George. The performance history was less happy as the two principal female singers, Faustina

Bordoni and Francesca Cuzzoni, both great singers, clashed on stage and were supported by audience factions. Handel was Music Director of the Royal Academy of Music.

Far from living a retired life as was claimed, for example, by the Jacobite Philip, Duke of Wharton in 1725, George also liked concerts and masquerades, being ready to resist repeated Church pressure against the latter. Interested in building, he was responsible for extensive work on Kensington Palace, including the completion and decoration of new state rooms and the remodelling of the grounds, where he liked to take long evening walks.

After having initially pursued a very divisive foreign policy, and accordingly coming to support ministers with divisive domestic views, George eventually, in the 1720s, helped to make the political system work effectively, bringing a valuable measure of political stability. The King played a formal role in the patronage process but one that was of consequence. Richard Arundell, an MP appointed Surveyor of the King's Works from 1726, wrote that year about Sir Thomas Hewet's death,

> upon which Sir Robert Walpole recommended me to the King, who has consented to give me his employment. Great endeavours have been used to make [William] Kent Comptroller, though to no effect, and he [Sir Robert] told me yesterday that he was obliged to make Ripley Comptroller to obviate the Duke of Devonshire's recommendation ... and that he had spoken to the King to put Kent into Ripley's employment, which was agreed to.[109]

George faced a major international crisis toward the end of the reign, with the confrontation in 1725-7 between the alliances of Hanover and Vienna threatening both Britain and Hanover with invasion (Britain was allied with France and opposed by Austria and Spain, which in 1726 won over Prussia from its alliance with Britain and France). The crisis threatened the Hanoverian order in Britain, with the prospect that the outbreak of war would lead to the recognition of 'James III and VIII'.[110] George took a detailed interest in the crisis and its international permutations.[111] Moreover, from 1726, there was a renewal in opposition parliamentary and press activity within Britain, with the opposition linked to the Austrian envoy.

Had the King died in 1726, then the situation would have seemed very bleak. George's father, Ernst August (1622-98), had lived to be nearly 70, older than George would be when he died, and Ernst August's health only began to fail in 1695. However, 1726 saw the death both of Maximilian Wilhelm, one of George's two surviving younger brothers, and of his divorced wife, Sophia Dorothea. George was one of six boys and one girl, none of whom lived as long as he did: three of the brothers died in battle comparatively young and the other two died not long beyond 60. The instructions to the French envoy in March 1726 noted that opponents of the alliance between Britain and France made no secret of their hope that George's death would bring changes.

The threat of attack from Austria, Prussia and Russia posed major challenges to Hanoverian security, which underlined Walpole's value to George, as Parliament rejected in February 1726 the opposition argument that the international crisis might lead to a war to defend Hanover, which would be a breach of the Act of Settlement of 1701. Instead, the ministry moved a motion promising George support if Hanover was attacked, which was carried by 285 to 107. George was 'overjoyed'.[112] He also sought to keep his allies in line, pressing their envoys accordingly to show the firmness he did.[113]

That George's position was seen as of great importance acts as a corrective to the assumption that he was somehow trapped by the rise of party, and in particular his reliance on Whigs, more specifically Walpole. Diplomats critical of government policy felt it worth trying to approach George through Hanoverian intermediaries, including the Duchess of Kendal, Friedrich von Fabrice, his Chamberlain, Bothmer, and Wolfenbüttel figures. George's Continental connections and diplomatic experience gave him at least some measure of independence from his ministers, who were also dependent on him. Under George I and George II a lot of the focus was on foreign policy, far less on domestic concerns beyond political manoeuvring and faction. This was important to the larger discussion of how these kings ruled, and it changed under George III from the early 1760s as foreign policy became less prominent, domestic and imperial policies more so. A sense of the significance of George I's presence in Hanover in 1725 can be glimpsed in a letter sent by Walpole from Richmond to Newcastle on his Sussex estate:[114]

> I was this moment interrupted in my diversions here with the inclosed pacquett [of documents] from Hanover, and as your Grace will see there is no possibility of my being your deputy to execute the King's commands, which I think cannot be delayed or should not be delayed an hour. I have ordered a set of horses to be at Grinstead this night... Pray be with us tomorrow night.[115]

In February 1727, Marshal Berwick, the illegitimate son of James II and a leading French general, remarked of the hostile Alliance of Vienna and Hanover: 'The King's dominions will be the first, and the most vigorously, attacked.'[116] However, the British opposition failed to mount a successful parliamentary challenge, while the international crisis moved toward negotiations rather than war. The easing of the mood was palpable. There were rumours of George breaking with Walpole, but they lacked weight. The febrile atmosphere that had surrounded the unsuccessful attempts by the Austrian envoy to establish a *secret du roi* or personal pro-Austrian diplomacy for George dissipated.

George II came to the throne in propitious circumstances, with Jacobitism weak and most of the Tories ready to join in a peaceful competition with the Whigs for royal favour. In part, this reflected a sense that he was more pro-British than the pro-Hanoverian George I.[117] Indeed, the response to the new King, which included

Tory peers going to Court to kiss his hand as a declaration of loyalty, was a clear comment on his predecessor. Edward Cooke, an Irish Tory, wrote from London:

> The people, as far as I can observe ... fancy they have got an English King again or at least one that has an aversion for foreigners, which is about half the character of a true Englishman. The Tories are all at Court to a man, and most graciously received... Not a word but English now at court, and a certain jeweller having shown the King a diamond of great value, and addressed him in French, His Majesty desired him to speak English for he had much rather hear him in that language.[118]

GEORGE II

When the Royal Couple came approximately in the middle of the Square [in front of Westminster Hall] ... these Cries of Joy began: 'Vivat, God bless the King, Vivat, God bless the Queen!,' by which all Men-Folk waved their hats, and all the Ladies their white scarves ... I forgot to swing my Hat myself, whereupon I got a Jolt in the Back from behind, and somebody started shouting 'Jacobite,' so I didn't hesitate to take off my Hat and swing it too... On one of these Benches I had my seat, but I had to take this Seat in the Evening at 7 o'clock before the Coronation day, stay there all night, and again till the next evening at 7 o'clock, because otherwise I could not have come there, and no one could get up from his Seat without fear of being thrown headlong into the Crowd, therefore one had to supply one's Pockets with something to quench one's Hunger and Thirst, and when you had to get rid of the Water, you have to cover yourself with your clothes and let it run down the Footboard, which was pierced with Holes, but the Rest you had to keep within you all the time.

Claus Seidelin, Coronation of George, 1727[1]

... to represent to the King the present state of the House of Commons, the difficulties attending this session, and

> the impossibility of operating without some solid settled consistent plan... That it is by no means proposed to engage His Majesty to anything, but only to learn upon what terms His Majesty may have the assistance of those who may be of use to his service.
>
> Duke of Newcastle, memorandum, 'State of the House of Commons', 18 April 1755.[2]

George II (r. 1727-60) had much in common with his father: his commitment to Hanover, warrior ethos, conflict with his son, and need to resist the Jacobite challenge. Yet, his reign was different. First, it was far longer; because he succeeded at a younger age and lived longer. Had George only reigned for as many years as his father then he would have died in 1740 and been succeeded by Frederick. If he had lived as long as George I, he would have died in 1750. In both cases, there would have been none of the triumphs from 1758 in the Seven Years' War of 1756-63, triumphs that ensured that George died bathed in glory.

The combination of his peaceful succession and the eventual failure both of Jacobite insurrection and of repeated French invasion attempts created a new basis for the understanding of the Hanoverian dynasty as the British monarchy, and a greatly successful one at that. This issue of the identification of dynasty and monarchy, and of dynasty with individual monarch, was highly significant to the practical grip of monarchical ideology, both in particular contexts and in the longer-term developments that helped cement the significance of the Hanoverian dynasty for British history.

Nevertheless, George II's reign saw a highpoint of concerns and tensions about the Anglo-Hanoverian link. In January 1737, a French agent reported on the widespread and unprecedented popular anger about George's absence in Hanover, with posters and seditious jokes daily,[3] while seven years later, Charles, 3rd Duke of Marlborough claimed in the House of Lords: 'It is not possible to mention Hanover, or its inhabitants, in any public place, without putting the whole house into a flame, and hearing on every hand expressions of resentment, threats of revenge, or clamours of detestation.'[4]

George Dodington was blunt in October 1743 when planning opposition tactics:

> I should think this a time to unite ourselves to the People by some signed Declaration of Standing by each other in certain constitutional points, and then, while the present impression is strong, and the partiality glaring, both to people and army, to move a separation of Hanover for ever. It must come to that, one day or another, or this nation must sink.[5]

Indeed, the Hanoverian link was to the fore when George I died in 1727, felled by a stroke and dying at Osnabrück on 11 June (22 June new style), en route for Hanover, his destination of choice throughout his reign. Bad news travelled fast. On Wednesday 14 June, towards 3pm, the news reached Whitehall. Walpole gave orders to double the guard throughout London and then left for Richmond, to inform George, Prince of Wales that his father had died. The following morning, George was proclaimed King as George II.

George's accession in 1727 was completely peaceful, but in 1745 he would face the most serious crisis of any for the Hanoverian dynasty. Having totally defeated the British army in Scotland at Prestonpans, Jacobite forces under Charles Edward Stuart (Bonnie Prince Charlie) invaded England via Carlisle and advanced toward London as far as Derby, reaching it on 4 December. They then turned back but were not defeated until the following April. The battle of Culloden in 1746 was very much a dynastic clash, reminiscent in many respects of the Wars of the Roses. Charles Edward Stuart, the elder grandson of James II and VII, was defeated by William, Duke of Cumberland, the younger son of George.

Throughout his reign, much of George's energy was directed to politics, where the King repeatedly felt boxed in. Yet, he was capable of change. Having shown scant favour to Walpole in the mid-1720s, George was widely expected in 1727 to back Spencer Compton for first minister, his Treasurer and the Speaker of the Commons since 1715. Instead, he rapidly came to support Walpole, Newcastle writing in his own hand on 20 June: 'The King is extremely civil to us, and as to foreign affairs, I firmly believe determined to go on in the same measures, as he has assured the Court of France and particularly the Cardinal in a letter from himself.'[6]

Tory hopes of favour proved mistaken, with George continuing the hostility noted in 1714.[7] The accession of a new monarch meant that Parliament had to be summoned, the Civil List (the annual grant paid to the Crown by Parliament) settled, and elections held for a new Parliament. With his proven track record as a parliamentary manager, Walpole made himself extremely useful, securing an enlarged Civil List of £800,000, an unprecedented sum for the start of a reign, as well as the largest jointure any Queen had ever enjoyed for Caroline, a sum Compton was apparently unwilling to seek. Thanks to this and other episodes, George was to acquire a reputation for being inordinately concerned about money. In 1732, he was accused of leaving places vacant in order to profit from the salaries.[8] The criticism of George II for being tightfisted can be misplaced, as in 1752 when his reluctance to spend more money to win the support of the German princes for the Imperial Election Scheme, a reluctance dismissed by Newcastle as 'for a trifle',[9] was fully vindicated by the very changeable nature of the political circumstances as well as the political sensitivity of these sums in Parliament.

In the general election of 1727, Walpole made full use of government interest in the boroughs, as well as of secret service money. After the election petitions were heard, the new House of Commons consisted of 415 ministerial supporters, 15 opposition Whigs, and 128 Tories, a government majority of 272, the largest since George I's accession in 1714. The comparable figures after the 1722 election were 389 Whigs and 169 Tories, a majority of 220.

Bar Compton, those close to George II as Prince of Wales were aristocrats such as the Earl of Scarborough who lacked much governmental or parliamentary experience, and none was a great borough patron. William Pulteney, the leading opposition Whig in the Commons, offered to help George obtain a major addition to the Civil List, only to be rejected, to be refused permission to stand for Parliament in the Court interest in the conspicuous seat of Westminster, and to be very coldly received. Charles Delafaye, an experienced official, felt able to adopt a relaxed tone in 1729: '... nor was ever king better pleased with his servants or more determined to continue his favour to them, and indeed more sensible of the injustice done them by the authors and abettors of those libels,'[10] the last a reference to the opposition press.

Rather than losing political significance during the reign, George achieved greater standing. The resignation in 1730 of Charles, 2nd Viscount Townshend as Secretary of State for the Northern Department, responsible for Northern Europe, while in some respects unwelcome to George, removed a highly experienced minister who had been Secretary of State for that Department from 1714 to 1716 and 1721 to 1730. Townshend shared George's interest in German politics and his views on Austrian policy. However, Townshend was inclined to be his own man and had fallen out with Walpole. Townshend's successor, William Stanhope, who held the post from 1730 to 1742 and 1744 to 1746, and became first Lord Harrington (1730) and, later, Earl of Harrington (1742), proved more pliable. George's favour for him was shown in Stanhope's appointment as Vice-Chamberlain of the Household from 1727 to 1730. The two men shared an interest in military matters that Townshend had not shared with George. Stanhope had fought in the War of the Spanish Succession, served as a colonel thereafter, and while Secretary of State also proceeded up the military hierarchy, becoming a Major-General in 1735 and a Lieutenant-General in 1739, finishing as a full General in 1747.

This was very much a minister in George's image and enjoying his favour, and it is significant that Horatio Walpole was not appointed, instead, as Secretary of State in 1730. While, like Harrington, well-experienced in diplomacy, Horatio was more opinionated and active in pressing his ideas,[11] less of a courtier, and did not have a military background. He was also prepared to keep George in the dark and was keen that confidential correspondence should not be read by him.[12] There was no warmth between Horatio and George. Yet it is striking that in 1747, Horatio, who had got to know George more when an acting Secretary of State, accompanying George to Hanover, was better able to assess the King than his more frequently quoted nephew, Horace Walpole. He observed that he 'has indeed an excellent understanding, sees things at first view, in the fullest, and clearest light'.[13] Less positively, Giuseppe Ossorio, who observed the King closely during a long embassy (1730-48), thought him honourable but overly prone to agree with whichever of his friends spoke to him last,[14] which contradicts the view that George was unchangeable, indeed was stubborn.[15]

Thomas, Duke of Newcastle, the Secretary of State for the Southern Department from 1724 to 1748, was less amenable than Harrington, and less pliable for both George and Walpole. In part, this was because Newcastle's frenetic and highly anxious personality did not lend itself to stable working relationships. A number of ministerial colleagues were to suffer accordingly, including Walpole in 1742 and Carteret in 1744.[16] In 1739, in a fair assessment that, typically, did not lead to any improvement, Newcastle admitted confidentially: 'My temper is such that I am often uneasy and peevish, and, perhaps, what may be called wrong-headed, to my best friends.'[17] Horace Walpole didn't mince his words, describing him as 'a Secretary of State without intelligence, a duke without money, a man of infinite intrigue, without secrecy or policy, and a minister despised and hated by his master, by all parties and ministers'.

Allowing for his tendency to exaggerate, the closeness between King and minister can be gauged by Newcastle's observation in a 'private' letter of 1747: 'the King, who daily sees and knows that I am the only man that has any hopes or expectations left' from the war.[18]

Although George, as Prince of Wales, and Newcastle had clashed seriously in 1717, the Duke appreciated the need to be accommodating once George became King. Moreover, he lacked George's direct knowledge of European developments and preferred to focus on electoral (not Electoral) politics, in other words British, not Hanoverian, affairs, a choice that suited the King. Newcastle did not go abroad until 1748, when he accompanied George to Hanover. This was a task Newcastle had always hitherto left to his co-Secretary of State, preferring to follow his annual practice of visiting his landed and electoral base of Sussex when George went to Hanover, an instructive preference.

George enjoyed considerable room for manoeuvre in foreign policy. It was not that his Secretaries of State lacked opinions of their own, and Newcastle, a major borough-patron (unlike Harrington), had a domestic personal political position of considerable weight. However, neither man was eager to push George in directions he did not wish to travel. Newcastle, intense and alarmist in his approach to foreign as well as domestic politics, was the most inclined to do so of the two. Nevertheless, the very concern with the domestic political situation, including at Court, that led Newcastle to try to dissuade George from certain policies, also left him disinclined to clash with the King unless the latter backed a minister or policy that would engender domestic political resistance. George's endorsement of Hanoverian neutrality in 1741 and his support for Carteret in 1744 were prime instances of such challenges as they threatened parliamentary support for the government. Newcastle learned to be careful of the King's moods, writing in 1755 to the Secretary of State with George in Hanover: 'I am sure you will take a lucky moment when *we* are in good humour, to lay the letters before the King.'[19]

Although Walpole managed George, the King also directed him. As a result of the politics of the Whig Split of 1717-20, when

George, then as Prince of Wales, had joined Walpole in opposing George I and his ministers, George II, who had then frequently attended debates in the House of Lords,[20] understood the significance of Parliament and the importance of its management. Yet, his appreciation of the place of Parliament did not mean that the monarch had no independent role in foreign policy. Far from it.

It is not easy to judge the King because, like his father and his two sons, Frederick, Prince of Wales and William, Duke of Cumberland, and very much unlike his grandson, George III, George II left few letters. As a result, his role largely emerges through the accounts of others. For the 1730s, the most influential have been the idiosyncratic memoirs of John, Lord Hervey, a courtier close to the Queen. Hervey disliked the King and treated him as a fool. As Hervey wrote well and is eminently quotable, his view has tended to prevail. This is ironic as the King was more experienced politically than Hervey, and notably so in foreign policy, of which Hervey had no experience.

Hervey's views have been made more credible because a similar approach was taken by others, including Bishop Hoadly, as well as another key source of memoirs, Horace Walpole, 4th Earl of Orford, the youngest son of Sir Robert Walpole. Horace Walpole is a major source for the 1750s, but he lacked the political experience of his father and, indeed, George, and was motivated in large part by malice, not least towards his own uncle Horatio as well as towards George and Newcastle. Horace Walpole was particularly poorly informed about foreign policy. However, his account has been read as a confirmation of the earlier judgements of Hervey.

In practice, George was the central figure in the politics of foreign policy, a politics that was dynastic as well as personal, for example in his suspicion of Frederick II, even when they were allies.[21] This centrality is underrated if attention is devoted to relevant archival sources left by his ministry, sources which focus on the office correspondence of the Secretaries of State. Instead, the monarch's role emerges more clearly from the private correspondence of ministers, notably Newcastle, and, even more, from the comments of foreign envoys, although, in turn, the latter may have overrated the role of the King. They spent time with him, sought to establish his views, and credited them with importance. While these elements were all true for the ministers, they had the added concern (and significance), that George did not have, of a frequent engagement with Parliament: George had regular and direct engagements at the opening of sessions, but he was not involved in the debates. The foreign envoys, in contrast, had no formal relationship with Parliament. Thus, the perspective taken and sources employed are of great consequence when evaluating opinions of George, as of each of the kings.

An interesting contrast emerges in the case of Louis XV. It would not have been credible to write of George, as James, 1st Earl Waldegrave, the British envoy, did of Louis in 1740: 'It is more for form's sake that we wait on him than anything else, for with regard to public affairs, our seeing him or not is much the same.'[22] At that stage, Louis appeared to have scant impact on French policy. (Waldegrave himself was an illegitimate descendant of James II, which raised the distrust of the Earl of Bristol that year.)

In 1733, in the aftermath of the Excise Crisis in which Walpole had been forced to withdraw a key piece of legislation, George's backing proved vital in steadying a growing opposition to Walpole at Court and in the House of Lords. Prominent Whig peers were dismissed from their posts for voting with the opposition, and George's clear and public favour helped to intimidate and silence other critics of Walpole. Delafaye, an Under Secretary to Newcastle, reported the King was 'resolved to stand by his minister (and to speak impartially, it is not easy to say how he could have been replaced, particularly with regard to the affairs of the revenue) there was no doing it otherwise than with a high hand.'[23] Between April and June, Bolton, Montrose, Marchmont, Stair and Cobham were dismissed from posts for voting with the opposition in the House of Lords. Chesterfield was sacked as Lord Steward on 13 April, after his three brothers had voted in the Commons against the Excise Bill. Lord Clinton, a Lord of the Bedchamber, was dismissed the same day. In the face of royal disapproval, Harrington, Scarborough and Wilmington proved unwilling to push their opposition to Walpole. The dismissals, therefore, were a significant public show of royal support, although they helped lose Walpole the backing of the clients and allies of those dismissed who sat in the Commons and also adversely affected the results of the 1734 general election, decreasing the government majority.

Despite differing with George over policy in the War of the Polish Succession (1733-5), Walpole retained the support, indeed the affection, of the King. Many attributed such support to Queen Caroline, such as Sarah, Duchess of Marlborough, who claimed 'as long as the Queen lives, Sir Robert will be minister.'[24] That view underplayed George's ability to reach his own decisions, and he supported Walpole not only in successive crises but also after Caroline died in 1737. Newcastle noted then:

> Sir Robert Walpole has seen him [George] often, and nothing can be kinder or more strong than his professions of friendship and regard for him, and dependence upon him, both as a friend and a minister, and if any are so vain as to flatter themselves with any hopes of a change from this fatal incident, upon a supposition of the King's sentiments being different from those of the Queen ... they are extremely mistaken.

Newcastle reported of his own meeting with George: 'It is impossible to show more regard for Sir Robert Walpole.'[25] The close nature of the relationship between George and Walpole was captured in an account given by Walpole to a minister he trusted, the Attorney General, Sir Dudley Ryder, claiming:

> That he had the only confidence with the King with whom he often talked freely. That the King often showed him letters and complaints which he had received privately against him, on which occasions he had frequently told the King that if

> His Majesty had the least imagination that he could be easier in any other minister he should with great satisfaction resign, and he should always endeavour to assist him. But the King always then flew into passions against Sir Robert's enemies.[26]

Having, however, failed to prevent the fall of the Walpole ministry in 1742 after its poor showing in the general election of 1741, George did not want to turn to the opposition Tories to support the ministry and, instead, wished to employ favourites such as John, Lord Carteret, a Secretary of State from 1742 to 1744. The emphasis on Carteret for those years can once again lead to an underplaying of George's role. The King was a key figure, in his own right, as King and, with far greater independence, Elector, and also because he provided Carteret with his support. George was a firm believer in defending his personal position. He showed himself capable of backing Carteret, a minister who did not possess a secure parliamentary position, and of seeking to follow a personal, secret foreign policy, a British version of the French *secret du roi*. Both backing Carteret and seeking to follow a personal foreign policy caused major political problems, and even more so because the two issues were believed to be related.

Serious instability within the ministry resulted, as the Pelhams (Newcastle and Henry Pelham), supported by the retired Walpole, opposed Carteret. This opposition was part of a multi-faceted process of manoeuvring for political advantage, and it made George even more prominent as competing ministers sought his support. George's stance also created major problems within the political nation, where the Hanoverian issue was pushed to the fore in the early 1740s to an extent greater than hitherto in the reign, or, indeed, since the mid-1720s. Thus 'Orator' Henley, who delivered lively soapbox-style harangues in London, claimed on 19 February 1744:

> 'The French fleet appearing upon our coast may be of great service to us by keeping a certain person at home who

> otherwise would run gadding abroad and surrender the nation's money.' Audience about 140. When anything was said that was insolent it was immediately followed with clapping of hands and beating their sticks against the ground in the same manner as is done at the Playhouse.[27]

This was not a one-off, and Henley's audiences included peers, such as William, 2nd Lord Talbot, who will appear anew in chapter six, and MPs. The cost that George as Elector charged for the Hanoverian troops committed to the war led to sarcasm about his generosity, for example from John Tucker MP, a protégé of the opposition politician George Dodington.[28]

Carteret was in opposition from 1730 to 1742 by necessity, not choice, and he had not then assumed the practice of decrying the extent of government authority or criticising the King. Indeed, Carteret was ready to make himself highly agreeable to George by backing his concerns in Continental power politics, not least his worry about the threat to Hanover from Prussia. In return, George saw Carteret not only as a gifted linguist but also as a highly able minister, of great knowledge and energy. This was a sensible view but one that did not capture Carteret's inability to manage colleagues and his marked inadequacy as a political leader, a situation also seen with Bute in 1762-3 and Shelburne in 1782-3. Carteret, who lacked Newcastle's interests as a borough-monger and manager of patronage, devoted much time to foreign policy. This pleased George, but the King also regarded as essential the 'Old Corps' Whigs, those who had wielded power under Walpole, who were implacably opposed to such favourites. George responded with his characteristic mixture of pragmatism and choler. As far as possible, he sought to maintain control of appointments.[29] In 1744-6, George failed in his efforts to keep Carteret in the ministry and then to bring him back, a situation that led to royal wrath[30] and distrust between King and ministers. Walpole, now Earl of Orford, advised that the Pelhams 'must not press the King so much at once, but bring his affection over by degrees'.[31] George's anger was well-known, news of it being spread by the press across the country.[32]

Following his father, diplomacy was a field in which George was particularly diligent, reading documents accordingly,[33] with strong concern about Hanover leading to a personal commitment to suspicious relations toward Austria and Prussia, one that could anger his British ministers. In 1737, Horatio Walpole noted that George was 'still extremely averse to do anything that squints in the least towards favouring the King of Prussia',[34] his brother-in-law Frederick William I. Poor relations continued with his nephew, Frederick II, and ministers frequently referred to George's anxieties about Prussian intentions.[35] They were a matter of concern as, continuing the pattern in 1726-7, Prussian pressure on Hanoverian interests was seen as a means to alienate British opinion from the King, and deliberately so.[36]

George took a close interest in diplomacy throughout his life. There were particular peaks during international crises, for example that of 1733 over the Polish Succession. More generally, diplomatic reports were carefully evaluated, instructions sent accordingly, and foreign envoys questioned, with George able to make intelligent reflections.[37]

There was a standard theme of George being restrained by his ministers, notably Walpole, but far from that view simply reflecting weakness on the part of George, it captured a creative tension in policymaking that was in the nature of a parliamentary monarchy.[38] Moreover, ministerial secret correspondence repeatedly makes it clear that it was not only over Hanoverian interests that George intervened. In 1747, when there was an attempt to negotiate a separate peace with Spain, in part by returning Gibraltar possibly in exchange for Ceuta, the Secretary of State noted: 'Gibraltar ... the King will not suffer to be mentioned either in a public or secret manner, and consequently His Majesty will not leave that matter in a state of discussion at what distance soever.'[39]

From another perspective, George's lengthy visits to Hanover, which were criticised in Britain,[40] as well as repeated public attacks on real or alleged Hanoverian influences and concerns, seriously compromised George's ability to present himself as British, or, rather, given his connections, English. Instead, that role was essentially left to Frederick, Prince of Wales, as well as to politicians able to claim that ground, notably William Pitt the Elder. In Tobias Smollett's *The History and Adventures of an Atom* (1769),[41] George was presented as the hot-headed Got-hama-baba who was devoted to 'the temple of the white horse', the established symbol for the Electorate of Hanover, the heraldic device of the ruling house. This made contentious reference to the 'pale horse' of *Revelations* that carried Death,[42] although, more positively, 'White Horse' chalk landscape figures were popular in the eighteenth century.

The Tory Smollett depicted Pitt as a fickle demagogue who in effect held George prisoner during the Seven Years' War (1756-63) by promising to help Hanover. George was certainly angry about the coastal expeditions against France that Pitt favoured, in part due to the diversion of troops from Germany but also because of the impact of failure on army morale.[43] The King was also associated during that war with instructions for prayers of thanksgiving for victories in Germany by the Army of Observation under Prince Ferdinand of Brunswick.[44]

George was much commented on by foreign diplomats who spoke to the King.[45] A French memorandum of 1744 claimed that George had two dominant passions: avarice and the wish to aggrandise Hanover.[46] Neither would please domestic opinion. George, however, can be difficult to recover as his own sources are limited. Referring to George's row with his eldest son, Frederick, in 1737, Lady Isabella Finch noted 'truth is hard to be come at' (a classic addendum to Elizabeth II's adage that recollections may vary). She also added that the King had less room for financial manoeuvre than his father as he had greater expenses, having a wife and many children.[47]

Keen on military matters and enjoying the company of military men, George participated in the battle of Oudenaarde in 1708 (one of Marlborough's victories), charging the French at the head of the Hanoverian dragoons and having his horse shot from under him, an episode that was to be referred to frequently, by both George and others. Thus, the 1727 Address of the Corporation and 'principal inhabitants' of Chipping Wycombe referred to George then as 'bravely engaged for the preservation of Europe, our religion and liberties'. At Oudenaarde, George fought alongside British units and his engagement with the anti-French cause in the War of the Spanish Succession was seen as soon as he arrived in Britain in 1714, when he complained about the fate of the once-allied Catalans. The French envoy then described him as only breathing war and as talking continually about the troops of the German Princes with which he drew parallels and the necessity of establishing studs to breed cavalry horses, as opposed to the hunters that he felt were useless for war.[48] George was closely linked to John, 2nd Duke of Argyll who had been one of Marlborough's commanders, including at Oudenaarde.

In 1734, during the War of the Polish Succession, rather than wait to settle the conditions of service over which Austria was creating difficulties, George, in a bold move, sent the Hanoverian contingent to the Imperial army to the Rhine at once, in response to reports from General Diemar, the Hesse-Cassel envoy, about the danger of France seizing the Rhineland crossing at Rheinfels.[49]

George commanded forces against the French at Dettingen in 1743, which was a victory, albeit not on the scale of Oudenaarde and one that was to be tarnished by controversy due to his alleged preference for Hanoverian over British troops. George was then 60. The battle brought him welcome prestige, and was applauded in Handel's *Dettingen Te Deum*, performed later that year at St James's Palace. George therefore could be depicted as a providential conqueror like the Biblical kings of Israel celebrated in Handel's oratorios. His father had done nothing to compare. George was delighted by Cumberland's victory at Culloden, which carried on the family's military triumphs: 'I never saw anybody in such glee as the King was this day at the Levee which was much crowded; he complimented the Duke of Argyll upon the behaviour of the Argyllshire men.'[50]

Cumberland was compared to Judas Maccabeus in Handel's oratorio of that name that appeared in 1747 and celebrated the defeat of the Seleucid Empire, with the chorus *See, the Conqu'ring Hero Comes!* soon after added to it.

George did not have battlefield commands after Dettingen, but he remained important at an operational as well as strategic level, notably in the '45, but also for example in sending instructions to the army in the Low Countries during the War of the Austrian Succession.[51] He played a key role in ordering the movement of units, as in ensuring there were sufficient troops in Britain to deter invasion. As the last was in line with the policy of his ministers, it is difficult to determine the direction of influence.[52]

George II was central to the process in which the monarchs sought to ensure professionalism in the military, emphasising competence rather than connections, rewarding success through promotions and honours, the latter linking the victorious conspicuously to the monarchy. Thanks to their personal experience, George I and George II were particularly adept at assessing competence, but under George III, this role was to be taken by his second son, Frederick, Duke of York. Visits to Hanover in 1729, 1732, 1735, 1736, 1741, 1743, 1745, 1748, 1750, 1752 and 1755 provided George II with opportunities to review troops, on which he spent many hours,[53] and also to hunt. Newcastle sent a 'secret' letter from Hanover to his fellow Secretary of State in 1752, noting that George had been delighted at the troop review, adding: 'I never saw the King in better health, or in better spirits.' William Murray was informed 'The King is in high spirits and perfect health and has been so ever since he went.'[54] An official reported in 1755 on his reviews, adding: 'His Majesty we had the satisfaction of seeing there in very good health and spirits, and able to pass many hours of the morning on horseback and on foot without being fatigued.'[55]

A strong constitution, notably physical stamina, was a feature of George I, George II and George III. A less benign account of

George's visits to Hanover, however, was provided by Henry Pelham in 1753, presumably derived from Newcastle as Pelham had not been there. That December, Pelham told Dudley Ryder that George 'passes his time there much in the same manner as here, and without any more spirit or cheerfulness, but gave rather a freer venture to peevishness when he was among his Hanover ministers than here.'[56]

It was alleged in 1755 that George became ill because he was upset at leaving Hanover.[57]

George also enjoyed troop reviews and hunting in Britain, and his troop reviews were public occasions.[58] He had begun doing so earlier in life, reviewing troops when George I was in Hanover.[59] George was very interested in military news from abroad,[60] questioning the Sardinian envoy in 1753 about French troop movements towards Italy.[61] In 1755, he suggested the Dutch general with whom there should be planning (which revealed that he was the key influence behind a recent ministerial meeting),[62] and in 1759, after the major victory over a French army at Minden, spent 36 hours reading the transcripts of captured documents.[63] Earlier that year, he told the Bavarian envoy that although as Elector he had a smaller revenue than the Elector of Bavaria, his peacetime army was larger.[64] George was very much concerned about war news, responding to victories with delight, as with that at Krefeld in 1758: 'It is not possible to tell how happy this battle has made the King,' who commented on the artillery's rate of fire there. George continued reviewing troops, including those sent abroad.[65]

George was proof against misplaced optimism, telling the Sardinian envoy in August 1760 that he anticipated a battle for Hanover and that the outcome of any battle was always very uncertain,[66] although, in 1755, he was reported as making an assessment based on respective naval strength and British popular support, favourable to war with France.[67]

Like his father, but totally unlike George III, George was far less interested in the navy and did not derive pleasure from reviewing it, but that did not mean that he could not praise the state and administration of the service,[68] and he was furious at Byng's failure to relieve Minorca in 1756.[69] John, 4th Duke of Bedford, the First Lord of the Admiralty noted in 1747, after George Anson's victory off Cape Finisterre: 'The King told me this morning at his levee that I had given him the best breakfast he had had this long time, and I think I never saw him more pleased in my life.'[70]

Instructions were of course in the King's name, as in June 1759, when, in the face of French invasion preparations, General Orders were issued to the fleet 'to impress for the King's service all seamen'.

Although affected by reverses which could throw him off balance,[71] George was inherently forceful and, even if reported indirectly, this stance was to be seen clearly, as in early 1748 when George, alongside Cumberland and Newcastle, backed a continuance of the war with France at a time when some of the ministers, notably Chesterfield, were keener on peace. In 1752, Newcastle wrote from Hanover that the King

> ... extremely approves the directions for fitting out, with the greatest expedition, a stronger squadron for the coast of [West] Africa, than the French will have there. In the present circumstances, there is no other certain way of doing with them, but by being stronger where we can.[72]

This was an approach to Anglo-French relations that was reliant on force, intimidation and deterrence as a background for negotiations, an approach also followed by Cumberland. George's instinctual militarisation of events was in evidence in June 1755 when, in the aftermath of clashes in the Ohio River Valley the previous year, Robert, 4th Earl of Holdernesse, one of the Secretaries of State, wrote 'entre nous' to Newcastle, that 'the King seemed overjoyed at the probable success of his measures in America,'[73] a reference to the decision to deploy more troops there and to attack French positions. That January, George had told the newly arrived French envoy that he sought a continuation of peace, but he also spoke to him with some passion about the situation in North America. Characteristically, George presented this in terms of honour and obligations, with the monarch appearing in the traditional light of a defender of his subjects, responding to repeated complaints from the colonists.[74]

George also had a sense of the tone of negotiations, one based on long experience. Thus, in 1756, Holdernesse informed Andrew Mitchell, envoy in Berlin: 'His Majesty was particularly pleased to observe the frank and confidential manner in which His Prussian Majesty had thought proper to open himself to you.'[75]

Professionalism was a wider issue for the King than simply in the army, and affected his attitude to politics, although social conservatism played a role. In 1756, George's concern with status as well as his own independence was on display when he told Granville, 2nd Earl Gower, the Lord Privy Seal, that he was wary about Henry Fox, the manager of government business in the House of Commons:

> The ambition of that man is not to be gratified. I have done more for him than any one person. He has power enough. I will give him no more. If he quits me now and throws everything into confusion, the whole world will blame him. I have made his brother [Stephen] an Earl [of Ilchester], over all the Barons' heads.

George, however, then had to listen to Gower explaining the uncomfortable truth about his need for Fox: 'He was ready to undertake His Majesty's affairs, provided a proper power was vested in him, but, without it, he would not pretend to carry on the business of the House of Commons.'[76] In short, the assumptions of the aristocracy had to yield to the needs of the Commons.

Not particularly grand, George liked ceremonial although without excessive effort. His relatively modest style of kingship anticipated that of George III. In the case of George II, this was linked to his persistent reputation for economy which, to critics, was meanness. Stubborn, George was also dutiful and sought to conform to the constitution as he knew it. George worked reasonably hard as King.

It is generally agreed that he was irascible. Thus, Edward Harley explained the political crisis of February 1746: 'The blame was laid on Earl of Bath's rashness in going to the King to irritate him against Mr Pitt being Secretary at War.'[77]

George was close to his wife, Caroline of Ansbach, but also had lovers, each of them for a number of years, which up to a point showed a need for stability and constancy that may be linked to being an adolescent whose mother had been absent. Henrietta Howard (*c.* 1688-1767) the estranged wife of the brutal Charles Howard, later Earl of Suffolk, was his mistress probably from 1713 until 1734, although in 1714 the French envoy, who also noted that Caroline was very popular with George, reported that Argyll had taken the Prince to a prostitute,[78] while in 1720, Mary, Countess Cowper suggested that Walpole had let George intrigue with his wife.[79] George presumably did not measure up to the undated quip sent Henrietta by Charles, 3rd Earl of Peterborough: 'Like my brethren the Whigs, I ever detested all passive obedience except from the lover to his mistress.'[80] In his 'Character' of the mistresses of George I and George II, Chesterfield suggested that George did not consummate his relationships as he did not want a bastard, claiming to Chesterfield that he could not make an illegitimate son what he ought to be. Chesterfield thought George mean and peevish, methodical, formal and not particularly bright, focused on dignity and minor matters such as punctuality.

In turn, after Henrietta, came Mary Scott, Dowager Countess of Deloraine (1700-44), the governess of George's two youngest daughters. Born Mary Howard, she was the daughter of Captain Charles Howard and had become a widow in 1730. She was followed from 1735 by the younger Amalie Sophie Marianne von Wallmoden (1704-65), who George met in Hanover, which helped to account for his visiting it again in 1736 and for a long period.

Indeed, an anonymous account in the Prussian archives claimed that Horace Walpole was sent to Hanover to bring her over so that George II would not go there so much, although there is no evidence for this claim.[81] Daughter of a Hanoverian general and niece of the Duchess of Kendal, she had married Count Gottlieb Wallmoden-Gimborn in 1727 and they had a son. In 1736, she had another son Johann Ludwig (1736-1811) who was said to be fathered by George but was not acknowledged and may have been the son of her husband from whom she had not yet separated. Coming to London in 1738 after Caroline's death the previous year, she acted as George's hostess, in 1739 was separated from her husband who was paid off, and in 1740 became a naturalised British subject and Countess of Yarmouth. Her relationship with George continued until his death, and she could act as an able intermediary between monarch and ministers. Yet, she could also challenge his relations with his ministers by serving as a conduit for advice from others, for example Carteret in 1745, a course that angered Newcastle.[82] She returned to Hanover after George's death while her second son, who was brought up in St James's and Kensington palaces, rose to be a Major-General and Commander-in-Chief of the Hanoverian army. After he died, George III acquired his excellent collections of antique sculptures and books.

George II matched his father in arguing with his eldest son, in his case Frederick, Prince of Wales. They had particularly poisonous relations from 1737 when they fell out over money. George conspicuously, indeed harshly,[83] refused favour to those who supported his son, which exacerbated relations, Thomas Pelham reflecting that July 'the breach seems to grow wider every day.'[84] George was not consulted on Household appointments by Frederick.[85] The government was aware through postal intercepts that diplomats followed the dispute.[86]

Frederick's support for the opposition in the 1741 general election helped cause Walpole's fall the following February. George did his best to ensure that Walpole did not suffer from the secret committee established to investigate his ministry. Frederick then became more accommodating, only to oppose the ministry anew, both in the 1747 election, which despite some predictions from hostile circles[87] the ministry easily won,[88] and until his death in 1751. George had followed the stance of leading figures in the 1747 election.[89]

In contrast to George's long life, the King's vivacious and highly intelligent wife, Princess Caroline of Ansbach, also born in 1683, died in 1737. Noting the great 'affliction' in which George had been left by Caroline's death, the French envoy commented on the very small group he was willing to see, the Dukes of Grafton and Dorset, Lord Harrington, and Walpole, three of whom were aristocrats. This was very much George's milieu.[90] Walpole then found business held up due to George's inaction: 'This is a season full of reasoning and speculation, and hopes and fears according to affections make up the conversation of the world... I have lost my sheet anchor, but I must do my best to weather the storms, that though not seen, will infallibly arise... I can have no support, but the approbation and assistance of my friends.'[91]

George then settled down into a domestic relationship with his already-established mistress, Wallmoden, whose role became similar to that of Melusine von der Schulenburg with his father. In a period of repeated political difficulties for George, she became an influential political force while giving him a welcome calm support, as Henrietta Howard had failed to do. Walpole's earlier position was essentially maintained.

In managing George, it was necessary to 'contend with his passions without ruffling his humour', the assessment offered by John, 5th Lord Berkeley of Stratton, the Captain of the Gentlemen Pensioners, concerning the success of the 2nd Duke of Grafton, the Lord Chamberlain of the Household from 1724 until his death in 1757. Berkeley provided a view of George in his later years, one in which the King was even more set in his ways, and for both good and ill. He was experienced and far more so than his ministers about international affairs, obviously so by the late 1750s, but remained irritable and peremptory. Berkeley criticised George for his fondness for Hanover and money, but also saw him as a monarch willing to respect the liberties of his subjects,[92] which was a ready contrast with the Stuarts and Jacobites.[93]

As with his father, his health remained reasonably good and he was able to travel to Hanover in his seventies, although, as his vision deteriorated, he wanted very black ink used for letters.[94] George III and George IV were also to suffer from poor vision in their later years.

There was no sense of George as a cipher. Indeed, the travails experienced by Pitt on his rise to, and in, office reflected George's strong suspicion of him as a demagogue hostile to the interests of Hanover. In 1748, Newcastle wrote to his brother Henry Pelham of an example of kingly intransigence:

> The King is extremely pleased with what has passed in Scotland; and I shall take this opportunity to press the Justice Clerk's warrant for life... The King has also said, he will give Dr Johnson [not the great lexicographer] one of the Church Preferments now vacant; but has absolutely refused to give Mr [Jonathan] Shipley either. [In a postscript] I have, with great difficulty, got the Justice Clerk's warrant for life. I am sorry, I could not prevail to get either of the vacant preferments for Mr Shipley.[95]

George's determination over patronage was a continuing feature of the reign and one that reflected his concern about his prerogatives, something shown by all rulers. At the same time, this concern was in part a matter of shifting priorities, with social position more significant for George I and George II than it was for George III. Thus, in 1756, George II would not 'suffer any but a peer of England' to be in the post of Captain of the Gentlemen Pensioners, and therefore turned down an Irish peer.[96]

An instance of the King's significance was provided by the fate of Carteret, now 2nd Earl Granville. In the face of strong political opposition, he had not been sustained in office in 1744 and 1746, but received the prestigious Order of the Garter in 1749, was made Lord President of the Council in 1751, and was regarded as a key player in foreign policy, notably in the support of the unpopular and totally unsuccessful Imperial Election Scheme.[97] In the mid-1750s, Carteret, now Earl Granville, was seen as having great influence.[98]

George's direct role in these and related matters is often obscure, although accounts of conversations with George are valuable, revealing his importance to diplomats and his ability to set out the international situation with clarity.[99] The flavour of a conversation was recalled by Sandwich, writing to Newcastle soon after, at a time when fighting on against France was a vexatious issue:

> As well as I can recollect the King's discourse to me about Peace, the strongest and almost the only thing he said to me was that he was not against a peace for that the present situation of affairs was too dangerous for him 'to engage in a measure which would not be supported by the people, which would be the case if he was to reject the offer of a negotiation'; upon my dropping some expressions relative to the danger there would be on the other side of our want of support if we should determine hastily in pacific measures, he entered hastily and fully into that reasoning, and concluded with saying he was determined that the negotiation whenever it was carried on should be managed by me.[100]

More distant references to his intentions, however, need to be employed with care. Thus, the suggestion that Newcastle's backing for the Imperial Election Scheme rested on his need for George's support against John, 4th Duke of Bedford, the rival Secretary of State,[101] has to be countered by an understanding of the degree to which Newcastle actively sponsored the Scheme because of his views on the European situation and his wish for stability. The prominence and length of the Scheme ensured that it was frequently the subject of conversations between George and foreign diplomats, and this provides an opportunity to see how George's views developed, as he sought to explain the problems facing the Scheme and its eventual failure. Thus, in 1753, he complained to the Sardinian envoy, a diplomat who had his confidence, about Austrian indifference, which became a slow-burn in the decline of the relationship, and also drew attention to a French weakness that he felt undercut the prospect of Prussian aggression. The envoy was convinced that George had not the slightest wish to risk an attack on Hanover.[102]

George's disappointment, sometimes rage, with Austria was frequent, a feeling of being used and taken for granted,[103] but he was also suspicious of Frederick II and hostile to France. George's frequent anger arose in part from a sense that a Continental alliance system was necessary but elusive and, if constructed, fragile. George's view about Austria was shared by many ministers and politicians.[104] Correspondingly, 'The master will not hear of Prussia, and the servants partly will not, and partly dare not propose it.'[105]

Policy and patronage were not the sole issues. An instructive instance of the clash between the 'public sphere' of free discussion and the Crown was offered in 1749 when Dudley Ryder, the Attorney General, was willing to consider prosecutions to deal with the opposition attempt, brought to his attention by Newcastle, to create a sense of uncertainty by suggesting that George was ill, which was not in fact the case. Ryder's letter revealed the concern for legality – and uncertainty as to what the law actually was – that characterised much ministerial judicial supervision of the press:

> As the publication of such false news of his Majesty has a tendency to disquiet the minds of his subjects, hurt public credit, and diminish the regard and duty which they owe him, I think the doing it with such views is an offence punishable at Common Law, and for which an indictment or information can lye. And the frequency of such publications is evidence of such wicked designs. But as every false report of this kind

> which may arise from mistake only cannot be charged as a crime, so it is very difficult to say how often must it be repeated in the same paper to make it criminal.[106]

George anyway remained significant politically, a situation and process enhanced by his role as Elector and by the fact that when in Hanover he was less under pressure from his British ministers. His visits there made him happier.[107]

As Elector, George had an insight into European power relationships. In 1753, Pelham was opposed to a peacetime subsidy to Russia, but Newcastle wished to please George who backed the idea; only for the Russians to reject the British counter-project, which the Austrian envoy in London thought as generous as Britain could afford.[108] In 1754, the new Secretary of State for the Southern Department, Thomas Robinson, a courtier who appreciated the nuances of German politics, was highly acceptable to George as well as Newcastle, while Pitt said that 'the King might as well have sent his jack-boot to govern the House of Commons as Sir Thomas Robinson.'[109] Encouraged by the surprise death of Pelham in March 1754, the risk that George could die at any time was mentioned in diplomatic correspondence.[110]

George's health led the Sardinian envoy in July 1754 to assess the royal family. He reported that Walmolden was still favoured by George but had no influence, that Cumberland and Princess Amelia caballed against Newcastle and had a political group in support, that Prince George was likely to resemble the King in being very careful about money and had a soft character and a mediocre education.[111] The last was inaccurate, but the sense of a legacy in difficulties was instructive.

The death of Pelham led George to reflect that he had hoped to finish his days in peace, but that he saw clearly that it would be impossible to do that now. This was a much cited remark,[112] and his being in difficulties as a result of Pelham's death was also expressed by commentators in a fashion that throws light on the relationship between ministerial stability and the Crown.[113] The subsequent political crisis and the move toward war with France found the King playing a crucial role both in the complex political negotiations and in foreign policy, for example pressing in 1755 for an alliance network that would include Austria, Bavaria, Russia and Saxony, and thus deter French and Prussian pressure on Hanover. At the same time, there was a hope – that was to be vindicated – that George's trip to Hanover would help win Frederick II round.[114]

In 1754, Newcastle complained to the Sardinian envoy about the difficulties of getting George to talk to Pitt, let alone find him the crucial role necessary to move government business forward.[115] Yet, from another perspective, there was support for George: 'Our affairs in Parliament have been a little disturbed, by the private views of some ambitious gentlemen, who have been desirous of more power, than the King intended to give them.'[116] He followed Parliament with care. In December 1755, George was reported 'too full of yesterday's debates to say anything to me on Lord Kildare's subject'.[117]

George faced an escalating international and domestic crisis in 1754-6, one in which he was unable to control allies and protégés. Aware of the formidable coalition taking shape against Prussia, Frederick II attacked Saxony in 1756, despite George's wish to see peace kept on the Continent, and the King was angered by the reactions of former close allies, Austria[118] and Russia; he found Prussia difficult for him, provocative to others, and a potential challenge to Hanover's position.[119] At the same time, George was challenged by a domestic disunity made more serious by its attracting foreign comments.[120]

That he was not close to Newcastle was a cause of great anxiety to the neurotic Duke. In part, this was because of the role of Carteret/Granville and of George having a Hanoverian minister with him, each providing a sounding board. Yet, Newcastle in reality enjoyed much of George's confidence,[121] and after the King's death Newcastle wrote described him as 'the best King, the best master, and the best friend that ever subject had.'[122] Carteret also thought him 'a most gracious and good friend'.[123] George's positive or negative attitude toward individuals, notably his dislike for Pitt, played an important part in political manoeuvres. This was underlined in Newcastle's repeated complaints, most particularly in 1755:

> If we either are forced to undertake measures, which from the circumstances and condition of the kingdom, we cannot carry through, or His Majesty will not permit us to have the assistance of those who are necessary for us, it will be in vain to attempt impossibilities. We wish we could do in the House of Commons, without troubling His Majesty for Mr Pitt and My Lord Egmont; but we cannot.[124]

Changes in George's attitude were significant, for example the vilification of Cumberland for military failure in 1757, which also affected the ministers close to him. Cumberland's failure to hold Hanover against French attack led to an occupation that cost George as Elector heavily, making him focus on compensation for the Electorate, an issue that held no weight for his British ministers. The costs ensured that George eventually left less money than would have been anticipated.[125] One of George's chaplains, Edmund Pyle, wrote on 21 November 1758: 'My old Master, the King, is not well: very far from it – he vexes himself – and no wonder, at the deplorable condition of his native country, that is undone in a cause it has no relation to.'[126]

Cumberland had been a major player in the debate within the ministry as well as attending Parliament.[127] Although without the constitutional basis of the King's governmental and political role, Cumberland's stance was of great political significance in part because he was not outside the governmental nexus, as was the case with so many Hanoverian princes. Aside from his closeness to the monarch, there was his position in the military, and his close links with specific ministers, notably Henry Fox. Other ministers regarded Cumberland's views as worthy of attention and comment. Thus, Robinson informed Newcastle at a time of escalating Anglo-French differences over North America that the government should fix France's imperial boundaries in North America and that once this was achieved, clear instructions should be issued to the British commander, so that 'he may not be liable to future reproaches from one or the other colony, or be sacrificed one day or other, to the clamours of merchants at home or their interested correspondents abroad.'[128]

Cumberland, showing the social conservatism also seen with George I and George II but less so with George III, appreciated the problems created by domestic political pressures, though in response he was inclined to dismiss or denigrate these pressures, an approach very different from that of Newcastle. Offering a harsh view of the transatlantic linkage in news and opinion, Cumberland's general conviction was that problems could, and should, be overcome through firmness. In 1755, he was presented by diplomats as a key political figure and blamed for deteriorating relations with France.[129] George certainly did not rein him in at this juncture.

Meanwhile, George was not known for his artistic interests and did not share the intellectual ones of his wife (who was allegedly criticised by Tories for talking too much).[130] Nevertheless, as King he was a patron of culture, although far less active in this field than George III was to be. For example, George II was the dedicatee of books such as Ferdinando Warner's massive *Ecclesiastical History to the Eighteenth Century* (1756-7), a work that emphasised the role of the monarch in defending religion. In his biography of Sir Thomas More (1758), Warner claimed that had his subject lived under the benign regime of George as opposed to that of Henry VIII, he would have survived, a fatuous point. Warner was to dedicate his *History of Ireland* (1763) to George III.

The verses of Nahum Tate, the Poet Laureate, for George I's birthday in 1715 had included reference to the succession, to George, Prince of Wales and his wife Caroline:

Yet long before our royal sun,
His destined course has run,
We are blessed to see a glorious heir,
That shall the mighty loss repair,
When he that blazes now, shall this low sphere resign,
In a sublimer orb eternally to shine.
A Cynthia too, adorned with every grace
Of person and of mind,
And happy in a starry race,
Of such auspicious kind,
As joyfully presage,
No want of royal heirs, in any future age.

The celebration of royal heirs was important as it countered the Jacobite theme of rebirth through a second Stuart restoration.

George's cultural impact was varied. He was not a major patron of architecture, but Henrietta, Countess of Suffolk, his mistress, was given £11,500 by him in 1724 to build and furnish an appropriate house. The result was the Palladian-style Marble Hill House, the garden designed by Charles Bridgeman, a leading figure in the field. Separately, in a fashion different to Frederick's cultural resonance, George later came to embody the greatly expanding British empire. In statuary, he was often depicted as a Roman general, in breastplate and leather shirt. Such a statue still stands on the Bargate in Southampton.

As later with George III, longevity brought its reward in terms of public acceptance and increasing affection and respect, a process not seen with George I and George IV. Born in 1683, George II was older from 1750 than his father (born in 1660) had been as King; a contrast underlined by the death of Frederick in 1751, of Princess Caroline in 1757, and Anne, George's eldest daughter, in 1759. His reign was longer than any since that of Elizabeth I (r. 1558-1603). As a result, there was not the sense of transience seen with intervening monarchs, one that meant that many of their subjects could remember more than one.

In 1756, as a crisis developed over Admiral Byng's failure to relieve Minorca, Holdernesse privately observed: 'In the midst of the storm, Our Royal Master keeps up his health and his spirits with amazing firmness.'[131] Two years later, William, 4th Earl of Essex, a Lord of the Bedchamber, observed from Kensington, 'The King was thank God in the highest spirits this morning I have seen him for many months,' while his wife Frances reported George II as reputedly 'younger than the Prince of Wales'.[132]

George's health had been good in his sixties (from 1743), although in 1746 he was ill and rested at Kensington rather than being available closer to the centre of government at St James's.[133] In the 1750s, alongside concern and reports about his health,[134] including very poor hearing by late 1753[135] and a persistent intermittent fever in 1758,[136] there was increasingly committed celebration of royal birthdays, and notably so later in the decade when the King was associated, as George III was to be, with national resolution, in the face of adversity and in triumph. Thus, in 1759, writing to his daughter, Carteret linked military successes over France to national morale and support for George: 'The good success of our fleets and armies of late has raised the spirits of the whole country and all people of what denomination soever pray most heartily for the King's long life and prosperity.'[137]

Moreover, from 1758, he largely lost the public perception of Hanoverianism, although that was posthumously revived in 1761-3 by those praising George III for disengaging from the Continental interventionism of the previous reign. Thus, the *Briton* in 1762 criticised the interventionism of the Seven Years' War, hoping on 10 July that 'the Elector of Hanover will never again have influence enough with the King of Great Britain' to take the latter into a costly conflict. His ministers certainly saw such influence, trying and failing to dissuade him from visiting Hanover in 1755, and in 1756-7 being vexed by the issue of Hanoverian neutrality. In 1759, Newcastle complained that George wanted to fight on only for compensation for Hanoverian losses due to earlier French occupation, adding that, if George could realise there would be none he would be as eager for peace as the ministry.[138] In large part, this was a question of a glorious opportunity to finish his rule, which was seen as a goal.[139] Yet, as Newcastle noted soon after, George still hoped to acquire Osnabrück and Hildesheim.

As Elector, George was a failure. Hanover suffered greatly from being the site of hostilities in 1757, and its conquest that year and damaging subsequent occupation[140] contrasted with the failed French invasion schemes for Britain. There was to be a similar contrast for George III.

From that perspective, George I was more successful, as a series of international crises, notably in 1717, 1720, 1723, and 1726-7, did not lead to an invasion of Hanover. Instead, invading forces actually landed in Scotland in 1719, while the larger-scale Spanish attempt of that year was only wrecked by storms. Hanover gained territory under George I and in George III's last years, but not under George II.

The private tributes paid to George when he died straining on the lavatory in 1760 after having had a hot chocolate, are striking, especially as it might not have been thought that the cantankerous monarch would have inspired such respect and affection. The 'bluestocking' Elizabeth Montagu offered a very personal assessment:

> With him our laws and liberties were safe, he possessed in a great degree, the confidence of his people and the respect of foreign governments; and a certain steadiness of character made him of great consequence in these unsettled times. During his long reign we never were subject to the insolence and rapaciousness of favourites, a grievance of all others most intolerable... His character would not afford subject for epic poetry, but will look well in the sober page of history. Conscious perhaps of this, he was too little regardful of sciences and the fine arts; he considered common sense as his best panegyric.

She had observed earlier that year: 'In politics great unanimity'.[141] There were particular lamentations from Dissenters, who had benefited from George's support of toleration for them.

Most, however, turned to the bright promise of a new, young and vigorous King, in the person of his grandson, George III, leading Sarah Stanley to note six weeks later: 'I cannot help regretting our late sovereign. If he had some defects, he had certainly many virtues, and he had experience, which nothing but time can give; yet he seems already to be almost forgotten.'

Ironically, this situation was to change when George III broke with the Whigs. He created the impression that he was echoing Stuart autocracy, and this helped to make George II more appealing in retrospect. So also did the political instability of the 1760s and the lack of a postwar prestige comparable to the Seven Years' War, which itself, in contrast to the repeated successes of 1758-60, became particularly controversial from 1761. The Rockinghamite Whigs of the 1760s and 1770s (in effect led by the very wealthy young aristocrat the Marquess of Rockingham) and their Foxite successors in the 1780s and 1790s, looked back to the reign of George II as a period of appropriate interdependence between monarch and nation, the latter represented by themselves. This approach suggested a lack of continuity between the two reigns, but in practice, both saw the adaptation by monarchs necessary for the working of parliamentary monarchy.

INTERLUDE: FREDERICK I

The monarchs who never were are important to dynastic history and often to that of a nation. They are always of great interest. These might-have-beens, which include contested successions, suggest how British monarchy might have gone in different directions. Aside from contested successions, death of course can intervene. Princes Arthur and Henry might have avoided the trajectories of their younger brothers, Henry VIII and Charles I, respectively. The swift departure of Edward VIII in 1936 and his replacement by George VI (r. 1936-52) was arguably important to British politics during the Second World War. Their father, George V, was the second son of Edward VII. Succession by grandchildren was less common but happened, with Richard II and not his father, Edward the Black Prince, replacing Edward III in 1377, and George III, not his father, Frederick, Prince of Wales (1707-51), succeeding George II in 1760.

As a might-have-been, Frederick is not easy to study as his extant papers are few, in part due to their destruction by his wife, Princess Augusta, but also because he was not a great correspondent. That sparseness was even more true for George I and George II, and it is only with George III that the papers become plentiful. Frederick is also somewhat obscure because his life was short and as a result of his not being king, which diminished the attention paid him, notably by diplomats.

Initially brought up in Hanover, Frederick was brought over to Britain in a major change of policy after the death of George I.[1] Frederick had fallen out with his father over money, and this broadened into a political division. In 1736, opposition Whigs, self-styled 'Patriots', congratulated Frederick on his marriage to Augusta of Saxe-Gotha, and the dispute soon after over his allowance from the Civil List was swiftly politicised. In 1737, George informed diplomats in London, via his Minister of the Ceremonies, Sir Clermont Cotterell, that it was his wish that they should not go to Frederick's Court, and subsequent instructions to envoys took note of these views.

Frederick very much presented himself as the British alternative to his father's Hanoverianism. John, Lord Hervey, a favourite of Queen Caroline, who had competed with the lascivious Frederick over a woman, as had Harrington, noted:

> The Prince I hear hating all German innovations on our old English customs and constitution, has ordered everybody not to call his daughter the Princess, but the Lady Augusta ... the two courts of the King and the Prince, over which a cloud has hung for some time, are at last quite separated by a storm.[2]

George made it clear that reconciliation would depend on Frederick renouncing his links with the opposition, 'the party contrary to the Court'. Foreign envoys and others were told not to speak to Frederick. George was also able to draw on royal patronage and funds, as well as on the political skill and connections of Walpole.[3] Frederick, in contrast, had the appeal of being the heir but also his electoral interest as Duke of Cornwall, the county most heavily represented in the House of Commons, with no fewer than 44 MPs out of 558 for Britain as a whole: now there are only six out of 650. As Duke of Cornwall, Frederick voted with the opposition in the unsuccessful parliamentary assault in March 1739 on the government's support for the Convention of Pardo with Spain (concerning trade terms and boundaries between Spanish Florida and the English colony of Georgia), a compromise agreement that was seen as humiliating.

As a patron, Frederick was much more important: he was a significant supporter of music, literature and landscape gardening, and an important and discerning patron of the Rococo style. Frederick was painted in 1733 by Philip Mercier, playing music with his sisters Anne and Caroline, while another sister, Amelia, listens with a volume of John Milton in her lap: he played the bass viol and, as shown in the painting, the cello. This looked toward his son George's interest in music.

From the mid-1730s, when Frederick took an active political role in opposition to his father and the latter's support for the Walpole ministry, there was a cultural dimension to the rivalry. This included the Prince's patronage of the Lincoln's Inn Fields theatre as a rival to George II's theatrical politics. Frederick displayed his 'rebellion' by supporting (according to some, co-writing) opposition plays put on in this theatre. Theatre was as much charged with Hanoverian dynastic politics as with Hanoverian politics. The recipients of Frederick's patronage included the Anglo-Scot James Thomson, who received an annual pension of £100 and contributed to the masque *Alfred* (1740), providing the words for 'Rule Britannia'. *Alfred*, which David Mallet wrote jointly with Thomson, was important among the literature of exalted patriotism inspired by Frederick's opposition to the Walpole ministry and patronised accordingly by members of his circle. In *Alfred*, the hermit predicted:

> ...the virtue,
> The great, the glorious passions that will fire
> Distant posterity when guardian laws
> Are by the patriot, in the glowing senate,
> Won from corruption.

This, an aspect of a more general Patriot Gothic,[4] seen for example in Thomas Lyttleton's *Letters from a Persian in England*

(1735), represented a very different role from that earlier taken by Frederick. His active love life had been the subject of James Miller's *Vanelia: or The Amours of the Great* (1732), the text of an unperformed opera that went through at least six editions. Frederick's pursuit of women was no secret. It was to set a pattern for all his sons bar George III.

Separately, the hunting of animals by Frederick was the subject of group pictures by John Wootton in 1729 and 1734. He was also a supporter of the creation of an academy for the arts, a project brought to fruition under George III. In 1739, Frederick was described as embracing 'every opportunity of promoting any branch of our manufactory',[5] a reference to his ostentatious preference for British goods, which included the arts.

Frederick's opposition had contributed to Walpole's fall in 1742 and, a frequent attender in the House of Lords, he was seen as in Carteret's 'system', 'as full as warm as his father for Lord Granville'.[6] Frederick had moved from opposition and maintained his new position in 1743-6, parting from Pitt as a result in 1744. He backed his father. In November 1744, when the King unsuccessfully supported the retention in office of Carteret (now Earl Granville) against the Pelhams, Hardwick reported that Frederick had told the Duke of Dorset: 'I am to talk to you and my Lord President, to convince you too, that if my Lord Granville stays in, and the others quit, you ought both still to continue in the King's service.'[7]

In 1747, however, still restless, and possibly motivated by jealousy of Cumberland's prominent role,[8] Frederick went into opposition to his father's ministers and, thus, to his father. Frederick's supporters were a motley group of opposition Whigs, but there was the possibility of more backing, and, that January the government won a division by only 184 to 143 over a motion to investigate the navy debt.[9] By the modern standards of disciplined parties, this was a clear majority, but in the eighteenth century, when disaffected or opportunistic Whigs could readily desert in order to encourage the reconstitution of a ministry, this was regarded as a weak majority that threatened instability.[10] Moreover, there was a developing crisis of public finances due to the burden of the war as well as scepticism about the prospect of military success, and worries about the content of peace terms and their political acceptability. All of these were seen as likely to challenge the ministry.[11]

To thwart Frederick, but also to enable the government to continue the war or negotiate peace, the ministry went for an early election: in 1747, not 1748, as would have been normal but was not essential under the Septennial Act, despite the pompous Speaker speaking 'constitutional paragraphs' against.[12] This was before Frederick had built up the necessary political alliances and worked at exploiting rifts within the ministry. Newcastle's explanation to Cumberland captured the significance of Frederick and Cumberland, who did not have a fraternal relationship like the Pelhams, as well as the link between dynasty and Whigs, at least in the eyes of the 'Old Corps' Whig leaders:

> The memory of their late deliverance, under God, owing entirely to your Royal Highness [victory at Culloden], and their obligation to the King for his goodness in making your Royal Highness the instrument of it, and for his royal protection and support, under the dangers this nation was so lately in, is at present too fresh, not to give us almost a certainty of choosing a good Whig Parliament this summer; The uncertainty as to the success of the war, and the terms of a future peace, will keep the people in suspense and hopes; whereas any reverse of fortune ... and ... almost any peace would undoubtedly give strength to opposition... The present *New Opposition*, is yet unsupported, unconnected, and not in high reputation; what the course of a year may produce, nobody can tell; unfortunate public events, or private disappointments, and personal views, may render that opposition formidable, which at present is far from being so.[13]

This did not address the long-term situation. Angry with his inconsequential political position, Frederick had not been particularly successful in the 1747 general election, the results of which did not 'make an opposition of consequence'.[14] Indeed, the ministry was left with a majority of 148 ('the old Tories are computed at 116, and the Prince's troop at 41,')[15] and another election was not due until 1754 or the accession of a new monarch.

Frederick was not kept informed by the ministry, although his wife allegedly was.[16] However, Frederick, understandably, as the reversionary interest, was regarded by foreign powers as worth cultivating[17] before and after his renewed break with his father. This was a two-way process, as he discussed foreign policy with diplomats.[18] This discussion included policy preferences. Thus, although rumoured to be pro-Prussian in 1742,[19] Frederick was generally reported as pro-Austrian, which was in line with George II's Hanoverian and British ministries,[20] whereas Cumberland was regarded as more favourable to Prussia. In late 1747, Frederick told foreign envoys and the Prince of Orange that there was a secret French emissary in London.[21]

Although there was division caused by the real or alleged Jacobitism of certain prominent Tories,[22] and Frederick was (unfairly) reported as a result to back candidates favourable to Jacobitism,[23] he was able to appeal to Tories who were loyal as well as to opposition Whigs. One, Tory, Velters Cornewall, pressed the case in the Commons in February 1748 for a naval war,[24] which was a criticism both of George II's Hanoverianism and of the ministry's commitment to Continental interventionism. In 1749, when the printer and publisher of the *Remembrancer* were arrested for their issue of 18 November accusing Newcastle and Pelham of corruption and manipulating George, and Cumberland of brutality in his administration of the army, Frederick proved willing to indemnify them. He was closely associated with the criticism, and, when George went to Hanover, was kept away from the 'shadows of him',[25] the Regency.

Frederick died of a burst abscess in one of his lungs, possibly the result of an old sporting injury. In a familiar pattern, Frederick's real and reputed political ambitions had been a cause of uncertainty before he died. Newcastle and Granville (Carteret) had been trying to recruit his support against Bedford and Cumberland.[26] Edward Bayntum Rolt, a member of his circle, noted: 'Two negotiations were carrying on with the Prince when he died. One by Dodington on the part of the Tories, the other by Lord Cobham on the part of Pitt etc.'[27] Tory disappointment about being let down by opposition Whigs in 1742 and 1744 was countered by a fear of redundancy if acting alone, combined with the total failure of the Jacobite option in 1745-6. Thus, alongside Tories who went over to the ministry, including Sir Miles Stapylton[28] and Henry, 3rd Viscount Downe, others were willing to look to Frederick.

Frederick had the capacity to challenge established links because he was able to attract support, or the prospect of support, across the political spectrum.[29] Increasing Whig-Tory co-operation was seen at local level, for example over the foundation of hospitals.[30]

What had appeared a possibly imminent succession became part of the history of speculations. There is a strong sense of potential not brought to fruition with Frederick. This potential now lay in Prince George, which came out very clearly in Bubb Dodington's journal.

Frederick's death more immediately helped bring forward political change in the shape of the consolidation of the ministry. That it was followed three months later by the removal of Bedford was no coincidence. Newcastle saw himself as strong enough to part with the Duke, and also believed it was necessary to act. One commentator observed: 'The two Dukes were like wrestlers waiting on opportunity of giving each other the trip and Mr Pitt moderating till the death of the Prince of Wales, which threw the power on the side of the Duke of Newcastle.'[31]

Far from sickly, Frederick, on the pattern of previous Hanoverians, including George I's parents, should have lived for many years. Moreover, had he done so for as long as his father, George II, the future George III would not have come to the throne until the late 1780s, and if for as long as George I, until the late 1770s.

In 1751, George II was still fit but, born in 1683, he was old by the standards of the age. With the unexpected death of Frederick that year Prince George's contacts and commitments were immediately of great interest. To a degree, these were the prince's response to his father's example, but they were also refracted through Frederick's subsequent reputation. Prince George was far more influenced than his three younger brothers (who were, in effect, children) by his father; but he added to the latter's strong sense of political responsibility and cultural commitment a religious devotion and sexual probity for which his father had never been noted and which also contrasted with his brothers.

The political code Frederick had repeatedly enunciated was scarcely novel, for both George I and George II had initially sought to rule without reliance on party, as had William III and Anne. Indeed, while Frederick's support for the enunciation of 'Patriot' kingship might have appeared novel, drawing as it did on the writings of 'Country Party' opponents of the 'Old Corps Whigs', most prominently Henry, Viscount Bolingbroke, in practice there was a very traditional aspect to Frederick's projected kingship, one that was to be inherited by Prince George. Similar arguments had been frequently made, both in the Middle Ages and more recently, by Henry VIII, Elizabeth I, Henry, Prince of Wales (eldest son of James I), Oliver Cromwell, and Charles II. In each case, this expression was stronger in some periods of a reign or life than others, and it often ran into the realities of politics and context, not least the difficulties of avoiding factionalism and an over-mighty minister. If Charles II had sought in the early 1660s and 1676-8 to rule in a 'national' fashion, the first attempt had fallen victim to the strength of the Anglican reaction and the second to politics domestic and international, leading to the Popish Plot Crisis of 1678 and the Exclusion Crisis of 1679-81.

Frederick had received a good historical education and sought to pass that on to his children. Given history to read as a child, being provided with the works of the 1st Earl of Clarendon and Gilbert Burnet, a Tory and Whig respectively, Frederick ingested historical presentations that located him within a benign portrayal of British monarchy. Nicholas Tindal, an Anglican clergyman, dedicated his translation of Paul de Rapin-Thoyras' *History of England* to Frederick, a work that prefigured Bolingbroke's presentation of the Patriot King:

> You will here see the origin and nature of our excellent constitution, where the prerogatives of the Crown, and privileges of the subject are so happily proportioned, that the King and the People are inseparably united in the same interests and views. You will observe that this union, though talked of by even the most arbitrary princes with respect to their subjects, is peculiar to the English monarchy, and the most solid foundation of the Sovereign's glory, and the people's happiness. Accordingly, you will here constantly find that in the reigns where this union was cultivated, the kingdom flourished, and the prince was glorious, powerful, trusted, beloved. On the contrary, when, by an arbitrary disposition, or evil counsels, it was interrupted, the constitution languished, mutual confidence vanished, jealousy and discord arose; and when entirely broken … confusion and civil wars ensued.[32]

History as a genre had grown in popularity among readers.

In 1751, Prince Edward, afterwards Duke of York, the second son of Frederick, sent Simon, 1st Earl Harcourt (the 2nd Viscount mentioned above), the head of the household for Edward and his older brother the future George III, a series of letters that included comments on his education in which history was presented through the lives of medieval monarchs:

> I go on very well with my Latin, as well as the history. I read this morning part of the life of King John, and must say, that

> though a King, he was a very sad fellow in private as well as public life. (22 June)
>
> I am now in the reign of King Henry the Third, who came to the throne in his minority; and therefore the Earl of Pembroke was Regent as well as guardian to the young King. The Barons were very angry in John's time that they had not got back again that which they had enjoyed under the Saxon Kings; and after Pembroke's death, being disgusted with the behaviour of the Regents, they sent to Rome to have the King declared of age before the usual time; but they were not long satisfied with their master, when they found that he did not pursue the wise and good measures marked out to him by Pembroke. (27 June)
>
> I am yet in King Henry III, whose life is very long, and I think very tedious. (2 July)
>
> I shall finish the reign of Henry the Fourth tomorrow, whose reign I think very intrigate [sic] (2 August)
>
> I am in the reign of Richard the Second, whose reign I both detest and abhor; firstly, because he gave himself up totally to his flatterers; and, secondly, because he had not the least grain of honour. (25 August).[33]

One of the first accounts of George is of his acting at the age of ten the role of the virtuous hero in a children's production of Joseph Addison's lay *Cato* (1711). Another Whig classic, Nicholas Rowe's *Lady Jane Grey* (1715), an account of exemplary Protestant virtue, was also staged by George and his siblings.

The role of chance was amply underlined in that Frederick's younger brother, William, Duke of Cumberland (1721-65), lived for a similar length of time but was still alive when George II died, having earlier prompted alarmist critical comparison with Richard III, who had usurped his nephew, Edward V, in 1483.[34] However, under George III, there were to be positive evaluations of Richard, notably by Horace Walpole in his *Historic Doubts on the Life and Reign of King Richard III* (1768), by Tobias Smollett in his *Adventures of an Atom* mentioned earlier (1769) and by John Wesley in his *History of England* (1775).

On 25 November 1752, *Old England*, an opposition London newspaper, warned about the danger of Britain becoming 'a military power', a reference to persistent distrust of the Captain General Cumberland, whose triumph at Culloden in 1746 was celebrated for years, for example with a banquet in York in 1784, while there were popular demonstrations of joy for some years after Culloden on his birthday.[35] He and George II were the 'only judges' of key military questions.[36]

Yet, there was also, prior to Culloden, scepticism about Cumberland's military ability,[37] and military failures on the Continent in 1745-8, notably at Fontenoy (1745) and Lauffeld (1747), were to boost this scepticism and lead to press attacks.[38] In 1756, George II initially sought not Cumberland to command an army to protect Hanover, but Prince Louis of Brunswick-Wolfenbüttel, the Captain-General of the Netherlands.[39] Like the later Frederick, Duke of York, Cumberland was a better planner and military bureaucrat than field commander.

Aside from his military ability, Cumberland was regarded as very well informed. William, Count Bentinck thought him free of artifice and with an understanding of the true interests of Britain, the Dutch, and the European system. To Bentinck, Cumberland, like him, was an exponent of the Williamite system.[40] In 1747, Newcastle claimed that without Cumberland's help, he would have failed to persuade the government to support the dispatch of troops to the United Provinces:

> His Royal Highness's great weight and authority; his knowledge of the fatal consequences in Holland, which might attend the two rigorously insisting here, upon what strict justice, and rules of proportion, might justify; his solid reasoning thereupon; and his showing (as His Royal Highness did), from demonstrable calculations, that the Republic had it in their power, immediately to complete their troops ...

> produced so good an effect, that, if all my brethren were not convinced, they, at least, acquiesced in His Royal Highness's opinion.[41]

Newcastle could be not only (characteristically) gushing, but also offer an unusual view of the government, writing privately to Sandwich: 'I am so happy as to agree in everything with His Royal Highness, and to act under him; so that it is unnecessary for me to trouble your Lordship with letters when I know you have the pleasure of hearing from the Duke.'[42]

Cumberland was kept informed of more general aspects of foreign and military policy[43] as well as of domestic measures.[44]

The suspicion of Cumberland's political intentions was not matched in the case of his great-nephew, Frederick, Duke of York, who was Commander-in-Chief from 1795 to 1809 and 1811 until his death in 1827, as well as Captain-General in 1799. Cumberland, however, was not a might-have-been monarch, for he had no intention of trying to displace his nephew, the future George III.

More mundanely, Newcastle also came to be troubled by Cumberland, seeing him as a supporter of rival members of the Whig élite, notably Bedford, Halifax, and Sandwich, and publicly expressing this support by relevant attendance in the House of Lords.[45] Nor did the unmarried Cumberland, who, like William III, was possibly a homosexual and certainly preferred male company, play a central role in marital diplomacy. He would spend much time at the races in Newmarket.[46] Nevertheless, Cumberland was an important member of the wider government in the late 1740s and early 1750s, reading and commenting on diplomatic correspondence and discussing policy,[47] his influence seen as agreeable to George II.[48]

In 1755, although not earlier, he was, as the Prussian and French envoys noted, a member of the Regency Council and took care to attend, as is clear from the minutes in which he was listed first.[49] Cumberland was reputedly responsible for the decision to take vigorous steps against France, a popular stance.[50]

In 1756, Cumberland was involved in planning for North American operations.[51] There were rumours in 1748 that a marriage might be negotiated with a Prussian relation in order to improve relations, and in 1749 that he might be intended for the Swedish throne.[52] Neither amounted to anything, nor did the idea that he might be made ruler of a secularised prince-bishopric, Osnabrück.[53] The marriage possibilities of the royal children and grandchildren attracted much attention.[54] George II himself took an interest in the marital prospects of other royal ruling families.[55]

Cumberland was particularly distrustful of Pitt, whom he regarded as the bridge between the 'young Court', that of Prince George, and the government. In 1757, Cumberland complained: 'I am very fully convinced that the Tory doctrine of a sea-war, which we are following, will be repented by our children's children.'[56] Both Pitt and the 'young Court' followed this doctrine and supported expeditions against the coast of France rather than backing Cumberland in Germany. Feeling that he was starved of support in his German command because of the influence of Pitt's ideas, Cumberland sought to condemn these ideas by labelling them as Tory, although that proved a difficult line to sell to ministry or public. In the event, Cumberland was linked to the most prominent military failure of the Hanoverian dynasty, defeat and overrunning by the French in 1757, and a humiliating neutrality convention.[57] Lord George Sackville was correct in thinking 'the game must be desperate.'[58]

Cumberland's position had been very difficult. Charles, 3rd Duke of Richmond wrote to his brother, George, a fellow officer, that the defence in the face of such numbers was 'madness' and Cumberland explained his agreement to the Convention on the same grounds.[59] However, the Convention, as the French had predicted, created serious problems in relations with Frederick II and in domestic British politics, and infuriated George. He told Newcastle that it was

> ... directly contrary to his orders. The King was pleased to say, that his honour, and his interest were sacrificed by it.

> That His Majesty had been by it given up, tied *hand and foot*, to France. That he did not know how to look anybody in the face, that he had lost his honour ... often saying that Providence had abandoned him, he hoped this nation would not forsake him.[60]

It is instructive that George made reference to Providence, frequently mentioned by George III in moments of crisis. Again, his mention of honour is noteworthy, for it was a major theme for the King.

Three weeks later, George returned to the charge, focusing on Cumberland: 'A scoundrel in England *one day* may be thought a good man *another*. In Germany, it is otherwise, I think like *a German*.'[61] George attacked the Convention when writing to reassure Frederick II that he would do all humanly possible to help him as King.[62] The French view that the Convention was good for Hanover,[63] which was probably correct, was one that did not suit George's wider circumstances. It was feared that Frederick might also seek a neutrality, which could leave Britain to face France alone, the situation later during the war of American Independence and for some of the French Revolutionary and Napoleonic wars. Cumberland, who had utterly failed to anticipate his father's response or to appreciate the British perspective,[64] ceased to be of political consequence during his reign, which very much affected the politics of the Seven Years' War.

George II also came to be disappointed with his eldest daughter, Anne, who in 1734 had married William IV of Orange, becoming regent on his death in 1751 for her three-year-old son William V. The British had moved naval and military units to provide potential support when the Orangists seized power in the provinces of Holland and Zeeland in 1747, and were very hopeful as to the consequences.[65] In the event, there was much disappointment and subsequently major differences between father and daughter over foreign policy, with Anne refusing to heed George's views, repeating the clash seen with James II and the future Mary II.[66] The assessment of William IV by Horatio Walpole, who had served as envoy at The Hague, is instructive about assumptions concerning rulers, and George I, George II and George III appear in a better light by this standard, though Horatio Walpole did criticise George II's commitment to Hanover:

> The Prince of Orange answers the notion I always had of him although I was in hopes that years and adversity might have checked his vivacity and ripened his positiveness with reasons. He has parts, but much more eloquence than judgment, and, as the late Queen [Caroline] said of him, they are the parts of a pedant and not of a Prince, and his self-conceit and ambition may prove perhaps almost as dangerous as the inactive flegm of an impotent Pensionary [the leading republican politician]. He will aim and push at more than can be done, as the other would not undertake, or venture to do so much as might have been done.[67]

The problems caused when Frederick, the Electoral Prince of Hesse-Cassel, who had in 1740 married George II's daughter Mary, converted to Catholicism in 1749, having already separated from Mary, enraged George.[68] The tendency to focus on George III's troublesome family could be contextualised by also looking at that of George II. George I had had problems of a different scale because he only had two children, and only one lived in Britain.

The focus on children demonstrates the importance of the international (Protestant) marriage market as a way to strengthen the Protestant succession and further differentiate the dynasty from the Stuarts. The role of king as paterfamilias is to the fore, one that was frequently more difficult than any political responsibilities.

An instructive parallel with Frederick was Louis, the Dauphin of France (1729-65) who died aged 36. The elder son of Louis XV, he was the only one to survive childhood. As with Frederick, as well as George III as Prince of Wales, Louis was kept from the battlefield, in his case with one exception. Like George as Prince of Wales, Louis was very devout, and this had a political consequence as he was linked to the *Dévots*, a group that wished to use the Crown to influence policy. Louis died of tuberculosis. It is difficult to know how far his succession might have eased French politics or avoided the Revolution. Louis' philanthropy and integrity certainly gained him popularity.

Louis XIV's eldest son, Louis (1661-1711), the 'Grand Dauphin', and eldest grandson Louis, the 'Petit Dauphin' (1682-1712) both predeceased him, dying of smallpox and measles respectively. The former had scant drive and limited ability, the latter, however, proving a more dynamic figure, again linked to the *Dévots* and, as with Frederick, was interested in a political transformation, in his case a governance through the Crown and the aristocracy rather than through ministerial agencies populated by members of the bourgeoisie. As with Britain, different paths were on offer. This was a repeated theme in British politics, a history involving choice and contingencies.

GEORGE III, A MONARCH IN CONTENTION

'I was astonished with the extent of information which the King displayed upon a variety of subjects.'

John Sinclair on his 1½-hour audience with the King after a Baltic journey. As a result, George wanted to read an account of Sweden.[1]

It is ironic but unsurprising that, as King, George is most commonly remembered today for being on 'the wrong side of history', the presentist view that bedevils our assessment of the past. For a while, attention focused on his health, most recently as a result of a play by Alan Bennett (1991), then film (1994), *The Madness of King George*. 'Mad King George' was his standard epithet. More recently, there has been a return to the earlier focus on his opposition to the American Revolution, a theme that resonates from Thomas Jefferson's text for the Declaration of Independence of 1776 to the more recent musical *Hamilton* (2015) by Lin-Manuel Miranda, which was based on the 2004 biography *Alexander Hamilton* by Ron Chernow. The criticism of George echoes that complained of by Dr Johnson in February 1784: 'The indecency with which the King is every day treated.' Johnson had been impressed by the King when they met in the royal library.

Clearly, it would be mistaken to ignore this opposition to American assertiveness and the resulting political and military failure, which indeed saw the British world divided as it was not to be again until independence for most of Ireland in 1922. The latter owed something to American support for the independence cause; and the more general role of America in supplanting and deprecating British imperialism highlights the consequences of George's failure and also the effect of the nineteenth-century Irish diaspora.

This failure was also very serious in the short-term. France and Spain, which joined in on the American side in 1778 and 1779 respectively, were thereby provided with opportunities to reverse their losses in the Seven Years' War whose glorious end in 1763 had crowned George's early years with repeated military success, notably the capture of Havana from Spain in 1762. This resumed war saw Britain threatened with invasion by France and Spain in 1779 as part of a military crisis that tested the empire, while the political system and public order in Britain were severely challenged in 1780, and there was a protracted governmental crisis in 1782-4.

It was not only George's failure of understanding and response that was responsible for the inept and unsuccessful reaction to demands for change which, despite the outbreak of fighting in 1775, did not amount to a quest for independence until 1776. Yet, he bore much of the responsibility, and George's attitude was not only one of the intellect but also in line with his instinctive responses to politics and indeed, life: a focus on order and continuity, and, at times, rigid conservatism, one feature of which was respect for institutions.

So also with George's response to the issue of Catholic Emancipation, with Catholic freeholders in Ireland granted the right to vote in 1793. He was far from alone in opposing this change, but what set him apart was his rigidity, and that against the advice of his experienced and talented leading minister William Pitt the Younger, who was his Prime Minister for the longest duration, beginning in December 1783. This reluctance, which led to Pitt's resignation in 1801, has been seen as responsible for the long-term weakness of Irish Catholic support for the parliamentary Union with Ireland that was one of the significant constitutional legacies of his reign. This may well exaggerate that weakness and underplay the significance of later developments in Anglo-Irish relations, but George's stance was certainly not helpful.

Failure as leader and individual is therefore a frequent analysis. It was also one found at the time, with George criticised in particular by those presenting themselves as Whigs. They argued that his failings arose from an authoritarianism that was reflected in an abandonment of the principles of the 'Glorious Revolution' of 1688-9 and, instead, support for a return to the Stuart autocracy that had been rejected then. George was therefore very much on the 'wrong side' of history, and, in every sense, a reactionary.

This is not exactly a hostile 'Black Legend' comparable to that which affected the perception of Philip II of Spain (r. 1556-98) or King John or Richard III. Yet, the account represented an invocation of an 'old order' that helped Whigs then and in the early nineteenth century to justify constitutional change in their interests, and their reform programme more generally. Moreover, the argument made the American Revolution appear less disruptive and radical; instead, as an essentially law-observing response to these reactionary features allegedly personified in George, a view taken in Britain as well as America.

In practice, this analysis was contested at the time and has been challenged since, revisionist works becoming more numerous over the last half-century. It might appear unnecessary to repeat the points amply covered in readily accessible works, namely that George was impressive as an individual, diligent as a monarch, and associated with success as well as failure. Writing about this George, however, confronts more of a problem of a strongly entrenched as well as anachronistic historiography than in the case of his two predecessors. For both George I and George II, there is a sense of discovery, or at least of a relatively unfixed historiography;

but for George III there is a very well-established discussion. To begin, as it were, at the beginning is to sell short those who are familiar with it, but probably will not convince those whose views are set in terms of the negative views of the time (Whigs, Jefferson) as reheated by the satire of the present (*Hamilton*).

That George reigned when Britain was at its busiest in the slave trade can also be significant for modern views, although George was also on the throne when the British slave trade was abolished. While sceptical about the consequences of Abolitionism and, more generally, concerned about the support of established practice, George was responsible for neither development, not an observation that conforms with the general tendency to ascribe too much to monarchs. Abolitionism takes on great significance given modern concerns but, for contemporaries, the French Revolution and the subsequent wars were far more important.

The focus on the monarch as the central figure understandably existed in George's case from the outset. His education emphasised the responsibilities of the monarch, presenting constitutional tasks in an intensely personal fashion. This drew on the legacy of George's father, Frederick, Prince of Wales, who sought to establish a party of opposition Whigs and non-Jacobite Tories to create a 'third force' that could offer a broad canvas, one-nation party, and correspondingly marginalise the other Whigs and Tories. Frederick achieved some success in 1741-2 as his movement helped lead to the overthrow of Sir Robert Walpole in 1742. However, he was subsequently outmanoeuvred and when he revived an opposition was unable to have comparable impact on the 1747 election. Frederick could not take the widespread interest in the reversionary interest forward to support an effective opposition before he unexpectedly died in 1751.

As a result, the ideas of a 'Patriot King' that had been focused on Frederick were inherited by George, his eldest son, born in 1738. Counterfactual 'what if?' approaches can only take us so far, but these concepts might have worked for George had he come to the throne later. George I lived from 1660 to 1727 and George II from

1683 to 1760, and George III was to live from 1738 to 1820; but Frederick only lived from 1707 to 1751, and his younger brother, William, Duke of Cumberland, from 1721 to 1765.

George is far from alone in being a monarch whose childhood is somewhat obscure. If the child was father to the man, George was not an immature boy-king, like Richard II, who in 1377 was the previous English/British monarch who succeeded his grandfather, or Henry VI and Edward VI, who succeeded their fathers. George's childhood was scrutinised at the time in an attempt to ascertain what he was likely to do when he succeeded, but this process only really started in 1751 with the sudden death of Frederick.

George was to repeat Frederick's pattern of moving from non-party rule to government by faction/party/connection; the choice of words, by both contemporaries and today, instructive in the specific case and also more generally for assumptions about politics. He had developed as a bookish and cultured young man, one who, to his chagrin, lacked military experience or any knowledge of 'abroad' (including Hanover), but who otherwise had been well-prepared for British kingship. Initially, George was brought by his father's death back into the orbit of his grandfather, for George II, although never the easiest of men, did not extend to his daughter-in-law Augusta nor to his numerous grandchildren the loathing he had shown for his troublesome eldest son. That Augusta was Protestant and came from a German ruling house, Saxe-Gotha, helped: there were echoes of Queen Caroline.

The education of the future King caused controversy in late 1752 when, with his household seriously divided, his Sub-Governor Andrew Stone, Newcastle's political factotum, was implausibly seen as pushing unwelcome Tory views. More credibly, the Pelhams saw Stone as a way to maintain their influence at the young Court.[2] In early 1753, Stone successfully defended himself before the Council from the charge of being a Jacobite, still a potent accusation; and an attack on the issue in the House of Lords was defeated by the ministry. The crisis indicated the continued traction of Jacobitism, the sensitivity of the topic of the future ruler's opinions, and also the ability of George II and the Pelhams to overcome attacks. In 1753, the new Governor, or head of the Prince's household, James, 2nd Earl Waldegrave, enjoyed considerable favour with George II and was close to the Pelhams.[3]

In the event, there was to be no regency as George II lived long enough for George III to reach his majority, as with William IV and Victoria in 1837. The main candidates for regent would have been Augusta and Cumberland, who were not allies. As a young and enthusiastic monarch, George was to be wrongly reported to be completely directed by his mother.[4] In the late 1750s, the prince represented to Hardwicke 'the succession' and his grandfather 'the possession', and Hardwicke argued that the support of the former for the latter was essential.[5] There were repeated divisions, but the politics of the period saw a growing success in holding them in check.

George III grew up into a rich cultural heritage. Aside from the strong influence from Frederick, Augusta was a patron of the architect Sir William Chambers (1726-96), who taught the young Prince architectural drawing, and was employed by Augusta to add to the gardens of her house at Kew. In 1757-62, Chambers erected a number of buildings there in oriental or Classical styles that had a great impact. George also learned much about painting while a young man, and also acquired musical skills.[6]

As a new King, George sought to negotiate peace with France in accordance with ideas of the Christian monarch as peacemaker,[7] and he sought domestic renewal of both politics and the Church, but he failed in all respects. Far from negotiations in 1761 bringing peace, the war continued while Spain came in on the side of France. In Britain, his ability to appoint bishops enabled him to advance ecclesiastical 'renewal', notably by preserving doctrinal orthodoxy and episcopal diligence, but he found the situation very different in secular government. From 1762, his policies and ministers were both attacked, and these attacks helped create a period of instability as he struggled to establish an effective ministry able to command a lasting majority in the House of Commons.

A regalist view was already present prior to the accession of George III, one that supported George II against the practices of the 'Old Corps Whigs'. This was seen with the *Con-Test* of 14 May 1757:

> Never did King better deserve the love of his people, than our gracious sovereign, and never were subjects more forward to express their loyal affection to the crown. They have, for many years past, beheld with concern the violence offered to majesty; they have seen the unworthy, by their powerful connections, and the intrigues of a cabal, force themselves into the administration; they have known a minister appointed in the morning, by the free election of the Sovereign, who has been seen to displace him before night, and submit to have the prerogative wrested from his hand by insolent usurpers: The reflections of distressed Royalty on that occasion, are not forgotten; and so far are the people from presuming to trespass on the regal right, that they wish nothing more than to see the sovereign use the free exercise of that privilege, which the constitution has wisely committed to his care.

This approach presages support for George III in 1783-4, with Charles James Fox as the 'insolent usurper'.

George took a very active part in the ministerial politics of the 1760s, and we can follow his activity because he left an extensive correspondence, official and private. This reveals from the 1760s a 'hands on' monarch, one who sought to direct his ministers and, to a degree, act, to use a later term, as his own Prime Minister. In contrast, there really had been a Prime Minister or would-be Prime Minister under George I and George II. In the 1760s, George III's disquiet about George Grenville and the Marquess of Rockingham, successive first ministers from 1763 to 1766, followed by the inability of the sickly Pitt the Elder and then the indecisive Augustus, 3rd Duke of Grafton to fulfil the role, encouraged him to act as a would-be directing figure.

Prior to his accession, there had been a conviction that the relationship with Hanover would alter under George. In 1751, the diplomat Sir Charles Hanbury-Williams had written:

> The grief at Hanover for the death of the late Prince of Wales [Frederick] is very great. They look upon themselves (and I hope with reason) as likely to become in reality a province subservient to the interests of Great Britain, and it is high time they should be so for during my stay at Hanover last summer I saw so much of the insolence of those ministers that it made me sick. But now I think the scene must change for 'tis impossible that a Prince [George III] not born there can possibly like such a poor scrubby town and such a barren and melancholic country.[8]

A broader shift in sentiment on international relations was anticipated by the well-connected Sardinian envoy in 1754, when he argued that birth in Hanover and frequent visits there had made George II naturally sympathetic to Austria, but that his grandson would be less so as he had never been there and had not been brought up by Germans.[9] Indeed, as heir, the future George wrote to his confidant, John, 3rd Earl of Bute, in August 1759: 'As to the affairs on the Weser they look worse and worse; I fear this is entirely owing to the partiality the King [George II] has for that horrid Electorate which has always lived upon the very vitals of this poor country; I should say more and perhaps with more anger did not my clock show it is time to dress for Court.'

George III's determination to act without a focus on Hanover was praised by some, a pamphleteer writing in 1762: 'What terrors can the most wayward imagination form of predilection and partiality to any foreign interests in the bosom of a sovereign who has so sensibly expressed his affection for this country when he boasted of his being born a Briton.'[10]

As King, George showed his determination to end Britain's involvement in the German part of the Seven Years' War:

> Though I have subjects who will suffer immensely whenever this kingdom withdraws its protection from thence, yet so superior is my love to this my native country [Britain] over any private interest of my own [Hanover] that I cannot help wishing that an end was put to that enormous expense by ordering our troops home... I think if the Duke of Newcastle will not hear reason concerning the German war that it would be better to let him quit than to go on with that and to have myself and those who differ from him made unpopular.

This shift in policy involved breaking with the expensive Prussian alliance, which greatly angered Pitt. In contrast, conscious of the importance of a different strand of popularity, George informed Bute in 1762 that he would 'never wish to load this country with' subsidies.[11] In the 1760s, George was not conspicuous as an advocate of Hanoverian interest or of British commitments to aid the Electorate. As a consequence, the King's views on foreign policy were not as politically contentious as those of his grandfather and great-grandfather had been. This owed much also to the dominance of colonial, commercial and maritime issues in foreign policy in the 1760s, and the political and public discussion of it. Compared to his two predecessors, George III had no diplomatic experience That, however, did not mean that George was not interested in Hanover, nor uncommitted to its interests. There were reports that he would visit Hanover, only to be thwarted by the demands of British politics.[12]

Figures with links to Hanover were important. Carl Heinrich von Hinüber (1723-92), who had been German Secretary in George's household as Prince of Wales, was described in 1772 by the experienced Bavarian diplomat Baron Haslang as a major favourite of George, his private librarian and his executor for all Hanoverian affairs.[13]

After 1763, foreign policy largely ceased to be such a consistently contentious subject of political debate. Domestic and American constitutional, fiscal and political issues diverted attention from foreign policy, with which it was difficult to link them, apart from India, where the role of France was significant. Those who challenged George or his ministers did not need to refer to foreign policy. The collapse of Jacobitism and the political shifts of the 1750s helped further to create a new agenda in which Hanover and the monarch played a far smaller part in foreign policy. This argument must not be pushed too far – foreign policy was not forgotten, and reference was made to George's views, but a substantial change followed his accession.

George's address to his first Privy Council revealed his determination to break with the past, and he made his views clear in his addition to the draft for his first speech from the throne:

> Born and educated in this country I glory in the name of Britain; and the peculiar happiness of my life will ever consist in promoting the welfare of a people whose loyalty and warm affection to me I consider as the greatest and most permanent security of my throne.[14]

This attitude led to concern among the 'Old Corps' Whigs. One of Newcastle's supporters, Charles, 2nd Marquess of Rockingham, first minister in 1765-6 and 1782, displayed such misgivings over the terms of a likely address from Yorkshire:

> I could wish that the words *Native Country* and *Truly English* were not echoed back from Yorkshire – as indeed it strikes me as carrying with it a signification that that was wanting in his late Majesty ... Queen Anne on the death of King William in her declaration set forth that *Her Heart was entirely English* which gave great offence to the Whigs at that time.[15]

Aside from George being keen to rule without party factionalism and determined to end the exclusion of the Tories, the leaders of the 'Old Corps' Whigs, especially Newcastle and Hardwicke, were ageing. A new generation of ministers was required, but, helping to provoke contention and instability, George neither waited for his grandfather's ministers to die or retire, nor took their advice on their successors. Newcastle in 1762 was the first of a series of ministers who discovered that an absence or loss of royal favour could be politically fatal: so also for Grenville in 1765, Rockingham in 1766, the Fox-North ministry in 1783 and the Ministry of all the Talents in 1807.

The 1760s was a watershed decade with a generational shift in political leadership that brought new people to the fore. But George struggled to find ministers who could maintain Parliament's confidence. The result kept a lot of issues, especially American ones, from being addressed effectively, and there were also distractions like the Wilkes crisis.

Many Tories came to court after the accession of George,[16] as they had done after that of his predecessors, but whereas they had been disillusioned in previous cases, that was not the case in 1760. Responding to the admission of Tories to Court office, Elizabeth Montagu thought that ministerial posts should and would be different:

> It is right that those who by their favour in administration are as it were accountable to the people for the execution of great and important offices should choose the men whose conduct they are to answer for, but as to a place in which nothing but court attendance is required, I see not why a king may not choose the person.[17]

This was not George's attitude. Instead, his policies destroyed the coherence and undermined the assumptions of the 'Old Corps' Whigs.

This break with his grandfather's ministers was intertwined with the break with the policies of the 1750s. It was not only that the alliance with Prussia was abandoned, but that the gap was not filled by an alliance with another major Continental power. The motives for such a course of action – royal anxiety about Hanover, ministerial concern about this anxiety, and the sense that defensive arrangements for Hanover could and should serve as the basis for a British alliance system – had been largely lost. So also had the interventionist habit of mind and the concomitant diplomatic assumptions. Newcastle had written of the response of the elderly George II to a Prussian victory:

> The King, who gives the tone to the nation, and is the foremost to extol and admire the great actions of this great prince, talks of this victory with the affection of a friend and near relation; the satisfaction of an ally, highly interested in the same cause; and with the praise, and admiration, of a general, who knows the real merit of it, and the extent of the genius which must, under God, have brought it about.[18]

The views of George III were very different. George, who had much better manners than his grandfather, might have been very gracious to Carteret soon after his accession, but he had only limited interest in the views that the minister had once stood for. In March 1761, Baron Haslang, the Bavarian envoy in London, pointed out that the prince-bishopric of Hildesheim, which George II had sought to acquire, was both vacant and actually occupied by George III's forces. George III, however, did not share his grandfather's views. Three weeks after reporting that Hildesheim was vacant, Haslang observed that the predilection for Hanover was no longer so strong and suggested that there would be no territorial cessions elsewhere to France in order to make gains for the Electorate.[19] This was at a time when the Electorate of Saxony was seeking territorial gains from the Archbishopric-Electorate of Mainz. George, however, took the nomination to the Prince-Bishopric of Osnabrück quite seriously: it went in 1764 to his second son, Frederick, Duke of York.

When, in June 1761, François de Bussy (a senior French diplomat who as agent 101 sold information to the British, and in addition might have been a double or triple agent) began peace negotiations with the British ministry, he was told by Carteret that the British had little interest in Hanoverian affairs. When Bussy told Pitt that France would expect compensation for her Hanoverian conquests, on the grounds that, in order to pursue her operations on the Continent, France had diverted resources from the defence of her colonies, Pitt replied that the argument would have had a great effect during the reign of George II, but that the situation had changed.

In turn, the criticism of ministers increasingly extended to the king, a process that with George III began in the early 1760s and became more striking, and more insistent than under George I and George II. 'Junius', writing in the *Public Advertiser* of 19 December 1769, caused a sensation with a bold letter to George claiming that he had never 'been acquainted with the language of truth, until you heard it in the complaints of your people'.

The situation appeared to change from 1770. George chose Frederick, Lord North, a longstanding friend, as First Lord of the Treasury and, far more politically accomplished than Bute, he held the office until 1782, despite his frequent requests in the face of bad news during the War of American Independence that he retire, requests George turned down until the crisis of parliamentary confidence after Yorktown. North's ministry endured a length of time not too different from that of Pelham (1743-54) and only recently surpassed by Sir Robert Walpole (1721-42). In the person of North, a moderate Tory, George had brought back the stability of the 'Old Corps' Whig system. Furthermore, with George's support, North delivered impressive electoral successes in 1774 and 1780, just as the 'Old Corps' had done. These suggested a winning and durable political system, and that George had implemented the ideas associated with his father with reasonable success. In this view, the earlier instability of the 1760s was an inherent aspect of the difficulty of bedding in a new system. In a different context, the same process of development could be seen in America from 1783 to 1815.

Mention of America is appropriate because George's success in the early 1770s, notably in Britain, in containing difficulties, was overturned not so much by the outbreak in 1775 of a revolution in the American colonies, but rather by the inability to settle it by repeated counter-attacks (1776-81), or negotiations (1776, 1778), or to limit it by preventing the war from spreading to include European rivals, as it did increasingly from 1778. It was this multiple failure that led North to political despair and George to its spiritual counterpart, for he saw these failures as proof of the anger of Providence, an anger that he attributed to both himself and the country.

The importance of religion to George is something that has emerged most clearly from some recent scholarship. He had a strong sense of the personal religious responsibility of the monarch and also of every human, and he was noted for the fervour of his responses to prayers. George took seriously his role in the appointment of senior clergy, and, as he told Johnson, enjoyed reading books of sermons. Both Lutherans, and influenced to a degree by the Pietist movement in German Protestantism, George I and George II had been more distant from the Church, although Queen Caroline was not. George III's emphasis on religious observance and moral conduct resonated with some facets of English High Churchmanship as well as with Methodism.

In a way that drew on a wider cultural change in tone,[20] the King's clear and well-understood religious commitment was linked to an overt moral stance. However, by modern standards, this was not to the fore in his response to slavery where his resistance to abolition reflected a preference for established practice which made him accept limits at times on royal authority. George was in favour of sobriety and opposed to blasphemy, gambling, late nights and indulgence, both personal and national. The last led to his hostility to the conduct of his sons, and this marked lack of personal sympathy was much clearer than in the case of essentially political estrangements between George I and the future George II, George II and Prince Frederick, and, to a lesser extent, George II and the future George III. Nevertheless, political estrangement was also important in the case of George III and his eldest son, the future George IV.

Morality was accompanied by purpose and by exemplary pastimes. A believer in the *métier* as well as responsibility of monarchs, George worked hard, as his correspondence amply showed. His pastimes were also designed to improve the country, not least in his personal interest in farming, one he showed at Windsor, although his spending more and more time there rather than in London also owed much to his enjoyment of riding, walking and hunting. To a degree, 'Farmer George' was a classic country gentleman.

Yet there was far more to his interests and role. He was very much a patron of opulence, as well as discernment, in his support for the arts, notably painting. There was an instructive development of his style in this respect with his favour for the painter Benjamin West, whom he made the second President of the Royal Academy, showing first a Neo-Classical and then a Neo-Gothic aesthetic. So also with George's architectural interests, which culminated in extensive work at Windsor, where George spent over £133,000 from his privy purse and helped make Gothic the national style and one conspicuously proper for major buildings. Among other cultural accomplishments, George played music and painted. George frequently went to the opera. The Court was a setting for cultural activity. On 1 January 1772, there was, as Frederick Hannecken, the Danish Legation Secretary, noted, a very numerous turnout at St James's for the King's levée and the Queen's circle, with the door to the Great Council Chamber left open so that it was possible to hear the performance of an ode composed by the Poet Laureate set to music by William Boyce, Master of the King's Music from 1755 to 1779.[21]

George's taste in literature was conservative, more sermons than novels. He praised seventeenth-century writers such as Robert Sanderson (1587-1663), a sermon-writer and chaplain to, and a favourite preacher before, Charles I, who lost his living and the divinity chair at Oxford because he refused to subscribe to the Parliamentarians' Solemn League and Covenant.[22] Johnson advised on the purchase of books for the royal family and was a beneficiary of George's largesse.

George had a pronounced historical awareness. When Henry, Duke of Cumberland married a commoner in 1771, his brother, the outraged and overwrought George, informed another brother, William, Duke of Gloucester, that such a step might threaten civil war, as he claimed that the fifteenth-century Wars of the Roses owed much to the intermarriage of Crown and nobility.[23] And George was reflective when he visited the tomb of the overthrown and murdered Edward II in Gloucester Cathedral in 1788, an event in 1327 appearing pertinent to him.

George also took a view on legitimacy that made allowance for the cause of the Stuarts, one that extended to providing financial support for 'Henry IX', the younger son of 'James III and VIII,' who was a theoretical claimant to George's throne. George had no time for the false report that 'James III', the 'warming pan baby' of 1688, was a changeling. Instead, George saw his own position, and that of future British monarchs, as resting not solely on dynastic right but also on parliamentary position and personal duty. He was mindful of what the 'Glorious Revolution' meant in terms of the rejection of unacceptable monarchy. Indeed, in his writings as a prince, George criticised James II and VII, arguing that the 'Glorious Revolution' had rescued Britain 'from the iron rod of arbitrary power' and praised Oliver Cromwell as 'a friend of justice and virtue',[24] a view somewhat different from the traditional Church presentation of Charles I. In 1799, an approach on behalf of 'Henry IX' led George to reflect that he had 'ever thought that (the) true solid basis' of Hanoverian rule was that 'it came to preserve the free Constitution of this Empire, both in Church and State, which compact I trust none of my successors will ever dare to depart from.'[25] George's views on legitimacy extended beyond allowance for the Stuarts. He remarked in the 1760s that abridging colonial charters was obnoxious and resisted suggestions for doing so in New England. His commitment to Parliamentary rather than dynastic monarchy also touched on legitimacy. These views limited options for dealing with America, both on concessions – what he could not yield – and on firm action.

In science, George had wide-ranging interests, particularly so in astronomy, which he supported financially, although he did not understand the complex mathematics that played an increasing role in it. This was an aspect of a commitment to discovery also seen with his engagement in voyages of exploration. The latter was linked to astronomy and, for both, there was an emphasis on practicality and application. George's interest in science included aspects of the British economy, such as canals and manufacturing. The King was very much an investigator of ways and means, as in his concern with clocks and other mechanisms. As Prince of Wales, George had visited the house of William Watson in order to see his electrical experiments.

George then was far from a dullard, but, instead, a committed individual with many interests. He was not a warrior-King, no Frederick II, 'the Great' of Prussia, but then it would not have been appropriate to have risked his life onboard a warship or in battle, as did Gustavus Adolphus and Charles XII of Sweden. Nor would it have helped the war effort. Instead, George took a great interest in supporting the navy, not only in visiting it but also in using patronage and oversight in order to reward appropriate conduct. The latter was particularly seen in terms of resolute command and brave conduct, for George believed in leadership through example, which was one reason why he repeatedly found his heir such a disappointment.

As far as contemporaries were concerned, he was more impressive than Louis XVI and more politically sage than Gustavus III of Sweden, the Emperor Joseph II or Christian VII of Denmark. Indeed, looking at other royal examples is instructive because it can encourage caution about being too damning of George. The weaknesses of monarchs were a matter not only of their personalities but also of their contexts. Thus, Peter III in 1762 and Paul I in 1801 were assassinated in Russia, but there was no other way there to alter policy and deal with the serious deficiencies of a ruler. In each case, as with earlier removals of monarchs, the solution was another monarch and not a republic.

George is relatively unusual in being a monarch whose subsequent reputation is so much more politically prominent than many others whose personality, instead, has been the main talking point. In part, this reflects the degree to which his lifetime saw the very position of monarchy become the issue, with republics declared in America (1776), France (1792) and Latin America from the 1810s, and republican views burgeoning elsewhere, albeit succeeding in Europe largely only through French conquest. In contrast, with the exception of 1649-60, republicanism had not seriously hitherto been on the agenda in Britain. Instead, the question had been one of restricting royal powers, as in 1215 or the early and mid-1640s, or of which dynasty, as in the struggle with the Jacobites begun in 1688 that had only really ended with French defeats in 1759.

Indeed, George was the first of the 'post-dynastic monarchs' in the sense that his reign was not defined by any struggle between dynasties or within the ruling house. There was a significant clash in 1788-9 over the regency for the apparently then irrevocably ill George. Yet the alignments of that dispute were not set by a rivalry between George and George, Prince of Wales, important as the latter was in the crisis, but rather between the government and opposition. Similarly, although facing criticism from a radical cousin, Louis XVI was not brought down by a dynastic challenge. Opposition to George III could not present itself through a dynastic alternative, and therefore needed a set of values different to that as well as to George, which in America meant republicanism.

Struggle, however, was the theme for his reign. Although the struggle that was to be highlighted by many was that over domestic politics, in practice it was war that was crucial, and this on a long-established pattern. During George's reign, Britain was at war with France in 1760-3, 1778-83, 1793-1802, 1803-14 and 1815, and with Spain in 1762-3, 1779-83, 1796-1802, and 1804-08. George never saw combat, but was not some passive

Above right: Queen Anne's failure to have children who survived her provided the Hanoverians with their opportunity. Portrait by Charles Jervas in the Royal Collection. (Public domain)

Below right: Electress Sophia and her daughter who became Queen of Prussia. (Courtesy National Library of Scotland, public domain)

Below: The Electoral escutcheon of Hanover. The two golden lions in red represent Brunswick, the blue lion on gold surrounded by red hearts represents Lüneburg and the white horse Hanover. (Wikimedia Commons)

George I in 1714 by Sir Godfrey Kneller, himself German-born. He came to England in 1676, was knighted in 1692 and created a baronet by George I in 1715. (Courtesy National Portrait Gallery, public domain)

George I in repose, which he rarely was, also by Kneller. In 1726, John Chamberlayne described the country as 'an hereditary limited monarchy, governed ... according to the known laws and customs.' (Courtesy National Portrait Gallery, public domain)

Above: George I silver shilling, showing the King in profile. (Wikimedia Commons)

Right: George II by Thomas Hudson, 1744. This captured the King after his triumph at Dettingen, at the height of his reputation. In London in November 1743, the novelty of a king returning as a conquering hero was joined to victory over the hereditary enemy. Church bells rang out, Handel did his stuff and bonfires and illuminations lit the night sky. (Courtesy National Portrait Gallery, public domain)

Above left: Henry Fox, 1st Baron Holland by John Giles Eccardt. (Courtesy National Portrait Gallery, public domain)

Above right: Amalie Sophie von Wallmoden, comforter of George II. Portrait held at the Herrenhausen Palace, Hanover. (Public domain)

Left: Caricature of John, 3rd Earl of Bute, alleged to have had an affair with Augusta, widow of Frederick, Prince of Wales. 'He doth bestride the narrow world like a colossus and we petty ministers walk under his huge legs.' (Courtesy Wellcome Collection)

Right: Portrait of Frederick, Prince of Wales by Philip Mercier, *c.* 1735-6. Although he saw himself as a leading political player, Frederick was very much in the hands of superior political intelligences and personalities who exploited his value to the parliamentary opposition. (Courtesy National Portrait Gallery, public domain)

Below: Portly caricature of William, Duke of Cumberland suggesting royal ambitions. (Wikimedia Commons)

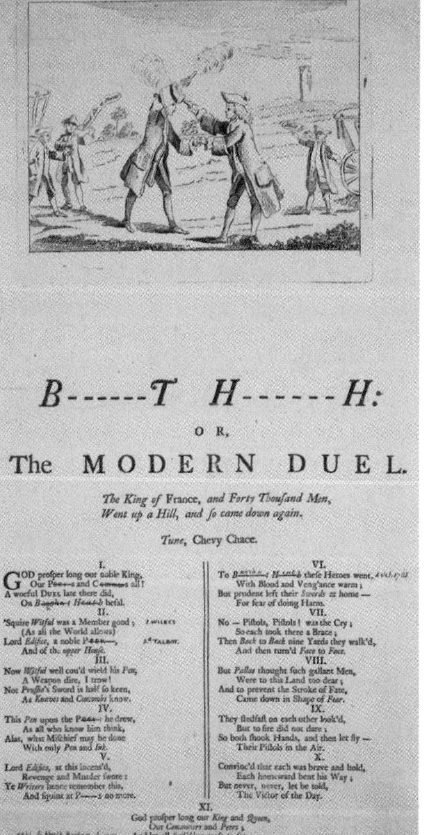

B------T H------H:

O R,

The MODERN DUEL.

The King of France, *and Forty Thouſand Men,*
Went up a Hill, and ſo came down again.

Tune, Chevy Chace.

I.
GOD proſper long our noble King,
Our P——s and C——s all!
A woeful DUEL late there did,
On *B——t H——h* befal.

II.
'Squire *Wilful* was a Member good;
(As all the World allows)
Lord *Edifice*, a noble P——,
And of the *upper Houſe.*

III.
Now *Wilful* well cou'd wield his *Pen*,
A Weapon dire, I trow!
Not *Pruſſia*'s Sword is half ſo keen,
As *Knaves* and *Coxcombs* know.

IV.
This *Pen* upon the P——r he drew,
As all who know him think,
Alas, what Miſchief may be done
With only *Pen* and *Ink.*

V.
Lord *Edifice*, at this incens'd,
Revenge and Murder ſwore:
Ye *Writers* hence remember this,
And ſquirt at P——s no more.

VI.
To *B——t H——h* theſe Heroes went,
With Blood and Veng'ance warm;
But prudent left their *Swords* at home—
For fear of doing Harm.

VII.
No — Piſtols, Piſtols! was the Cry;
So each took there a Brace;
Then *Back* to *Back* nine Yards they walk'd,
And then turn'd *Face* to *Face.*

VIII.
But *Pallas* thought ſuch gallant Men,
Were to this Land too dear;
And to prevent the Stroke of Fate,
Came down in Shape of *Fear.*

IX.
They ſtedfaſt on each other look'd,
But to fire did not dare;
So both ſhook Hands, and then let fly—
Their Piſtols in the Air.

X.
Convinc'd that each was brave and bold,
Each homeward bent his Way;
But never, never, let be told,
The Victor of the Day.

XI.
God proſper long our *King* and *Queen*,
Our *Commoners* and *Peers*;
And let all *Scribblers* ceaſe to ſet
The *Nation* by the Ears.

Above: 'Solomons Glory or the Rival Mistresses', 1749. The Duke of Cumberland as the subject of salacious comments with Windsor Castle in the background. In fact, the unmarried Cumberland generally preferred the company of officers. (Courtesy LOC)

Left: The duel on Bagshot Heath between John Wilkes and William, 1st Earl Talbot, the Lord Steward. Neither was hit. This caricature suggests the duel was a stunt. (Courtesy the British Museum, public domain)

Frederick, Prince of Wales by the Neapolitan Jacopo Amigoni, 1735, who worked in England from 1730 to 1739. Painted in a lush palette, his work reflected the openness of English high society to Italianate styles. (Courtesy the Royal Collection Trust, public domain)

Augusta of Saxe-Gotha by Charles Philips, who died young like Frederick, Prince of Wales. Painted in 1737 when Philips also painted the Prince, as he had already done in 1732. (Courtesy National Portrait Gallery, public domain)

'The Music Party': Frederick, Prince of Wales and his sisters by Philippe Mercier, 1733. Frederick is shown playing the cello. Born in Berlin of Huguenot background, Mercier arrived in London probably in 1716 and was appointed Principal Portrait Painter by Frederick in 1729. (Courtesy National Portrait Gallery, public domain)

George III, 1754, by the Genevan painter Jean-Étienne Liotard who visited London in 1753-4 and 1772-4. This was commissioned by Princess Augusta and showed George in a gorgeous red coat that has, however, faded. Soon after, his grandfather George II refused George's wish to serve in the Seven Years' War. (Courtesy Scottish National Gallery, public domain)

Above: George III's procession to the Houses of Parliament, showing the new state coach (probably by John Wootton, 1762-4) designed by Sir William Chambers and first used on 25 November 1762 for the state opening of Parliament, replacing the Baroque-style state coach made for Queen Anne. The decoration of the coach included references to Apollo, Mercury, Britannia and Neptune. (Courtesy the Royal Collection Trust, public domain)

Right: Queen Charlotte by Thomas Gainsborough, 1781, who also painted other members of the royal family. George III hung the painting in the Dining Room at Buckingham House. (Courtesy of the Royal Collection, public domain)

George III and Napoleon as rival gardeners. Caricature by Charles Williams, 1803. George is shown as a more honest and successful gardener. (Courtesy LOC)

George III's statue in New York being pulled down in 1776. (Courtesy LOC)

James Gillray caricature of George III repelling the French invasion, 1793. Pontefract, identified on the map, was noted for the production of liquorice, then used as a laxative. Gillray produced a number of depictions of George. The King wears a fool's cap labelled 'Northumberland', which suggests that Gillray wasn't entirely convinced that mere bluster was enough when it came to the security of the realm. (Public domain)

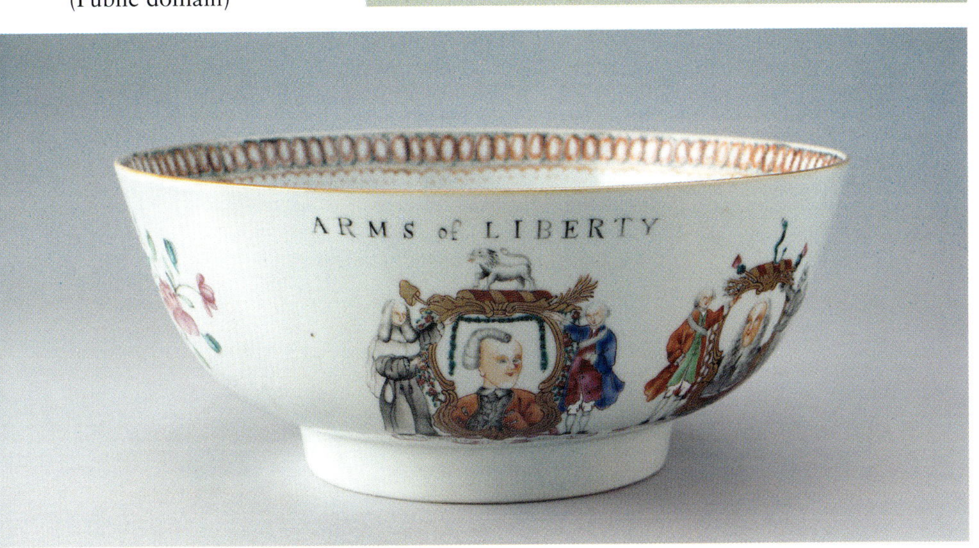

'The Arms of Liberty' punchbowl, produced in China for the American market. The portraits are copied from a broadside printed in London in June 1768, depicting John Wilkes (left), an advocate of political reform and American liberty, and Lord Mansfield (right), who tried to silence Wilkes with charges of libel. Mansfield appears with George III and the devil by his side. (Courtesy the Art Institute of Chicago, Bequest of Frederick S. Colburn)

The 1780 Gordon Riots in London saw George take a firm stance, saying in Council that 'the magistrates had not done their duty, but that he would do his own'. Engraving after a painting by Francis Wheatley, commissioned by the publisher John Boydell, 1790. (Public domain)

Queen Charlotte with her two eldest sons by Allan Ramsay, *c.* 1765. The two sons were the future George IV and Frederick, Duke of York. (Courtesy of the Royal Collection, public domain)

Right: George IV as Prince Regent by Sir Thomas Lawrence, 1814. (Courtesy National Portrait Gallery, public domain)

Below: Buckingham House. Bought by George in 1762 for £28,000, this had been built in 1702-5 for John, Duke of Buckingham and included many Baroque features that George found unwelcome, such as a row of statues on the skyline and angle pilasters, which were removed. (Courtesy of the Royal Collection Trust, public domain)

Caroline of Brunswick by James Lonsdale, 1820. He was commissioned to paint a portrait by the Lord Mayor of London and after that he was appointed her official portrait painter. Queen Caroline's wedding ring was displayed in order to stress her role as a wife at a time when her reputation was under attack. (Courtesy National Portrait Gallery, public domain)

Princess Charlotte of Wales by Sir Thomas Lawrence, a standard, idealised presentation of a child. Her father, the future George IV who was estranged from her mother, refused to allow Charlotte to be brought up at Windsor under the care of George III. The whole painting is shown opposite.

George IV, double sovereign obverse, 1823. The reverse features the standard George and Dragon design. This was the first circulated double sovereign in history as the 1820 double sovereign struck under the reign of George III was not for circulation purposes. (Courtesy LOC)

Caroline, Princess of Wales and her only child, Charlotte, by Sir Thomas Lawrence, 1801. The absence of the father, George, later George IV, is appropriate. (Courtesy of the Royal Collection, public domain)

Left: 'The Stool of Repentance; the Scorn of the World!!' A hand-coloured etching published by William Benbow, January 1821. Britannia is central, Queen Caroline and George IV underneath. Wellington is behind Caroline. George, Caroline and the Cabinet are mocked by the four Continents. Below, a waterfall of corruption falls to pollute polite society and Westminster. Benbow was a keen supporter of reform and a printer, publisher and bookseller, who got into trouble with the law. (Courtesy LOC)

Below: The Governor's Palace, Williamsburg, Virginia. Destroyed in a fire in 1781, it was rebuilt in the early twentieth century with funds from J. D. Rockefeller Jnr – with the Hanoverian coat of arms prominent, as in the original. (Courtesy LOC)

bystander, as ministerial correspondence made clear. In 1761, when Pitt the Elder proposed a pre-emptive attack on Spain, Newcastle recorded:

> The King told me, Lord Anson [First Lord of the Admiralty] was of the opinion that the ships could not be ready in two months and His Majesty says Lord Anson promised him to give this opinion in Council, which cuts short, at once, any consideration of immediate operations.

In peacetime, he was assiduous in troop reviews and being portrayed in military uniform.[26] In 1777, George III wrote to John Robinson, Secretary to the Treasury, about the threat from American privateers:

> I trust the different vessels that hover round the island will be put on their guard particularly to protect Liverpool, Whitehaven, the Clyde, and even Bristol, for I do suspect that the rebel vessels which have been assembling at Nantes and Bordeaux mean some strike of that kind which would undoubtedly occasion much discontent among the merchants.[27]

Two months earlier, George had suggested that a few vessels stationed on the coast of Virginia might be able to control the tobacco trade from the Chesapeake. Indeed, leaf prices rose tenfold in Europe.

On a pattern that was widely shared, George typically saw divine support as well as human action as important. In October 1778, he expressed to North his trust that the navy would be in a state to cope with both France and Spain:

> Lord North must feel as I do the noble conduct of the three fifty gun ships that with so much bravery have driven off separate ships of far superior strength; I doubt not whenever

it shall please the Almighty to permit an English fleet fairly to engage any other a most comfortable issue will arise.[28]

A month later, however, correctly concerned about naval factionalism, George pressed for a new head of the Admiralty Board in place of John, 4th Earl of Sandwich: 'In a war and more so in the present which is a naval one, it is highly advantageous to have in the Cabinet a person able to plan the most effectual manner of conducting it.'[29] There was to be no replacement, nevertheless, until the fall of the North ministry in 1782 when Sandwich was succeeded by Augustus, 1st Viscount Keppel, a veteran and Whig dismissed in 1779 in the politicised aftermath of the disappointment of the battle of Ushant with a French fleet the previous year. (The battle was an indecisive mess, leading to two courts-martial in Britain and the resignation from the French navy of Louis Philippe II d'Orléans, a French *Prince du sang*, Prince of the royal blood, who took part in the action.)

The King's identification with the navy was demonstrated with his third son, William (later William IV), born in 1765, entering naval service in 1779 and in 1780 becoming a midshipman and seeing active service. He was to be the 'Sailor King' from 1830 to 1837. George also visited the fleet in 1778 (both Chatham and Portsmouth) and 1781 (the Nore), paying minute attention to the naval review of 1778, following Keppel's court-martial (Keppel's acquittal was a defeat for King and ministry) and pressing for a battle with the combined Franco-Spanish invasion fleet in 1779, even though it was larger.

In what was a protracted military and political crisis, George displayed generally resolute leadership and proved an impressive figure in a crisis. It would therefore be misguided to contrast him too readily with George II during the crisis caused by the Jacobite invasion of England in late 1745, although George II did not go on to rely on divine providence as his grandson was to do.

When North resigned in March 1782, having lost parliamentary support over persisting in the war in America, George, to his readily apparent fury,[30] was forced to turn to the Rockinghamites, a group he distrusted, who were pledged to independence for America. After Rockingham died, William, 2nd Earl of Shelburne was appointed to head the ministry in July 1782. His opposition to party or, in his words, faction, greatly attracted George, even though his interest in parliamentary reform was unwelcome, and Shelburne a Chathamite (a supporter of William Pitt, 1st Earl of Chatham). George's failure to choose the new leader of the Rockinghamites, William, 3rd Duke of Portland, led to the resignation of prominent members of the group, especially Charles James Fox. Nevertheless, George's determination to defend his prerogative of choosing his own ministers was widely accepted. That did not help George move toward the policies of his new ministry. Indeed, Shelburne complained to the French envoy that hitherto ministers had not made George understand the position of the country, and that redressing the issue was not easy.[31]

Not a Newcastle or a North, Shelburne lacked the ability and support to sustain his position and parliamentary defeats led to his resignation in early 1783. With the crisis affecting Geroge's health,[32] this provided an opportunity for Fox and North, former enemies, to form a coalition ministry headed by Portland, in April 1783. This was regardless of any claim by the King to choose his ministers and despite the bitter disapproval of George, who had failed to persuade William Pitt the Younger to form a government.[33]

George played a key role in undermining the new ministry, helping defeat the East India Bill, a crucial item of government business, in the Lords in December 1783. Regarded by some as unconstitutional, this move was countered by a collective resignation of some office holders, George saw himself as 'on the edge of a precipice'.[34] Commons defeats in January 1784 led the new First Lord of the Treasury, Pitt, to think of resigning and George to reiterate his (privately expressed) willingness to abdicate. In the crisis, public opinion moved toward the free exercise of the royal prerogative in choosing ministers. Over 50,000 people backed Addresses from counties and boroughs to that end. Parliament was dissolved when Pitt felt able to face a general election; and the elections, many of which were contested on national political grounds, were very favourable for the ministry.

An intimation of a rallying round the Crown had been seen in July 1783 when John, 2nd Earl of Buckinghamshire, a former diplomat, took time off from admiring the bathing beauties at Weymouth to question his assumptions in the face of the lack of a 'firm' administration:

> The state is now circumstanced as a human body in the last stage of a decline, Whig as I am and sufficiently vain of my descent from Maynard and Hampden [opponents of the Stuarts], it sometimes occurs to me that something might be obtained by strengthening the hands of the Crown.[35]

George had handled the political crisis well and in 1784 helped ensure a stable ministry under Pitt, who remained in office until 1801. He took a close interest in the elections, being concerned to balance loyalty and service, as with his attitude to David, Viscount Stormont, a longstanding former diplomat and Secretary of State, who had served as a minister in the Fox-North ministry. George decided with reference to the election of Scottish representative peers to the House of Lords that 'if Lord Stormont would be quiet he had no objection to his being in the government list, but if he interfered and canvassed for other opposition Lords the case was widely different.'[36]

It having been a major issue in the deterioration of relations, George helped manage reconciliation with America. George had been pleased to be away from London when the humiliating peace that acknowledged American independence was proclaimed in 1783, but he struck an appropriate note of wise and honest courtesy, on 1 June 1785, when he received John Adams as the first American envoy to the Court of St James's. A delighted Adams recorded George as saying:

> I have done nothing by the late contest but what I thought myself indispensably bound to do, by the duty which I owed to my people... I was the last to consent to the separation; but the separation having been made, and having become inevitable, I have always said, as I say now, that I would be the first to meet the friendship of the United States as an independent power ... let the circumstances of language, religion, and blood have their natural and full effect.[37]

Not everything, however, was so benign. The following March, Jefferson, on a visit from his embassy in Paris, was received by George. There are no detailed contemporary accounts of the meeting, although in his autobiography, written 35 years later, Jefferson was very critical. Claiming that he had been ungraciously received, Jefferson added: 'I saw, at once, that the ulcerations in the narrow mind of that mulish being (George III) left nothing to be expected on the subject of my attendance.'[38] Ironically, the two men in fact had much in common, from an interest in architecture and applied science to a disdain for luxury and a tolerance for slavery.

The sense of the King as a working monarch, and certainly no fool, is one that very much arises from his correspondence. Thus, in December 1783, George wrote to his new Foreign Secretary, Francis, Marquis of Carmarthen, offering guidance to the new young minister:

> The Marquis of Carmarthen has conducted his conference with the French Ambassador as stated in the note he has sent me with the greatest propriety; discretion is the first requisite in treating with foreign ministers, of which a smaller share is not desirable with the one from so intriguing a court. The remark that good offices and guarantees are not synonymous was happily stated; undoubtedly our mediation to heal the differences between the Russians and Turks is natural; but the taking up the character of guarantor must be at the invitation

> of the Courts concerned, not our own offer. The having acquainted Mr Simolin [Russian envoy] with the whole of the proposal made by France was very proper; Russia must be the judge how far she approves of the idea.[39]

George, is nevertheless today better known for his mental health problems than his diplomatic acuity or work ethic. Conscientiousness, and the sense of responsibility that the King strove to inculcate in his children, can be related not only to George's piety and sense of morality, but also to his mental health.

In the mid-twentieth century, at a time when personality traits were linked to psychiatric conditions, not least repressed sexuality, there was a widespread failure to consider the relationship between mental illness and physical causes. One American psychiatrist discerned 'manic-depressive insanity' arising from an inability to tolerate his own timorous uncertainty. Subsequently, there was a shift in psychiatry towards looking more closely at the relationship between mental disorder and physical health, and a focus on the effects on George of the disease porphyria. That shift also went too far, and there was insufficient attention to his mental state during the bulk of his reign when he was not ill. Noting four bouts of mania, it is possible that George suffered from manic depression, which would account for his compulsive characteristics, although much should also be attributed to his hard-working interpretation of the *métier* of kingship.

No simple explanation is satisfactory: George's desire for order may have owed something to his personality, or even to his concern about his own irritable anxiety when faced by disorder. Nevertheless, his beliefs about his role are also pertinent. An emphasis on order certainly affected George's relations with his family.

The extent to which George's serious illness in 1788-9 contributed to a major political crisis was strong evidence of his continued political, constitutional and symbolic importance, for his symptoms of insanity precipitated the Regency Crisis. George's health had generally been good, but in late October 1788 he began to talk rapidly and uncontrollably, becoming delirious in early November. At the time of the attack, George was fifty, and the auguries for a long life were not good, as his father had died at the age of 44, and of George's eight siblings, six died before the age of fifty. The alternation of apparent madness with intervals of lucidity, of paroxysms of rage with hours of calm, proved particularly disconcerting, and not only to others for, when lucid, George was aware of his situation.[40]

It was clear that if there was to be a regency, George, Prince of Wales, now of age, would be regent. The situation was different from that under George I with the unwillingness to have George, Prince of Wales (the future George II) act as a regent when the King visited Hanover. This illustrated the differing meaning of the term regent. In 1788, the ministry would change, as the Prince was close, politically and personally, to Charles James Fox. The extent of the Prince's likely powers as regent, however, was unclear, and the political interest and inherent drama of the occasion attracted intense public interest. The conduct of the Prince and of the Whigs, who were eager for power and hopeful of George's death or continued madness, aroused much criticism, which, greatly encouraged sympathy for George.

The King's doctors disagreed as to whether he was likely to recover, until a new doctor, Francis Willis, who declared that George would recover, came to the fore. His methods relied on enforced 'calm', including the use of a gag, a straitjacket and a restraining chair, which were designed to end the over-excitement that he believed caused madness, and the majesty of monarchy was ignored as George was bullied and coerced. Recovery took time and led to much discussion of medical options with the cricket-loving and womanising John, 3rd Duke of Dorset, ambassador in Paris, offering a cure that reflects the extent to which in health, as in so much else, the notion of a division between a modernising enlightened élite and the bulk of the population, was, and is, misleading:

> I have always had little or no hopes of the King, I have sent however by this day's courier a remede which they tell me est sure. It is tout simplement the blood of a jack-ass which after passing a clear napkin through it two or three times is given afterwards to the patient to drink. I really hope Willis will try it.[41]

In the meantime, Pitt's attempts to restrict the power of the Prince as Regent caused great constitutional and political controversy – only for George's restoration to health in February 1789 to pre-empt the Whigs. This recovery may only have been partial; but, as far as the public was concerned, it was complete – necessarily so, as assumptions about the structure and practice of royal authority required the King's mental and physical health, in both appearance and reality. A new phase of the reign began, inaugurated by the service of thanks for his recovery, held on 23 April 1789.

GEORGE III, FATHER OF THE NATION

'Eighteen years ago the World at our feet, but alas! now we die at the feet of the World.'

Lord George Herbert, 1779.[1]

The ideas and realities of George as, successively, Patriot King, King who Lost America, and the National Symbol against Revolutionary France, captured the strengths and tensions both in the general situation of British monarchy and in the particular character and position of George. After the Regency Crisis of 1788-9, George was no longer seen primarily, at least in Britain, as the ruler who had lost America, for that defeat receded into the past, not least as there was no movement for revanche.

George's summer travels after his recovery in 1789 drew even larger crowds than those in 1788 and, alongside growing signs of division in France, this burst of royal popularity, one that was to last, generated confidence in the British system, marking a major change in attitude from the early 1780s. There was a rallying of the social élite and of much opinion around Country, Crown and Church that prefigured the loyalism of the 1790s in opposition to the French Revolution and the attendant radicalism in Britain.

Seeking to strengthen his recovery, in 1789 George's made his first visit to Weymouth, where he found the sea air and bathing 'certainly agrees'. The King's trip there gave a new curative significance to his travels, but also confirmed his tendency to visit southern England. He visited Weymouth every year bar three from 1789 to 1805, but never Liverpool, Manchester, Leeds, York, Newcastle or Norwich, let alone Hanover, Ireland, Scotland and Wales. Whereas George I had taken the waters at Pyrmont in Germany, George III took those at Cheltenham. Yet, unlike his predecessors, he also toured industrial sites, including a pin manufactory at Gloucester, a carpet works and a china factory at Worcester, the carpet works at Axminster, and the canals and cloth industry near Stroud.

George's journeys to and from Weymouth provided an opportunity to see such sites, but primarily, to visit stately homes such as Longleat, the seat of Viscount Weymouth, and the Earl of Ailesbury's Tottenham Park. Such visits offered not only an opportunity to converse with the aristocracy but also to be seen by the local public, and in their thousands. This was a royal progress very different from those in London. George's visits to the West Country included going to naval dockyards, notably Plymouth in 1789 which he combined with staying in John, 2nd Lord Boringdon's house at Saltram,[2] and to towns where loyalty could be paraded in addresses, for example at Exeter and Lymington.

George's travels looked to his wider interests. Visiting Worcester Cathedral in 1788 for the Three Choirs Festival, of which he became patron in 1788, George added his own private band to the orchestra. The festival brought together many of George's concerns, as it was intended for the relief of the widows and orphans of the clergy and included a cathedral service, and his visit provided him with an opportunity to display royal bounty: he left ten guineas for the workmen at the china factory he visited, £50 for the poor of the city (with another £50 from the Queen), £200 for the clergy widows and orphans, £300 to liberate debtors, and his pardon to deserving criminals awaiting transportation. The

King thus demonstrated concern about the moral and physical welfare of all, which, alongside Christian charity and care for others, was a counterpart to celebrating the nation's triumphs. George's stance looked forward toward the strong later emphasis in the royal family on charitable philanthropy, one that continues to bring together religious and social roles.

George had urged diplomatic caution in the aftermath of the War of American Independence, writing in July 1784: 'Till I see this country in a situation more respectable as to army, navy and finances I cannot think anything that may draw us into troubled waters either safe or rational.'[3] There had been such a recovery, and, in light of this, Britain had taken a more assertive role in international affairs from 1787. Breaking out in 1789, the French Revolution, however, found the government cautious anew, and that did not really change until late 1792 when French expansionism increased tension.

In response to the Revolution, George thought that if the escape of the royal family in 1791 succeeded, it would be providential,[4] but he was no ultra and was not an enthusiast for Louis XVI. Nevertheless, George, Earl Gower, the Ambassador in Paris, felt it appropriate to write privately to the Foreign Secretary when decrying Louis:

> I am going to write private truths which might be unpleasant to a royal eye. If this country ceases to be a monarchy it will be entirely the fault of Louis 16th. Blunder upon blunder, inconsequence upon inconsequence, a total want of energy of mind accompanied with personal cowardice have been the destruction of his reign. In this last affair when he had undertaken to escape from Paris … he ought to have effected his plan or perished in the attempt… It has always been the fate of this unfortunate monarch that whenever the enemies of his government have begun to suffer in the public opinion he has adopted some measure which has reinstated them.[5]

This was not only a critique of Louis but also implicit praise for George, although the Danish envoy, in contrast, thought that George suffered because his ministry obliged him, against his wishes, to adopt the same system of inconsequence that had hit Louis.[6]

George was correctly wary of claims about the scale of royalist support in France, and did not press for the restoration of the Bourbons as a war goal. Yet, although unenthusiastic about fighting on for them, he came to agree that Jacobinism could not be destroyed 'unless Royalty is re-established'. George wanted France beaten and, whether Britain experienced victory or defeat in the war, he pressed for resolve in the struggle. In James Gillray's 1793 caricature 'A new Map of England and France. The French Invasion; or John Bull bombarding the Bum-Boats,' in which the French threat is dispersed with excremental force, John Bull was given George's face. This was to become a characteristic link of nation and king through patriotism. John Bull, who required personalisation, could also be portrayed as Farmer Bull, thus providing a link with land and agricultural prosperity.

'No King' appeared as a slogan on London's walls.[7] Yet, George benefited from the revivification of royal ideology in the light of French developments. The execution of Louis in January 1793 led to the use of the January sermon in Westminster Abbey before the House of Lords, the Sermon on the anniversary of the execution of Charles I, for the delivery of a powerful attack on revolutionary theory. Stressing royal authority and religious duty, Samuel Horsley, Bishop of St David's, a favourite of Pitt, presented the constitution as product and safeguard of a 'legal contract' between Crown and people, and strongly attacked both executions.[8] The sermon drew applause from the congregation.

George kept a close eye on military policy and made informed comments. Unlike most of the leading ministers of the period, the King had had experience in directing a war (if on the losing side), that of American Independence. George was prominent in the celebration of victory. In 1794, George hastened to Portsmouth to congratulate his commanders after the Glorious First of June, a naval victory over the French, giving Howe a diamond-hilted sword on the deck of the *Queen Charlotte* and presenting the admirals involved with gold medals. In 1797, in response to naval mutinies, George wanted 'any neglect that may have given reason' for discontent remedied, but was also keen on the enforcement of 'due subordination,' and was worried:

> The spirit seems to be of a most dangerous kind, as at the same time that the mutiny is conducted with a degree of coolness it is not void of method; how this could break out at once without any suspicion before arising seems unaccountable ... it must require a cruise and much time before any reliance can be placed on a restoration of discipline.[9]

The original mutiny ended when many of the demands were accepted and a royal pardon was granted, but in May there were renewed disturbances reflecting the failure to fulfil governmental promises, George noting the unfortunate consequences of Parliament's delay in increasing naval pay.[10] Not all naval opposition was politically radical.

Later in 1797, the unpopularity of the astonishingly brutal and unpredictable Captain Hugh Pigot of the *Hermione* led to a mutiny and the killing in Puerto Rico of Pigot, whose career had been helped by being the son of an admiral, and nine other officers. Encouraged by George who was concerned about 'the discipline of the navy,'[11] much effort was devoted to hunting down the mutineers. (The Navy eventually captured 33 of them, 24 of whom were hanged and gibbetted, one was transported, and eight were acquitted or pardoned. The ship was recaptured from the Spanish, to whom the mutineers had turned it over, and in 1800 was renamed HMS *Retribution*.)

George took an approach to appointments that reflected his social values and the prevalence of patronage, but a patronage in which merit played a genuine part. Thus, after the capture of a

French frigate in 1795, George applauded the promotion of the Captain and the First Lieutenant, adding:

> As the Second Lieutenant, Mr Maitland, conducted himself very well, I trust he will soon meet with the same favour, being a man of good family will I hope also be of advantage in the consideration, as it is certainly wise as much as possible to give encouragement if they personally deserve it to gentlemen.[12]

Frederick Maitland, the grandson of an Earl, was indeed a brave officer and was to have a distinguished naval career, including being Napoleon's captor in 1815.

Ill-discipline was a particular issue in 1797 due to the crisis of British naval power and the threat to Ireland. George felt it necessary to affirm his 'confidence in naval skill and British valour to supply want of numbers. I am too true an Englishman to have ever adopted the more modern and ignoble mode of expecting equal numbers on all occasions.' In the event, victories at Cape St Vincent and Camperdown enabled the British to transform the situation that year. That December, George III took the leading role in the Naval Thanksgiving held in St Paul's Cathedral after he had processed in state through the thronged streets of London, while captured flags were paraded through the streets by sailors and then deposited in the cathedral. The association of the Crown with repeated victory was an important legacy of George's reign and one that stood it in very good stead in its domestic position and international reputation. Defeats and setbacks could be attributed to divine punishment of a dissolute and sinful people.

King and ministry united in pursuit of victory, but there were tensions. Facing France's repeated military successes from 1794, George shared his ministers' dissatisfaction with the allies,[13] notably Prussia and Austria, but the ministry, much to George's concern, was more willing than he was to begin negotiations with Paris. This repeated the tension between George and North, albeit in a different context. George doubted that a lasting peace could be negotiated with an outlaw regime that lacked legitimacy and he believed that France had to be defeated before there could be a basis for fruitful negotiations, an attitude that adversely affected his response to negotiations in 1796 and 1797. George agreed with Edmund Burke's *Letters on a Regicide Peace* (1796) which opposed Pitt's quest for peace.

In addition, George characteristically adopted a moral tone and feared that seeking peace would weaken Britain: for the King, the issue of negotiations was one in which honour and integrity were as much to the fore as were aspects of prudence. The failure of negotiations in 1797, which eased tensions between King and ministry, left George hopeful that if Britain acted firmly it could win an honourable and lasting peace, helped by factional struggles in Paris and the exhaustion of French resources. He read Burke's *Reflections on the French Revolution* (1790), which had become a key conservative text, and said that every gentleman should read it.

Negotiations with France proved an issue that could be settled, but over Catholic Emancipation, the removal of Catholic disabilities (Catholic freeholders in Ireland had the vote from 1793), George was unwilling to match the ministry and brought up his coronation oath to protect the established church and the confessional state. In his case, inherent conservatism was linked to a stubborn determination to support the constitution and the Church of England, and, thus, the traditional, as well as legal, character of authority and power. He did not give enough weight to the Catholic loyalism seen after the Jacobite risings in 1715-16 and 1745-6, nor to the formation of the Catholic Committee in Dublin in 1757, the loyalty proclamation by the Catholic bishops in response to the War of American Independence, and the opposition of the Catholic Church to the French Revolution.

George's dispute over this issue with Pitt, First Lord of the Treasury from 1783 to 1801 and 1804 to 1806, however, was not to the fore as far as the public was concerned. Instead, the monarchy had become a potent symbol of national identity and continuity in response to the French Revolution. In 1801, in dedicating the works of his father to George III, James, 1st Earl of Malmesbury, a Whig who had switched to support the government, fixed both ideological framework and recent history: George's 'life and reign have been an uniform practice of religion and virtue. To Your Majesty Europe is indebted for whatever is still preserved to it of social order and legitimate government,'[14] this a reference to holding firm against France.

George benefited from the strength of a patriotism based on hostility to France, of loyalism, in the sense of an active opposition to democratic and republican tendencies, and of adherence to non-partisan principles of constitutional propriety and support for the established order. Opposition criticisms failed to gain political or popular traction.

The monarchy played a greater role in political ideology than it had done between 1689 and 1746 when it had been compromised by serious differences over the legitimacy of the dynasty, as well as the contentious nature of constitutional arrangements after 1688. From the 1790s, no such problems undermined an emphasis on monarchy on the part of conservative elements, and this contributed to the stronger conservative ideology of the period and to the repurposing of monarchy in terms of an active national patriotism, one in which far less attention was given to the Hanoverian link.

This did not mean that George had no interest in Hanover. He actively pursued the interests of the Electorate, although he was not responsible for it becoming a much-expanded kingdom in the post-Napoleonic peace settlement. There were differences, tensions, between ruler and British ministers over George's backing for Hanover, notably in 1785-6, when an Hanoverian alignment with Prussia cut across the attempt by the ministry to improve relations with Austria. However, there was no public controversy equivalent to those under George I and George II. There was a continuance of the situation from the beginning of the reign, from Pitt the Elder's support for a German commitment from 1758, but one that was particularly significant during the French Revolutionary and Napoleonic wars as the potential room for republican sympathy and agitation within Britain was thereby reduced.

There was a more general shift in the British monarchy under George: the union of the Westminster and Dublin parliaments, the establishment of British power in India, and the competition with Napoleon, who made himself an emperor in 1804. For less obvious shifts, there was not only the ageing of George and, as a result, his more symbolic role, but also the extent to which the greater scale of government, not least as a result of the war that began in 1793, made the degree of oversight George had attempted earlier no longer feasible. Government became more formal, with the growing role of the Prime Minister and of cabinet methods lessening the significance of individual links between monarch and ministers. The longevity of the ministries of Pitt (1783-1801, 1804-6) and Robert, 2nd Earl of Liverpool (1812-27) accentuated this tendency. The Prime Minister became in effect an office unto itself, with its own particular set of responsibilities, and was no longer an *ad hoc* addition to being First Lord of the Treasury or another officeholder. In contrast, under North, individual ministers saw their first loyalty as to the King, rather than to the Prime Minister or Cabinet. Edward, 1st Lord Thurlow, Lord Chancellor from 1778 to 1783 and 1783 to 1792, was one of the last to hold and act upon this view, and in 1792 Pitt forced his resignation.

So, a major change over the nineteenth century was the reduction of the governmental and political significance of the royal role. This made it easier for the empire to have an imperial monarchy of pomp, but without, for example, the highly active even intrusive role that might make the personal responsibilities and views of the monarch a stumbling block in ensuring that self-governing colonies did not follow the North American route. In contrast, imperial monarchy in France was much more a matter of the views and policies of first Napoleon I and later his nephew, Napoleon III (like Louis XVII, Napoleon II did not rule), and was eventually, accordingly, a failure.

Already, under the long ministry of Pitt there had been a growing contrast between problems for the ministry, for example legislative defeats in 1785, and the different and, to a degree, at least less controversial, stance of the King. Thus, Shelburne, now 1st Marquess of Lansdowne, reflected in 1785: 'The fate of the Irish Propositions has been no doubt a subject of mortification to administration, but I do not conceive it has left the King under any *real* difficulty as to men or things.'[15]

The distancing of George from the daily processes of a government expanded from 1793 to fight a war with France of unprecedented difficulty increased. This distancing, which characterised the Pitt years, also contributed to George's growing popularity. This was particularly so as the ministry gained cohesion round Pitt, not least with the grudging dismissal of Thurlow by George in 1792, the last major 'King's Friend'. Unpopular decisions were now blamed on the ministers, while the Crown demonstrated its largely non-partisan usefulness by standing above parties in defence of the constitution, including the constitutionally Established Church, and was thus the guardian of what had become popularly known to its defenders as 'the Protestant constitution'.

George himself contributed to this positive image, not by making a special effort to change, but by being himself. A series of gestures underlined George's commitment to the country. These included the payment of £20,000 from his Privy Purse to the Voluntary Contribution of 1798, and the extension of taxation to the private income of the Crown resulting from the passage of the Crown Private Estates Act of 1800. Yet, alongside this distancing, George continued to take an active interest in government activity, for example that of the navy. His was a rulership both active and symbolic.[16]

If in 1742, 1744 and 1782, the British monarchy had appeared one of the weakest in Europe, its rulers unable to sustain in office ministers who enjoyed royal confidence – Walpole, Carteret, and North respectively – by 1810 it was the strongest in Europe, other than the Romanov regime in Russia, and Napoleon's monarchical dictatorship, which lacked comparable legitimacy. In contrast to the cold shoulder George V turned toward his relatives the Romanovs of Russia once they were overthrown in 1917, under George III (prefiguring the stance taken in 1940 toward the rulers of Norway, the Netherlands and Luxembourg) other European rulers, such as Louis XVIII of France, the Kings of Naples, Portugal and Sardinia (ruler of Savoy-Piedmont), and William V of Orange (first cousin of George), took shelter in Britain, or sought protection behind British forces, especially the navy, as in the cases of Ferdinand IV of Naples in Sicily, Victor Emmanuel I in Sardinia and John VI of Portugal in Brazil.

In this resistance to France, George might appear to be somewhat inconsequential. He had survived bouts of ill-health in 1801 and 1804, but now in his sixties, his vigour was fading and his eyesight going; he was, in some respects, becoming yesterday's man. His political importance, however, was pushed to the fore as a consequence of the revival in the 1800s of ministerial instability as well as royal resolve. George played a central role in the downfall of Pitt, the most powerful Prime Minister of his reign, in 1801. George's opposition to Catholic Emancipation was crucial in this episode.

The establishment of a new ministry under Henry Addington, Viscount Sidmouth, a man for whom he had much time, gave George the opportunity to take a more active part in government, which was necessary if a stable ministry was to be created. This ministry remained in power until 1804, a far shorter period than Pitt's but longer than the short ministries of 1782-3. The son of Pitt the Elder's doctor, Addington had been Speaker of the House of Commons and was an instance of George's preference for those who were not at the apex of society. Indeed, George had scant time for some of the great families, especially those with a Whig heritage, notably the Cavendishes and the Russells, the Dukes of Devonshire and Bedford respectively.

Helped by his hostility both to the French Revolution and Napoleon, George remained convinced that politics was a struggle of good versus evil, one in which Providence played a key role. On 31 January 1805, Sir Nathaniel Wraxall recounted a story told after dinner by Captain Francis Sutton, whose father, Charles Manners-Sutton had been selected by George to become Archbishop of Canterbury. George had long supported Manners-Sutton, who was Dean of Windsor, and that month had had a row with Pitt who had sought to interfere. (Manners-Sutton was to christen the future Queen Victoria in 1819.) The story highlighted George's piety and respect for the Established Church. Sutton had just come from Windsor where George was preoccupied with the upcoming installation of Knights of the Garter, planned for St George's Day, 23 April. When George was discussing the installation, Philip, 5th Earl of Chesterfield, who had recently received the Garter and was one of the knights to be installed, asked 'with some levity' whether they were not to take the sacrament before the ceremony of the installation:

> The King immediately changed countenance and assuming a severe look, 'No,' replied he, 'that institution is not to be mixed with our profane ceremonies. Even at the time of my coronation, I was unwilling to take the sacrament. But, when they told me that it was indispensable, and that I must receive it, before I approached the Communion Table, I took off the Bauble from my head. The Sacrament is not to be profaned by our Gothic Institutions, my Lord.'
>
> The severity of the King's manner completely silenced and confounded Lord Chesterfield, who had not a word to reply, but fell back rather confused. This trivial anecdote may serve to confirm the deep and awful impression which the King always entertained of the sanctity of an oath, to conform or accompany which he had received the sacrament. We cannot afterwards wonder at the Repugnance and unconquerable aversion which he manifested in 1801 to break what he esteemed his Coronation Oath respecting the Catholic Laws of Ireland.'[17]

George's commitment to the greater good did not provide an easy basis for policy and politics. Concerned to do the proper thing, George sought to accommodate gradual change to accustomed order, and, as a consequence, he was opposed to what he saw as unnecessary governmental innovation. At the same time, George continued to be a hardworking monarch, and his oversight of government enabled him to make qualitative, well-informed statements about the conduct of business, as well as to respond to the management of individuals.

The monarchy maintained public magnificence where necessary, and private modesty, the latter in accordance with 'middle-class' mores and cultural aspirations, and with that part of the aristocracy adhering to Christian and modest standards. Alongside accounts of George as an accessible individual, walking, riding and travelling without pomp, indeed any protection (especially outside London), came the reporting of Court life, which presented a very different resonance. Tone and accessibility did not mean that George's lifestyle was that of the middling orders, for he was head of society in what was very much an aristocratic monarchy, which made Court routines very important. At the same time, the tone now was very much that of responsible and, ultimately, accountable monarchy, of the ruler as diligent servant.

George's Court was glorious and yet mocked by the fast set as pedestrian and lacking in glamour. This was not a Court for gambling or indulgence. Thus, for his meals from 1788, the period that has benefited from detailed analysis, his most consumed dish was chicken broth. George did not usually dine alone, but when he did, his choice was roast chicken and then cherry pie. Dining in company, George had richer food, including beef and lobster, but also vegetables, notably artichokes, asparagus and spinach.

George and his family were closely associated with the war effort. On 26 and 28 October 1803, George reviewed 27,000 volunteers in Hyde Park, in each case in front of an estimated half a million people. Through his sons, the royal family played a role in the war effort, notably Frederick, Duke of York, his second son, Commander-in-Chief from 1795 to 1809 and, after a scandal involving his mistress selling commissions that had led to his fall was eventually overlooked, from 1811 to 1827. Although a failed campaign commander in Holland in 1799, a campaign commemorated in a popular ditty about his marching his troops up and down hills, York was an effective and impressive administrator, and his care for merit in the army matched his father's for merit in the church.

Despite his naval career, the more limited William, Duke of Clarence, his third son, later William IV (1830-7) did not put to sea during the war, but Ernest, Duke of Cumberland, the fifth son, served with Hanoverian forces, gaining a justified reputation for bravery, while Edward, Duke of Kent, the fourth son, a Major-General, took part in the capture of Martinique and St Lucia from France in 1794. The youngest brother, Adolphus, Duke of Cambridge, served as a volunteer with the forces in the Low Countries, and later held command positions, and George's nephew, William, Duke of Gloucester, fought with distinction in the Low Countries.

More generally, the strains that lengthy warfare placed on British society, as it did to its European counterparts, encouraged an enthusiasm for symbols of identity. These were particularly significant as nationalism became more important. In the British case, there was no longer a rival dynastic claimant, 'Charles III' having died in obscurity in 1788, and 'Henry IX' doing so in 1809. Moreover, although the War of American Independence might have left George associated with failure, this was not in fact the case, in part due to his successful emergence from the political crisis of 1782-4. And the more extreme fears that the loss of America would lead to the collapse of the entire empire proved grossly exaggerated.

During the French Revolutionary and Napoleonic wars, George was fit for the role of symbolic war leader, was needed for this role, and was willing to take it. In turn, George's role helped set the pattern for that of a war leader who was not on the battlefield, even though members of his family would be, a pattern that has continued to the present. This role proved very important for the reputation of the monarchy, both in general and with reference to George's reign and its aftermath. In terms of the shifts noted in his reign, there was an important one in the reaction to the Regency Crisis of 1788-9 and, more lastingly, to the long-term war from 1793, which engendered greater popularity for the monarch.

In modern terms, this role in the conflict with France is seen as less significant than the transatlantic slave trade, which, like the transportation of convicts and the treatment of aboriginal peoples, explains why George's reign invokes an ambiguous reaction at the very least across parts of the world. The anniversaries of claims of territory for the King, under whom James Cook reached Australia, and, later, of a British base established in Botany Bay in 1788, are especially controversial in Australia. The material George retained for his private working library indicates his personal interest in the transoceanic world. It includes Cook's original drawings for the survey of St Pierre and Miquelon islands off Newfoundland, as well as a set of topographical drawings of the new Australian colony. The King financed Cook's first voyage to the Pacific and supported the establishment of botanic gardens – at Kew, Calcutta and St Vincent – in order to increase botanical knowledge.

George was happy to approve transportation of felons for life to Botany Bay as a way to build up the new colony. In 1789, he was concerned when three convicted felons chose death instead of transportation: 'It is shocking that men can be so lost to every sentiment of gratitude not to feel the mercy shown them in sparing their lives,' a rejection of a royal act of mercy. They were cajoled into changing their mind. To George, crime represented a defiance of divine guidance that required admonition. This was a heavy duty, and one that he found increasingly difficult to undertake optimistically, referring in 1802 to those who were to be transported: 'As to the reforming the morals of those who have deserved that punishment, the King, from now a long experience, is not sanguine in expectations on that head.' Seriousness, a firm sense of morality and an awareness of duty were all clearly present in George's attitude to his role in confirming death sentences. The King was willing to be merciful, responding favourably to recommendations for mercy, especially for first offences, and influenced by the youth of the convict – unless the crime be murder – but he could also reject them. He believed in the exemplary nature of punishment and was concerned for due process in the shape of maintaining the authority of the judiciary.

The acceptance of the King's role as the head of state and nation was seen in the willingness of many, both institutions and individuals, to focus on him. This included communities he had never visited. For example, in 1795, John Nichols, the printer to the Society of Antiquaries, dedicated the first volume of his *The History and Antiquities of the County of Leicester*, published that year, to George.

After his attack of mania in February 1804, George's health did not return to its previous equilibrium, and he remained easily agitated, leading Pitt that March to avoid meetings likely to upset him. Due to his ill-health, George was unable to attend the spectacular Jubilee fête held in 1809 at Frogmore, only a mile from Windsor. Instead, a portrait of the King was displayed in the temporary temple erected for the occasion. The Jubilee provided a major opportunity for the display of respect and affection for the King as a central part of patriotism; and celebrations were held not only in Britain but across the empire, although there were, unsurprisingly, criticisms of the occasion from radicals.

George's health permanently broke down towards the close of 1810. As late as 18 October, he was able to write to Charles Yorke, the First Lord of the Admiralty, approving a promotion and adding: 'The King is truly sensible of the affectionate manner in which Mr Yorke has noticed the distress under which His Majesty suffers from the precarious state of his dear daughter.'[18] The shock of the fatal illness of his last-born, his favourite daughter Amelia, proved crucial to George's deterioration. It was initially thought that he would be alright despite her illness, but the fact that she did not die quickly helped cause the crisis, and they both declined together. George frequently questioned her doctors on her progress and was popularly supposed to have been pushed over the edge when Amelia gave him a mourning ring containing a lock of her hair. Symptoms of insanity were obvious by 25 October, the day of his last public appearance.

The ministry moved quickly. On 10 December, Spencer Perceval, the Prime Minister, introduced a Regency Bill based on Pitt's Bill of 1788. The Regency Act passed on 5 February 1811, with royal assent signified by a commission, and George, Prince of Wales was sworn in as Regent on 6 February. The Act and the resulting oaths emphasised the possibility of recovery and for the first year, at the insistence of Perceval, and against the wishes of the Whigs, the Prince's powers were accordingly limited. Separating the Regent from custody of his father, George's care was entrusted to Queen Charlotte under the Regency Act, a trying responsibility. On 1 June, Dr Robert Willis took over the total management of George's health, and this change extended to the King's personal circumstances: his pages were replaced by Willis's keepers. George was again to endure the 1788 system of seclusion and restraint, a policy that made him increasingly isolated. The deterioration of his condition in July meant that he was physically restrained. Despite the opiates he was given in the form of laudanum, sleep proved difficult, while he ate little, and his awareness of the world around him was limited. This included such triumphs as the battles of Salamanca and Waterloo, and a major gain in prestige, royal status for the Electorate of Hanover, proclaimed by the Prince Regent in October 1814.

In 1812, after the Council had been told by George's doctors on 4 February that their patient was insane, the Prince Regent gained the full prerogative powers of the Crown. He was to follow his father in stressing patriotism, duty and the wish for an inclusive ministry, and determination not to reward the Whig opposition.

Elderly, blind and deaf, George was far less fit than he had been in 1788-9, and there was to be no recovery. Kept in his apartments in Windsor, and out of touch with the world, George no longer recognised his family and took solace in imaginary conversations, for example with Lord North. Disconcerted by his state, most of his relatives showed scant interest in him, Princess Augusta preferring to remember him in earlier times rather than to see him as he now was. Charlotte was in effect a widow. This situation remained largely unchanged for the last years of his life, although, on Charlotte's death in 1818, Frederick, Duke of York, was appointed Guardian, which again kept the Regent at bay. This gave Frederick a postwar role appropriate to his status. George's declining health left him unaware of the deaths of those close to him. The portrait entitled *George III during his last illness*, attributed to Joseph Lee, was, despite the richness of the background, of a man far removed from grandeur.

The King died in seclusion in his room overlooking the North Terrace at Windsor, of pneumonia, on the evening of 29 January 1820, aged 82. Having lain in state for two days, he was buried in St George's Chapel on 16 February, a building on which he had lavished so much attention. Large numbers attended the funeral of a man who had seen so much history and who had been the King of the overwhelming majority for their entire lives. Despite the glory of his burial place, George returned to the common clay as he always knew he would.

By 1820, George's reputation was justifiably different from what it had been in 1766, 1776 or 1783. In each of those years, the general tone had been that of failure, a failure both by George and one forced upon him by others. The situation was very different at the end of his life. He himself was a man who was no longer able to rule, but the total defeat of Napoleon in 1815 had brought a national sense of triumph. So also with the ambivalent (at best) reputation of the Prince Regent, one that made George III appear more honourable, pleasant and majestic; rather ironically, as George II's posthumous reputation benefited from George III's unpopularity in the 1760s.

This has been a positive reappraisal of George. It can be argued that it underplays the King's failure to respond in time to the pressures for new political settlements in America and Ireland, the latter through Catholic Emancipation. Certainly, George got both wrong, as did much of the governing élite and the population: Catholic Emancipation was strongly opposed by most public opinion. It was not only the King's stubbornness that prevented flexibility but also his constitutionalism and the complexities of each issue. His stubbornness and constitutionalism could be seen as nationally representative: he was the voice, as well as the father, of his people.

Ultimately, the King played a crucial role in stabilising dynasty, kingdom and empire. He avoided the very different fates in his lifetime of such varied dynasties as the French Bourbons, Spanish Bourbons and Habsburgs. George helped establish an image and practice of constitutional monarchy, not the directing one his father Frederick had sought, but, instead, a more effective, practical and flexible rulership that was to last.

GEORGE IV

> There is perhaps nothing in the case of the Prince of Wales which ought to affect us more than the influence it will have on foreign nations. The London Gazette goes to every court of Europe. What must be the feeling of every foreigner, when he sees the Heir Apparent of the British dominions advertising a dividend to his creditors of one shilling and ten pence farthing in the pound!
>
> *Newcastle Chronicle*, 19 May 1787

Both as Prince Regent (1811-20) and as King (1820-30), George IV was about show, not power, and a ruler who found it difficult to measure up to the expectations of the monarchical system. In part, this reflected the degree to which the character of the man was judged a central feature in the quality of rule, and George was found wanting. This judgment was a longstanding pattern and one in which George consistently suffered from comparison with his father. Indeed, George III lived sufficiently long for George IV to be cast in the shadows. He was able to recover from the trauma of the loss of America and the constitutional strife of 1782-4, from the Regency Crisis of 1788-9, and from the repeated military failures, fiscal strain, social disquiet and political difficulties of 1793-1801. By staying alive until 1820, George III also shadowed the fame George IV might have won, however unworthily from the victorious final stages of the Napoleonic Wars in 1812-15.

It was somehow appropriate that George IV, who was ill with pleurisy anyway, was not the chief mourner at his father's funeral (monarchs did not go to predecessor's funerals). The role was taken by Frederick, Duke of York; but a Duke of York in such a place was not going to be the basis for a royal coup, in some sort of repetition of 1460 (by Richard, Duke of York), 1461 (by Edward IV), 1471 (by Edward IV), and 1483 (by Richard III). Similarly, the antipathy between George IV and his father, while difficult, had been less traumatic politically than the comparable rifts under George I and George II. The idea of a monarch deploying force to achieve his own goals would have seemed bizarre. Radical critics made hostile comparisons, but it was the King-in-Parliament, not the King alone, that was the centre of such criticism, as had also been the case for the American Patriots.

Born in 1762, the future George IV became King at 57, having waited longer than virtually any previous heir to become monarch, although not as long as William IV, Edward VII and Charles III. As a result, George became King not only long after he was estranged from his wife (as was also to happen for Charles III and his first wife), but also after the death of his only legitimate child, which meant that, given the then unlikely event of the death of his wife, he was not going to have a legitimate child unless he remarried, which meant an equally unlikely divorce. Unlike William IV and Charles III, but not Edward VII, George IV succeeded at a time when he increasingly suffered health problems that sapped both energy and will, and that marked him out as unlikely to make old bones, a situation shared with Louis XVIII.

George's alienation from his father had added to the sense of exasperation and urgency with which he pursued the trappings of monarchy. This had been very obvious during the Regency Crisis of 1788-9. Already, prior to that, there was tension as a result of the Prince's debts that spilled out into politics and public discussion.[1] In turn, political differences affected the money, for the King's advisors, hostile to any ministry under Fox, were opposed to giving the Prince more cash as it would increase his political power, which was then focused on supporting Fox.[2] This was ironic in that Fox, Burke and their allies had alleged that the deficit on George III's Civil List was the result of buying political influence and of political subterfuge, for example expenditure on the press.

The costs posed by the Prince were heavy. George III had to pay £5,000 to buy back the love letters that the prince had written to his mistress, Mary Robinson, a prominent actress whom he had seen playing Perdita. She was also given a life annuity of £600 and £200 for her daughter (who predeceased George) in return for surrendering the prince's promise of £20,000 when she came of age.

The prince's secret marriage in 1785 to Maria Fitzherbert was far more serious as it risked compromising the succession and was in defiance of the Royal Marriages Act of 1772 under which descendants of George II could only marry before the age of 25 with royal permission, thereafter they had to give a year's notice to the Privy Council, and Parliament had not expressly to disapprove of the marriage. Occasionally unfaithful and more consistently difficult, the prince stayed with Maria until 1794 when he left her for his new mistress, Frances, Countess of Jersey. Maria was given a settlement of £3,000 a year.[3]

In 1795, the prince married his first cousin Caroline of Brunswick-Wolfenbüttel, a choice that delighted George III. Motivated almost entirely by the desire to clear his debts, he had expressed no preference, and when they first met, recoiled, drank a brandy, and fled. She lacked a royal demeanour and suffered the consequences of her failure to wash, while he was fatter and more ill-natured than she had anticipated.

George's choice of Lady Jersey as a lady-in-waiting was tactless, as Caroline correctly suspected she was his mistress. A disastrous honeymoon, greatly affected by George's preference for alcohol over his new wife, was followed by steadily deteriorating relations in which the position of Lady Jersey played a major role. Caroline's demand for the dismissal of the mistress from her office was rejected by George. In 1797, Caroline left Carlton House and set up an independent establishment in Blackheath. Critics of the prince presented Caroline as a wronged woman who had suffered at the hands of a debauched husband, but Caroline herself was no saint or moral exemplar.

Meanwhile, Lady Jersey had lost George's favour in 1798, although she was swiftly replaced by Elizabeth Fox, the mistress of Lord Egremont. By George, Elizabeth had a son, George Crole, who received £10,000 and an annuity of £300 after George's death.

George meanwhile hankered anew for Maria Fitzherbert, and they lived together again from 1800. From 1807, George's favour for Isabella, Marchioness of Hertford put this relationship under strain and in December 1809 it came to an end.

George's several children established his fertility, but only one, Princess Charlotte, born in 1796, was legitimate, although that was 'better' in dynastic terms than his brother and successor, William IV, who had many illegitimate children by his relationship with Mrs Jordan (another actress), but only two legitimate ones, both of whom died very young, by Queen Adelaide. Married in 1816 to Leopold of Saxe-Coburg, Parliament having voted him £50,000 a year, Charlotte died aged 21 in 1817 after she gave birth to a stillborn son, her death the cause of great public grief. George had left no spare because of his rift with his wife. That pushed the dynastic duty of the succession onto his brothers, two of whom, William and Edward, parted from their mistresses and married rapidly afterwards. The second fathered Queen Victoria. Thus George IV, in a pattern that was all too familiar in his case, pushed his responsibility off onto others.

Once Prince Regent, and later King, George was not a man able effectively to resist the trend toward a lesser political role for the monarch, however much he might spasmodically insist on his reiterated views of his own importance. His stamina was already weakened by his weight, poor health, laziness and self-indulgence. George lacked his father's strong sense of duty, as well as his moral concern. An analysis of his meals up to 1813 reveal a predilection for rich food including deep-friend potatoes – and deep-fried cream. Melted butter was a very common sauce. While keen on women, George did not have the personal capacity nor political ability to manage scandal in any effective way.

George's personal limitations indicated a more general problem with monarchy, its dependence on individual aptitude and application. He was not alone in such faults, while, in part, the distinctively shared nature of the British governmental and political system helped limit the consequences and even, to a degree, were strengthened by the faults, as they led to an increase in the practice of Cabinet government. Moreover, just as the prince's pre-1810 antics had aroused sympathy for George III, his later faults directed attention away from the ministers. In contrast, there were many problems in other states caused by monarchical weaknesses, as with Louis XVI. In 1787, Joseph Ewart wrote to a fellow-envoy about Frederick William II of Prussia (r. 1786-97), a relative of George III through the latter's grand-aunt, about his

> ... excessive jealousy of his authority, and, in reality, his principal defects proceed from the idea of his doing everything himself being joined to his constitutional bent to indolence and pleasure. Besides, his real talents and judgement, whose existence no person who has had access to know him can dispute, actually tend to increase the evil arising from this circumstance, since they prevent him from sufficiently employing the abilities of his ministers, to whom weak and ignorant princes naturally resign their authority.[4]

George was conscious and envious of the military reputation enjoyed or adopted by other monarchs, including relatives, notably the Princes of Brunswick, two of whom died in conflict; the first, Charles William, the husband of George III's elder sister Augusta, receiving a fatal wound at Auerstädt (1806), and his heir at Quatre Bras (1815). George liked to set a military tone and was painted in 1792 wearing the uniform of the Grenadier Guards.[5] He commanded the Prince of Wales's Regiment of Light Dragoons. His pretensions could verge on the ridiculous, especially in 1811 when he made himself Field Marshal, designing a uniform in scarlet that, with its weighty gold embroidery, was reported to weigh 200 pounds, and in which he was buried. When in 1816 he visited his daughter on her honeymoon, George spent two hours describing the details of uniforms to her new husband, which was seen by Charlotte as a sign of his good humour.

In 1792 and 1814, he had himself painted in uniform, and later in life liked to tell people that he had been at the battle of Waterloo and would seek confirmation from Arthur, Duke of Wellington, winning the tactful reply: 'So you have told me, Sir,' but, in truth, angering him, as he also did by falsely claiming to have played a major role in winning the battle of Salamanca (1812). In 1821, while en route to Hanover, his sole visit there as King, George was shown the battlefield at Waterloo by Wellington, the King being interested to see where Henry, 2nd Earl of Uxbridge, now Marquess of Anglesey, had lost his leg near the close of the battle.

Sir Thomas Lawrence painted not only George as a Field Marshal, but also the portraits of those who had secured the defeat of Napoleon that line the Waterloo Gallery at Windsor Castle. An instance of the imperial artistic patronage of George's reign, Lawrence was well rewarded for this work, while, as a sign of favour and prestige, in 1820 he also became the fourth individual to be President of the Royal Academy, succeeding George III's protégé, Benjamin West, on the death of the latter. Lawrence had also enjoyed George III's patronage from 1789, succeeding Reynolds as 'Painter-in-Ordinary to His Majesty' in 1791, and his commissions for George IV included Princess Charlotte and Walter Scott.

Having been closely linked politically and socially to the Whigs as a young man, notably during the Regency Crisis, George shifted his position from 1807 and more particularly in 1811. He became more conservative, with a greater concern about the Church of England and opposing the Whigs' pressure for negotiations with France. As Prince Regent from 1811, George did not want to accept the restrictions of the Regency Act, but was outmanoeuvred by Spencer Perceval, the Prime Minister, who was stronger in Parliament. Perceval's assassination led Robert, 2nd Earl of Liverpool to become Prime Minister after a protracted crisis in which George had shown his opposition to his former Whig allies. Perceval was shot by the merchant John Bellingham. In his statement to the court he said:

> Gentlemen, when a minister sets himself above the laws, as Mr Perceval did, he does it as his own personal risk. If this were not so, the mere will of the minister would become the law, and what would then become of your liberties? … Gentlemen, my life is in your hands, I rely confidently on your justice.

He was hanged three days later.

Although posing difficulties in his petulance, which could be childish and was rarely majestic, George followed his father in stressing his patriotism, duty and wish for an inclusive ministry. In his first message to the Cabinet after he assumed his full powers in 1812, George stated his wish to pursue goals 'common to the whole nation'. Although that was the norm, and the speech would have been written for him, George was also expressing a position he shared. As postwar differences were to underline, there were no such goals.

The Whigs accused George of being a turncoat and overly influenced by Tory associates, notably Isabella, Marchioness of Hertford, but, as with the criticism of Walpole and Bute in earlier reigns, this underestimated George's capacity to make his own decisions. In 1812, George tried to bring the Whigs into what he hoped would be a widely inclusive ministry, but he refused to accept their liberal views on Catholic Emancipation and the war.

He also, with familiarity, became satisfied with the ministers he had inherited, a course eased by the clear competence of Liverpool as Prime Minister and by George's disinclination for work. He certainly did not match his father.

A supporter of the government during both the war with Napoleon and of the post-war socio-political discontent, approving, after the events, 'Peterloo', the deadly military action against a pro-reform crowd in Manchester in 1819, George created political problems in 1820 in his personal life. He wished to divorce his first cousin, Caroline of Brunswick(-Wolfenbüttel), whom he had married in 1795 but who had left him in 1797 due to his boorishness and infidelity. In 1820, her cause was taken up by radicals, while ministers sought to avoid public scandal. The entire episode was very different from that which had faced George I, not least because it was played out in Britain, whereas George I's difficulties with his adulterous wife Sophia Dorothea had been contained to Germany, occurred twenty years before he came to the throne, and had been largely private. She was held under comfortable house arrest until she died.

The small majority in the House of Lords for the divorce Bill led the government to withdraw it rather than face a stormy passage in the Commons, much to the fury of George. The press lapped up the sexual details and engaged in a vicious and personal debate as to whether Caroline was a wronged woman or a disgrace to her sex. As support for Caroline was a popular cause (in part because the government was so unpopular), and a useful means of attacking the undoubted libertine ways of the King, the entire debate lent focus and interest to political controversy, and it did so with profit, causing a boom in newspaper sales. The major dailies took sides, *The Times* supporting Caroline, while the *Morning Post* attacked her.[6] George, however, benefited from growing popular disquiet about Caroline's personal life, especially the evidence that she had had affairs with foreign servants, notably her major-domo, Bartolomeo Bergami. As a result, the Commons rejected by a large majority an opposition motion that Caroline's name be restored to the liturgy.

She was also refused entry to the lavish coronation that George had planned. In this, the crown was enhanced by an unprecedented number of borrowed jewels, and George wore ornate and heavy clothes. These included on his entry into Westminster Abbey a black velvet hat carrying a large plume of ostrich feathers from which a heron's plume emerged. His gold-bordered crimson velvet train was so long and heavy that nine pages were needed to support it. This was an ironic echo of Napoleon's bombastic coronation as Emperor in 1804 and prefigured that of Charles X as King of France at Rheims in 1825. Charles revived the practice of touching for scrofula at this coronation, whereas George IV did not seek to touch; Charles Edward Stuart had also touched for scrofula.

Although radical sentiment remained strong, there had also been a rallying of support to George by the time of his coronation. Caroline died three weeks later, George remarking on 'the blessing which the protecting Hand of God, in his mercy, has bestowed upon me, in this recent event ... it has literally turned one almost quite topsy turvy.'[7]

He did not remarry in order to secure the succession with children of his own. Whereas his brothers, the Dukes of Clarence and Kent, had put aside their lovers in 1818 in order to make marriages that were acceptable in dynastic terms, George was unprepared to do so.

George's coronation was followed in 1821-2 by highly popular visits to Ireland, Hanover and Scotland; the first to Ireland and Scotland by the monarch since the seventeenth century. In Wales, in contrast, he only visited Thomas Burgess at Abergwili near Carmarthen and Plas Newydd, the seat of the Marquess of Anglesey, en route to Dublin, as he had continued the Hanoverian pattern of having no inauguration ceremony as Prince of Wales. George's visit to Ireland saw him at his best, able to respond to people and circumstances and to present himself in a benign and accessible fashion. Very much enjoying the fuss, George conspicuously associated himself with Irish themes: on his royal entry into Dublin, he carried a hat decorated with a big bunch of shamrock, while he requested the wearing of Irish goods at the drawing room held in the Viceregal Lodge. A triumph of showmanship, George's visit enabled him to see his mistress, Elizabeth, Lady Conyngham, visiting her twice at Slane.[8]

Adopting a similar stance to his father, George showed no willingness to respond to the address from the Catholic bishops and move toward Catholic Emancipation. Indeed, a careful distinction was drawn between the addresses from the Established Church, Dublin Corporation and the University of Dublin, all of which were to be presented to George while he was on the throne. Those from the Presbyterians, the Catholic bishops and the Quakers were presented in the Closet, ie privately.

The last stage of George's trip to Ireland was spoiled by poor health – 'an attack in his bowels' – and by George's anger about the movement of Caroline's body through London. Viscount Sidmouth, the Home Secretary, complained:

> The King is in a very uncomfortable state of mind. The circumstances attending the Queen's funeral he is frequently recurring [sic] to, in a manner which shows a degree of chagrin, and irritation beyond what I have ever observed in him. These feelings have not affected his general behaviour, and deportment, so as to attract the observation, except of a very few; the actual expression of them has not been so confined, and limited as could be wished.[9]

Having returned from Ireland, George swiftly moved on to Hanover. In Brussels, en route, his ability as a mimic enlivened dinner with William I of the Netherlands. In Hanover, George's skill in making himself agreeable to a new audience was seen with his facility in speaking German, but his precarious health soured the trip. George had to convalesce, but soon recovered sufficiently to take part in the social round expected of him, one reminiscent of the social pressures of modern kingship:

> The King is well enough to receive company at dinner – Tomorrow he will have audiences – Friday he is to visit his stud, and manege, which is upon a very large scale, and on Saturday His Majesty will take leave by showing himself at the theatre. As the King proposes to stop at Gottingen on his way the disappointment occasioned by his illness will have been in some measure repaired.[10]

In an echo of the past, George's visit provided an opportunity for diplomatic discussion with other leading figures, as the Austrian Chancellor Metternich visited Hanover. However, as a sign of the times, Metternich was there to see Robert, 2nd Marquess of Londonderry, the Foreign Secretary, formerly Viscount Castlereagh. Whereas on the last visit by a monarch, by George II in 1755, the King had played a central role in the negotiations handled at Hanover, that was no longer the case.

In 1822, George visited Scotland. He sailed in his yacht, the *Royal George*, from Greenwich to Leith and back from Queensferry, and therefore he did not have to face the long journey through England. As a sign of changing times, steam tugs were used to help the *Royal George* cope with contrary winds. In Scotland George visited Newbattle Abbey, the seat of the Marquess of Lothian, and not Glasgow. Wearing Highland dress of a lavish and very expensive type, George favoured Scottish music and dances during his visit, as well as Glenlivet and Atholl Brose: the previous year, he had enjoyed Irish whisky punch. What George made of the sermon he heard preached by the Moderator of the Church of Scotland, against lust and in favour of marital harmony, is unknown, but the King was innured to the varied and often hypocritical consequences of his position as a public defender of the moral order. George Cruickshank's caricature, *Results of the Northern Excursion* (1822), showed George in a ridiculous Scottish outfit that showed his thighs, using a road post to 'cure the itch', a reference to fleas. Yet with George shown scratching his hand in front of his sporran, there was a reference to venereal disease.

The expectation that responses to George in Edinburgh, as in Dublin and Hanover, would be more favourable than in London, the centre of English disaffection, was proved correct.[11] This echoed the enjoyment that George I and George II found in their visits to Hanover, as well as the lack of a comparable experience of popularity for George III, who had passed up the chance by not going there. George III, nevertheless, had found that leaving London in order to travel through southern England brought him into contact with a very supportive public, prominent figures, from aristocrats to town councils, and the mass of the public who made up the crowds that applauded him.

After his tour of his kingdoms, however, George retreated from the public face of monarchy. Indeed, from 1823, he made no public appearances in London except for the ceremonial opening and proroguing of Parliament. Instead, George spent most of his time at his favourite haunts of Brighton and Windsor, much of it in the company of his mistress, Elizabeth, Lady Conyngham.

The daughter of a self-made Yorkshire businessman, she was considered a parvenue and a gold-digger. She replaced Lady Hertford as favourite in late 1819 and gave George, who, in a familiar pattern, was initially intoxicated by her, a new optimism. Her husband, Henry, Viscount Conyngham, was appointed Lord Steward of the Household in 1821, the year in which her relationship with George was closest, which aided their contact, although propriety was maintained to the extent of George and Elizabeth not living under the same roof. He also became a Marquess. The lavish presents and clear public regard that George showed for Lady Conyngham was such that the relationship was no secret. Indeed, the King insisted that she sit close to him throughout the coronation. Her presence was rewarded with repeated looks that struck some as indecent.

Lady Conyngham, however, was peremptory and could irritate the King, who was eventually to complain that she bored him. Both were quite easily bored. George's affections were not restricted to her, although, with increasing age, he seems to have been seeking affectionate company rather than sex. Lady Conyngham was no youngster: she was 57 in 1823.

In July 1822, George wrote as 'a most affectionate friend' from Carlton House, possibly to a 'Mrs M.'; the recipient is unclear:

> You may easily imagine, warm & sincere as my affections are towards you, I have had but little rest, since we separated last night. The [sic] feel, that I may, possibly & unfortunately in a hurried moment, when my mind & Heart being torn in fifty different ways from fifty different causes have let an unjust or a hasty expression escape me to any one (but most especially to You, who I so *truly love* & who are so *invaluable* to *Me* as my *friend*) is to *me*, a sensation much *too painful* to be *endured*; therefore, let me *implore* of You, to come to me, *be it but for a moment*, the *very first thing* you do this morning, for I shall hate myself until I have the opportunity of expressing *personally* to You, those pure & Genuine feelings of affection for You, which will never cease to live in *my Heart*, so long as that Heart, itself continues to beat. I am much too unhappy to say more[12]

One of the reasons why George showed himself so rarely in London in his later years as King was that he was very unpopular there. He also felt ridiculous as a result of his girth and was affected by poor health, two problems later seen with Edward VII. He had been badly ill with a chest infection when he became King, Sidmouth noting: 'The situation of his present Majesty was extremely alarming during the greater part of Tuesday night: but the formidable symptoms have gradually given way, and all apprehensions of a fatal result appear to be over.' The fear, however, of 'a fresh attack, to resist which his constitution may have become unequal' led to action: 'The quantity of blood taken from him in the course of twelve or thirteen hours by the advice of Dr Tierney[13] was enormous, and to that advice the preservation of H.M.'s life is, through the blessing of Providence, to be ascribed.' Ten days later he added, 'The King's health gradually improves but there are very painful obstacles to a rapid recovery.' Renewed ill-health led Liverpool to write in July 1820, 'The King's progress to recovery is but slow.'[14]

Principally due to the death of Princess Charlotte, his only child, in 1817, George's life was sad. His reign was, at times, a ludicrous postlude to the more flamboyant days of his career, when, as the leader of fashionable society, he had created a new, alternative image of royalty and a new standard of English and international elegance: the Brighton Pavilion stands today as testimony to his idiosyncratic taste, but this was no longer the prince who had built so grandly and strove in his own fashion to compete with Napoleon.

Initially, as Prince of Wales, George's building had essentially been for private purposes, and it was decorative rather than a work or projection of state. Carlton House on Pall Mall, which George had been granted in 1783 as his first independent residence, required restoration, but George had it extensively rebuilt by the architect Henry Holland and the building was also lavishly decorated, providing a setting for impressive and always expensive entertainments. This expenditure contributed substantially to the Prince's debts.

On the site of what is now Carlton House Terrace, Carlton House was designed as the end of the ceremonial route that John Nash created from Regent's Park via Regent Street. A magnificent residence, Carlton House was demolished in 1826, in part as a result of a focus on developing Buckingham House but also because Carlton House was affected by subsidence.

From 1783, the Prince spent summers at Brighton, newly fashionable as a result of the belief that sea bathing was healthy. Needing a residence, George had a house transformed into a villa by 1787. Subsequently, the Brighton Pavilion was enhanced with fresh construction and exuberant decoration. The Dome, built from 1804, was designed in what was seen as an Indian fashion, and the metamorphosis of what had been a classical villa into an oriental pleasure palace was also accomplished by the furnishings, which again were in an Indian style.

As King, George was responsible for the rebuilding of Buckingham House and also supported John Nash, the architect there, in his work on what became Regent's Park and on the building of Regent Street. George also backed Jeffry Wyatville in the rebuilding of Windsor Castle.

George was a supporter of the new National Gallery and proved a great and lavish patron of painters and collector of artistic treasures. As a child he was able to explain the historical references in the paintings in the royal collection, including of victories over France, which indicates that they had been used to teach him.

Initially, as King, George set himself up in considerable style. The list of courtiers and servants requiring lodging at Phoenix Park in Dublin in 1821 was impressive:

His Majesty – requiring for his private apartments a Bedroom, a Sitting room adjoining, and a Page's waiting room.
4 Pages of the Backstairs in constant attendance
4 Pages of the Presence (2nd class of servants)
4 Footmen
Sir Benjamin Bloomfield
Valet
2 Footmen
Equerry in Waiting
1 servant
Gentlemen of the Wine Cellar, Confectioner, Pastry Cook, 2 Master Cooks, Table Decker, and from 10 to 12 Cooks and servants belonging to the Kitchen.
The above must be lodged where the King resides.
The Lord Steward of His Majesty's Household
The Lord Chamberlain
The Master of the Horse
The Groom of the Stole
4 Valets and 8 Footmen

4 Lords of the Bedchamber
4 Valets and 4 Footmen
4 Grooms of the Bedchamber
8 Equerries and Aide de camps
4 Gentlemen Ushers
16 Servants
Secretary to the Lord Steward
1 Clerk
1 Servant
Secretary to the Lord Chamberlain
1 Clerk
1 Servant
Clerk Comptroller of the Kitchen
1 Servant
3 Clerks
2nd Gentleman of the Wine Cellar
2nd Confectioner and his Assistant
2nd Table Decker
3 Silver Scullery Men
4 Principal Cooks
3 Apprentices
Physician, Surgeon, and Apothecary to the Person
20 Gentlemen Pensioners and 4 Officers
Stable Department – numbers not known.[15]

This was different to the style of George III when travelling, although George IV's purpose in Dublin was very different from that of George III in Weymouth. And there could be a splendour to George III's court, one that led to newspaper reports such as the lengthy one in the *London Packet* on 21 January 1795 describing what had been worn at St James's for Queen Charlotte's birthday. Once he became reclusive, George IV cut a far less impressive figure, but he still spent heavily, including on German musicians and French cooks, and had five yachts. His immense debts, which had angered Sir Benjamin Bloomfield, his Private Secretary from 1817 to 1822, meant that in 1822 George gave Sir William Knighton, the newly appointed Keeper of the Privy Purse, effective control of his financial affairs, which he managed with some success. Knighton brokered George's friendship with literary types.

Like his father, George's range of interests was impressive. He founded the Royal Society for Literature and chartered 25 other bodies in his reign including the Royal Asiatic Society, the Society of Geology, Edinburgh Academy, McGill University in Canada, St David's College Lampeter and King's College London. In each case, his support was significant. Bishop Burgess said that George ought to be remembered for these more than other things. He backed the Literary Fund's support for indigent writers, had literary interests, secured the return of the Stuart papers to Britain, sponsored the copying of a collection of papyri found at Herculaneum, a parallel to Napoleon's interest in Egyptology, and was interested in animals. His menagerie reflected the spreading sway of British power and included kangaroos, an ostrich, a zebra, a leopard, and a giraffe presented in 1827 by Mehmet Ali, the Pasha of Egypt.

A more lasting tribute was the invitation to Jane Austen to dedicate *Emma* (1815) to George, who was a fan of her work. Her reluctance was overcome and the dedication was duly carried in the book. This dedication would have been commercially valuable, and probably, in the event, a psychological help. Recognition was doubtless more important to her than is now apparent. *Emma* was a conservative work, Austen referring critically to schools teaching 'upon new principles and new systems'. George's librarian, James Stanier Clarke, advised Austen in 1815 on the subject for her next novel. George was also a fan of Walter Scott, who turned down the Poet Laureateship in 1813. After the publication of *Waverley* (1814), he was invited to dine with the King and made a baronet in 1820.

Politically, George benefited from the stability of the Liverpool ministry (1812-27), in much the same way that George III had benefited from that of Pitt the Younger. George followed his father in being the target of Whig and radical criticism. For the Whigs in particular, they were later versions of the dastardly Stuarts. Thus, criticism of the Stuarts could be conflated with criticism of both men, which had not been the intention of Whig writers under George I and George II.

After Liverpool had a stroke and retired in April 1827, however, George found politics very troubling, facing the same problems as his predecessors after longstanding ministers fell, notably Walpole, North and Pitt the Younger. The crisis of Liverpool's succession was resolved by making George Canning head of the government, against the initial wishes of the King and to the anger of many Tories. In turn, Canning's death that August undermined political stability one more. Keen not to turn to Wellington, whom he distrusted politically, the even-more-than normally petulant George helped to put in a government under Frederick, Viscount Goderich, a former Chancellor of the Exchequer. However, the agreeable Goderich was weak and could not control his colleagues. Disillusioned with Goderich, whose willingness to blubber did not impress the King, George accepted his resignation in January 1828 and finally turned to Wellington. George insisted that the government should not push through Catholic Emancipation; indeed, he had obliged Canning to appoint a Chief Secretary for Ireland who did not support it.

Wellington, however, saw Emancipation as necessary in order to reduce political tension, and pressed George hard on the issue, urging him to ignore the contrary advice of his brother, Ernest, Duke of Cumberland, the fifth son of George III. As George, who, in his anger, threatened Wellington with abdication, had no alternative ministers to turn to, he finally agreed, under pressure from the Duke and a Cabinet resignation, to sign the Catholic Relief Act on 13 April 1829. The willingness of George to bow to necessity defined this last stage of his reign, but it left him bitter and deflated. This weakening of a Protestant church-state, if not monarchy, qualified the legislative context established in 1701 for the Hanoverian succession, but, like that, it was a parliamentary act and as such, a product of the Revolution Settlement after the 'Glorious Revolution'.

George might have been earlier described as the 'First Gentleman in Europe', but as monarch he lacked charisma and was widely believed to have no sense of integrity; even if he has recently benefited from some moderately sympathetic reassessment. His reign was a lost opportunity for assertive monarchy. In some respects, the history of the British monarchy has often been such. James I and VI failed to unify England and Scotland, and his Stuart successors found it impossible to create a domestic consensus or to win glory abroad, while the 'Glorious Revolution' did not produce an uncontested succession, nor lead to the accession of vigorous monarchs with children.

Whereas Georges I, II and III were not without success, under George IV, especially after the royal visit to Scotland, the British monarchy blatantly lacked flair, and George himself acquired a general and sustained unpopularity that was greater than that of the earlier Hanoverians. No later British monarchs, including Edward VIII on his abdication in 1936, had been so unpopular on the eve of their death as George was when he died on 26 June 1830.

George's primacy, as Prince Regent and King, helped focus unpopularity on the dynasty as a whole. In 1818, the anecdotes of the Jacobite William King (1685-1763) were published, which included Walpole's remark, 'I have two cursed drawbacks, Hanover, and the *** avarice.' Peter, 7th Lord King, in his *Life of John Locke* (1829), included notes from his ancestor who had been Lord Chancellor from 1725 to 1733. His preface asserted that:

> Abundant proof will be found in the following pages of the disproportionate importance attached to German politics, during the reigns of the two first Princes of the House of Brunswick, who were more interested in the welfare of their Electorate, and in making some petty addition to their German territories, than in that of Great Britain, which they neither valued nor understand.[16]

The deaths of his brother Edward, Duke of Kent in 1820, and even more Frederick, Duke of York in 1827, had a damaging effect on George, helping turn his continual hypochondria toward thoughts of mortality. These deaths also brought problems to sort out. Wellington wrote to George's confidant, Sir William Knighton, after Frederick's death:

> Before I would take charge of the enclosed paper I was made certain that there was no male by which the unfortunate person to whom it related could bring under His Majesty's notice unless I could interest you in her favour; and I shall not think it proper that I should know of the circumstances therein stated without at least giving you the option of laying before the King, knowing as I do His Majesty's affection for his late brother, and how keenly he feels everything that can affect his reputation and honour.[17]

Close to his end George was suffering from breathlessness, bladder inflammation, arteriosclerosis, and failing sight, and was heavily drugged with laudanum; but he still ate and drank heavily and ignored his doctors. At this stage, alongside eagerness for news of the results of races and for details about horses he wished to buy, came signs of religious devotion. George read the Bible frequently, took solace in receiving the sacrament, and declared his repentance of his youth, saying that he hoped the mercy he had shown others would be offered him.

The King's decline took several months, during which he displayed considerable courage and calm, while in great pain and breathless and dependent on a chair that doubled as a bed. In his last moments, he looked at Sir Jonathan Wathen, his physician, who was holding his hand, and said 'My boy, this is death!'[18] He then fell back dead in his chair; the rupture of a blood vessel in his stomach had killed him. George bequeathed his plate and jewels to Lady Conyngham, although she refused them.

The funeral, in Windsor on 15 July, saw few signs of grief. The Unitarian *Monthly Repository's* obituary declared: 'He was too regardless of the decorum which his father so steadily maintained for it to be decent in religionists to become his apologists.' *The Times* acidly observed: 'What heart has heaved one throb of unmercenary sorrow?'

BRITISH MONARCHS AND THE OTHERS

'Each tries to save his house [dynasty] the best he can.'

George II, 1743.[1]

The position and development of the British monarchy appears distinctive, and was so, seen against the backdrop of contrasting styles of monarchy across Europe and the world. Moreover, comparisons throw light both on contemporary perceptions and on subsequent views. The former were particularly important because of the way in which British hopes and fears were thereby explained and played out. Comparing George II with Louis XV of France, or George III with Gustavus III of Sweden (who suppressed the Swedish 'Age of Liberty' in 1772), made a very different point from contrasting George III favourably with Napoleon. The latter comparison was pushed to the fore when Napoleon made himself Emperor in 1804, and was encouraged when the death of Pitt in 1806 led at first to a ministry of 'All the Talents'. That was a coalition and anyway not an exemplary contrast as far as many patriots were concerned. Subsequent prime ministers did not provide an appropriate contrast to Napoleon. None had the reputation of either of the Pitts. Indeed, the symbolism of power focused on Crown not Parliament, still less ministry, and this did not really change until the reign of Queen Victoria.

Who made the comparisons was salient, and also the extent to which they accorded with or refracted ideological norms. Thus, in 1728, a leading opposition newspaper praised the Pope's decision to stay in Rome and not go to his summer palace at Albano, where the papal palace of Castel Gandolfo served as a summer residence. This was a clear reference to attitudes to George II going to Hanover.[2] In 1744, 'Orator' Henley challenged the norms in comparing Britain with France: 'We have a pretender to the Crown, so has France, for the King of England calls himself King of France… In France the King rules by arbitrary power – I don't say that is quite the case here yet.'[3]

Irrespective of the politics, many of the views held about foreign rulers could be mistaken. In 1749, Joseph Yorke, the British envoy to France, noted:

> I confess nothing since my coming into this country has surprised me more than to find the French King [Louis XV] spoke of with so little regard, which is so contrary to the notion one generally has conceived, of their outward at least affection for their monarch; but it is certainly much otherwise at present.[4]

On Charles Edward's invasion of England in 1745, he spent too much time with a small cadre of advisors. His failure to take the Highland chiefs with him, which led to them forcing him to abandon the invasion, forms an ironic counterpoint to George II's difficulties with the 'Old Corps' Whigs in 1744-6. In a very different context, George was better able to adapt.

Comparisons were implicitly suggested as monarchs were discussed. Thus, the British envoy reported of the new ruler of Spain, Charles III (r. 1759-88), who in some respects anticipated George III:

> The Catholic King is indefatigable in his application to business: he passes many hours alone in his Closet every

> morning before the arrival of the ministers; as His Catholic Majesty rises constantly at five, no matters are postponed, as formerly, from day to day, and then often left unexecuted.[5]

Conversely, praise for Frederick II (the Great) of Prussia (r. 1740-86)[6] could provide an implicit comment on respective success, and George II was jealous of his cousin.

It was less common to make comparisons between other aspects of the political system and those abroad, although in the 1730s British critics had a habit of referring to the Westminster Parliament and the *Parlement* of Paris, a comparison driven home by calling the latter the 'Parliament'. This was a way of criticising Walpole, but said nothing substantive about Parliament, and still less monarchy.

The rulers themselves were able to make informed comments about domestic circumstances in other countries. In 1753, George II commented to Perron, the Sardinian envoy, on the bad state of France and the weakness of its ministry.[7] It was more common to look for Classical comparisons to British governance, a readily understood parallel for a public culture in which there were frequent references to the Classics. The usual comparison was with the Roman Empire, and notably the early Emperors. They ranged in their presentation from figures treated generally positively (Augustus) to those regarded as villains (Caligula, Nero, Domitian). In 1715, William Cookson, a former Mayor of Leeds, produced a Jacobite broadside, *Nero the Second*, comparing George to Nero. The French envoy saw this as an instance of the impunity with which rulers could be maligned in Britain – but Cookson was imprisoned.[8] Part of a long-lasting pattern, seen in particular in earlier opposition to Spain and France, a different type of monarchy was outlined in the idea of a 'universal monarchy' posed by a European hegemon.[9]

In Ancient Rome, the key political relationship, that between Emperor and chief minister, meant that rulers could be presented as misled. Thus, discussion of George II and Walpole in terms of Tiberius and his murderous minister Sejanus meant that the King escaped a measure of criticism. The evil ministers trope is an old one, as with Wolsey for Henry VIII and Richelieu for Louis XIII, then Bute for George III. In 1718, Charles, 8th Lord Cathcart, who was close to the Prince of Wales, reflected on the rift between the latter and his father: 'The principals in this quarrel can nor ought to have no separate interest. I am afraid the seconds of both sides mind themselves more than anything else.'[10]

Any focus on evil ministers provided monarchs with a measure of protection and made constitutional sense of the existence and practice of opposition. On 30 December 1726, the *Craftsman Extraordinary* attacked Walpole in the guise of Cardinal Wolsey, a comparison also used in William Hogarth's print *Henry VIII and Anne Boleyn* (*c.*1728-9). Attacks on evil ministers in plays such as *The Fate of Villainy* (1730) and *The Fall of Mortimer* (1731) were unambivalent.

Yet, the relationship could still be one that could become a stick with which to beat the monarch. Attacking George III's favourite, Bute, on 3 July 1762, the *North Briton*, the most prominent opposition publication, referred to the reign of Edward II (r. 1307-27)

> ... distinguished in history as the reign of favourites: to his unbounded affection for them may be ascribed the various misfortunes that afflicted this country at that time; and by those attachments, the affections of the Old Nobility were so alienated from his that he became involved in disputes which terminated with the loss of his crown and life.

The relationship between monarchy and ministers became a focus for differing views, not only of the constitution, but also of society. Defending Bute, the *London Chronicle* of 21 December 1762 printed a dialogue in which Richard Candor, 'an honest tradesman in London,' asks:

> Do'st thou think that Will Thimble the tailor, and Ned Anvil the smith, would not be much better employed in shaping a

> coat, and shoeing a horse, than in puzzling their own pates [heads], and misleading others (ignorant as themselves) in matters vastly above their weak understandings?

This was a reference to the Peasants' Revolt of 1381.

As a very different defence, William, 1st Earl Talbot fought a duel with the journalist John Wilkes due to the *North Briton*'s attack on his management of the royal household as Lord Steward, a post he held from 1761 to 1782. Talbot had been close to Frederick, Prince of Wales. Both men survived the night-time pistol duel without a scratch. Literature also played a role, as on 18 January 1718 when the pro-government *Weekly Journal or the British Gazetteer* urged the Prince of Wales to follow the contrite example of 'Prince Hal'.

In 1733, in the aftermath of the Excise Crisis, Henry Pelham, who was not generally an alarmist, warned his brother Newcastle: 'The whole country almost is poisoned. Very little regard in the common people for the King or Royal Family, less for the Ministry.'[11] The ministry was to go on to win the General Election of 1734, which offers some qualification of Pelham's observation, although the representative system was scarcely a democracy in modern terms.

Critics of the alleged pusillanimity of successive governments bruited the efforts of glorious past rulers, particularly Edward III (r. 1327-77) and Henry V (r. 1413-22) with regard to France,[12] and Elizabeth I (r. 1558-1603) with reference to Spain, as with Samuel Johnson's *London* (1738) and Smollett's *The Reprisal* (1757). On 1 October 1757, the *Monitor*, an opposition paper, made reference to Elizabeth's leading minister, with George having 'committed the reins of government to men of true British virtue, who with the spirit of a Burleigh, are ready to assist the oppressed so far as it may coincide with the interests of Great Britain'.

The example of past rulers such as Henry III and Edward I was used to criticise Hanoverian monarchs fighting abroad, as in *Old England* of 14 January 1744, when the analogy was clearly with George II:

> It appears from the whole stream of our history that the great care of our ancestors was to root from the breasts of their kings every principle of vainglory, which the more ridiculous it is, becomes the more expensive to the nation; and every partiality for foreign interests, ever bootless, if not destructive to England.

Comparison with Classical rulers was frequent, as with the pro-government *Weekly Journal* of 18 October 1718 defending naval action against Spain in the Mediterranean as a pre-emptive projection of naval strength to protect maritime strength: 'This was the practice of the Romans; and this has been the policy of His Majesty's royal predecessors, the Kings of England.' The example given for the latter was Edward I in opposition to Philip the Fair of France. For Rome, the example was not the Empire but rather the Republic in its long conflict with Carthage.

Comparisons with past English monarchs included ones long in the past, notably the ninth-century Alfred of Wessex, who was presented as a heroic and successful defender of the nation, which helped explain the interest in him of Frederick, Prince of Wales, who supported a production of a masque, *Alfred*. In the 1730s and 1740s, merely to mention Alfred was to make a political point about the need for national integrity and the defence of national honour in the face of (foreign) Hanoverian influences, those associated with George II and extrapolated backwards onto the Vikings.[13] A parallel with John and Magna Carta in 1215 was drawn over the resignation of ministers when in 1746 the King was obliged to abandon his attempt to bring Carteret back into the government:

> This was called a factious measure by some, who compared it to the violence offered to the kings by the barons of old; and was universally condemned by all, when it appeared that the public had no concern in the dispute; that instead of obtaining a second Magna Carta ... they had only made a new provision for themselves.[14]

This criticism was wide-ranging and helps provide a context for the later favour for the Gothic seen with George III and George IV at Windsor. *Common Sense*, a leading opposition London newspaper, in its issue of 15 December 1739, provided a historicised context for the criticism of the very different Rococo style prevalent under George II:

> Methinks there was something respectable in those old hospitable Gothick halls, hung round with the helmets, breastplates, and swords of our ancestors. I entered them with a constitutional sort of reverence and looked upon those arms with gratitude, as the terror of former ministers and the check of kings. Nay, I even imagined that I here saw some of those good swords that had procured Magna Carta... And when I see these thrown by to make way for tawdry gilding and carving, I cannot help considering such an alteration as ominous even to our constitution. Our old Gothick constitution had a noble strength and simplicity in it, which was well enough represented by the bold arches and the solid pillars of the edifices of those days. And I have not observed that the modern refinements in either have in the least added to their strength and solidity.

This contrasted with the idea of a 'Norman Yoke'.

Comparisons were less common with non-Western rulers, for example the Ottoman Sultan of Turkey and the Manchu Emperor of China, but they were made. Interest in Persia (Iran) in the 1730s led to comparisons with its politics, with Nader Shah (r. 1736-47), earlier the general Tahmāsb Qoli Khan, a figure of great contemporary interest to Britain. Taking the item from the *Daily Advertiser* of 27 February 1734, a Londoner recorded in his diary:

> The Secretary to Kouli-Kan the Persian General having proposed to him to raise a sum of money, by setting to sale all posts in the government and army, that general replied

> in a passion: 'Employments are the reward of virtue. Your councils therefore tend to rob honest men of their rewards, and myself of the honour of bestowing them where due; in either case you merit death.' So ordered him immediately to be put into a sack and thrown into a river.[15]

In 1737, a pamphlet praising the voluntary nature of British public finances, commented:

> It is not probable that the greatest absolute monarch could, in most extensive dominions, raise by voluntary contributions, a loan of 50 millions of money. And yet France, Turkey, Persia, India, and China severally yield much larger annual revenues than Great Britain.

However, in these states, the pamphleteer added, the security for the public loans on which Britain relied 'would be as the breath in a man's nostrils'.[16]

Separately, and on a longstanding pattern going back to the Ancient World, it was possible not only to compare monarchy with tyranny, but also to contrast it with republicanism, notably the Roman Republic. That contrast was given a modern twist with the successful Dutch Revolt against Spanish rule in the late sixteenth century and (very differently) the unsuccessful republican experiment in Britain in 1649-60, and then taken forward in different forms with the American and French revolutions.

Republicanism enjoyed very little traction in England, Scotland and Wales, but was seen in Ireland in the 1790s. Prior to then, it was the other British monarchy, in the shape of the Jacobite claimant, that attracted more attention. The degree of Jacobite sympathy and support in the country is a matter of contention, but the claimant represented a potent alternative, at least in diplomatic terms and with reference to Scottish sympathies. This put pressure on the Hanoverians, who needed to determine how best to defend their international and domestic position and to advertise their claim to political virtue. Ruling with reference to the constitution and in defence of Protestantism provided ways to do so, as with winning military success.

British commentators were free and easy in their comparisons, but so also were diplomats. Prince Antioch Cantemir, who had been Russian envoy in London, once he had moved on to Paris in 1738 told his friend, the Genoese envoy to London, that George II was not only affable but also did not seek to infringe the rights of his subjects, the latter a point more generally made.

The defence of the Jacobite claim could be punished with executions.[17] 'James III and VIII' appeared an unimpressive alternative to the Hanoverians, and the loyal press focused on this, as in the *St James's Weekly Journal* of 2 January 1720: '... the Pretender is neither able to fight nor pray for himself.' His alleged illegitimacy was also a factor.

After the battle of Culloden in 1746, a decisive and bloody dynastic triumph for the Hanoverians in the person of William, Duke of Cumberland, the dynastic clash with the Stuarts was no longer of much relevance in domestic or international politics, although in 1747, 'in a little sort of private conference', George told Simon, 2nd Viscount Harcourt, whose loyalty had been shown by his raising a regiment in 1745 to serve against the Jacobites, of the recent violent display of Jacobite sympathies at the Lichfield races: 'He must and ought to consider that company as his declared enemies.'[18] In the 1748 peace settlement, Louis XV agreed to recognise the Protestant Succession and to expel Charles Edward Stuart.

Nevertheless, Jacobitism remained, not only as a claim and movement but also as a state of mind, an expression of anger, and an element in anti-British international relations. And the British government took the abortive Elibank Plot of 1751-3 to kidnap (and maybe assassinate) George II and his family seriously.

In Britain, there remained, as a result, a lingering paranoia. On 18 March 1755, Theophilus Lindsey feared that 'our sportful neighbours had a mind to play *Perkin* again upon us,' a reference to the unsuccessful Yorkist pretender Perkin Warbeck (*c.* 1474-99), noting a rumour that Charles Edward Stuart had been seen in Paris.[19] That year, the British government sought to win international support for pressure on Pope Benedict XIV to expel the British consuls at Ancona and Civitavecchia who acted on Jacobite commissions.[20] Under Benedict, Charles Edward's brother Henry (1725-1807) had been created a Cardinal-Deacon in 1747 and ordained a priest in 1748, which of course meant he could not marry.

Nevertheless, Jacobitism then appeared redundant to the French ministry[21] and was only of very limited political consequence in Britain. As early as 16 August 1755, the *Monitor* had referred to 'the obsolete name of Jacobitism'. In 1756, there was an invasion panic, but Rouillé, the French Foreign Minister, referred to the Pretender as a 'fantôme' and said that only the British people could overthrow their government.[22] *A Letter to the King of xxx* [France] claimed: 'If a love of liberty, zeal for the commerce and glory of Britain, and for that basis of it, the Protestant Succession in the illustrious House of Hanover, are criterions of Whiggism; we are a nation of Whigs.'[23]

When Cumberland was disgraced in 1757 for military failure, it was for defeat at Hastenbeck at the hands of the French and the subsequent neutrality convention for Hanover, and not due to any Jacobite triumph. Yet, as a reminder of conjunctures, the situation would have looked very different had the French invasion attempt in 1759 succeeded; unlike in 1744-6, the French were not at war with Austria and Sardinia (Piedmont). As in 1744-6, their navy had not yet been defeated. Andrew Mitchell reflected in 1759: 'The French have begun to play off the Pretender, which will only serve to make them more hated and Jacobitism more contemptible, if possible, than it was before.'[24]

The Jacobite court in Rome became inconsequential and Italianized. When 'James III and VIII' died in 1766, his elder son, Charles Edward, who had become a Protestant on a secret visit to London in 1750, was not recognised as king by Pope

Clement XIII.[25] Charles Edward was succeeded by his younger brother, the last Stuart in the direct male line, Henry, who was also not recognised as a king but instead as the Cardinal-Duke of York. When he died in 1807, Henry left the famous marble busts of the Stuart Kings of England to George III.

Already, in 1792, in face of the growing threat from Revolutionary France, the Vatican had for the first time referred to George as King of Great Britain and Ireland, rather than, hitherto, as Elector of Hanover, and had sought British naval help. Whereas the seizure (and maybe assassination) of George II had been important to the Jacobite Elibank Plot of 1751-3, a plot betrayed by Alistair MacDonell, the British agent Pickle, by the 1790s it was pro-French radicalism that was of significance.

Another frame of reference was provided by the kings themselves, for as Electors of Hanover they were able to comment from a different perspective, feel freer from British politics, and indeed keep British ministers in the dark.[26] In 1734, replying to remarks from the Spanish first minister, the British envoy Benjamin Keene remarked that rulers with different possessions 'governed them after different maxims'.[27] In 1752, accompanying George II to Hanover, Newcastle noted that George had commented about an acquittal in London of a disaffected printer linked to the controversy over Parliament's decision in the contested return for the Westminster by-election of 1750: 'He had read, set out the newspapers: he ran into one of the usual, but strongest declamations against our laws, that punished nobody.' Newcastle's comment linked this anger to George's wish to be as independent as possible of his ministers:

> This spirit in the juries and the City [of London] which the King had flattered himself was almost entirely spent, and at an end... From these His Majesty fears that that quiet which he thought himself sure of, is not so certain, and that he may still be more obliged to follow the advice of his ministers, than he has of late thought himself.[28]

George was 'extremely well satisfied', however, with the Lord Chief Justice, Sir William Lee, who had given 'strong direction' to the jury.[29]

More than opinions alone were at stake, for the kings also used their position as Electors to advance policies; and for Britain as well as Hanover, with Hanover's neighbour Prussia a key focus.[30] Thus, in 1757, George II, in an audience with Joseph Franz Xavier, Count Haslang, the experienced Bavarian envoy, in which only the two men were present, expressed his concern about the future of the German Empire if Frederick II, the Great, was defeated and the balance of power thereby lost. This fear led George to propose that the Electors of Bavaria and the Palatinate should try to mediate between Austria and Prussia,[31] which would entail them not supporting the Holy Roman Empire in its military action in support of Austria.

George's emphasis on secrecy in this and other matters[32] was in part directed against his British ministers, but keeping them in the dark resulted in tension and uncertainty. In 1757, this led the Pitt-Devonshire ministry, fearing Hanoverian neutrality, to press George to realise that the defence of Hanover could not be acceptable without the Prussian alliance.[33] The significance of the Hanoverian link meant that trips to the Electorate were regarded as indicators of policy, for example in 1755 of whether Britain was on the eve of war.[34] Aside from their international relevance, there were domestic complications. Newcastle certainly made clear that he was opposed to George going to Hanover.[35]

Moreover, there were divisions in the royal family, with Cumberland's backing for a British-financed army in Germany opposed by Prince George, who was in favour of expeditions against the French coast, a strategy designed to win over Tories and opposition Whigs by being seen as not linked to Hanover. Members of the family reacted differently to the argument that as 'good Germans'[36] they should pursue or support particular policies or stances.

The alignment of domestic and international affairs was shown in April 1757. The ministry fell with Pitt's dismissal on 6 April.

Eight days later, Cumberland disembarked at Stade in response to George's determination to have the Hanoverian government take a resolute line in common with Britain, which was a parallel to George I's removal of Townshend from his Secretaryship of State in 1716. Holdernesse commented in 1757: 'His Royal Highness's presence at Hanover will alter the face of affairs, and vigorously carry into execution His Majesty's commands.'[37] The problem more generally was posed by the King's 'two bodies': 'The Court of Vienna has an affectation of treating with the King in his Electoral capacity only, and at the same time propose conditions to him directly repugnant to some of his engagements as King.'[38] Hanoverian vulnerability was a theme throughout the century, and one that led the rulers to more urgent interest in power-politics and to be active participants, even discussants, regarding matters with foreign envoys.[39]

Hanover also presented a way to look at British monarchy, such as the argument made in Parliament in 1733 that German rulers had used their armies to end popular liberties.[40] The threat of attack on Hanover could be paralleled with that of Jacobitism for Britain, although the *Monitor* expressed doubt on 7 April 1759: 'The threatening to march an army to Hanover is now almost as stale a piece of politics, and as little regarded as the contemptible trick of playing off the Pretender, on every bickering between France and England.'

There was tension between the constitutional nature of the state as a parliamentary monarchy and the diplomatic dual entity of Britain-Hanover. This created multiple political pressures and issues of perception, both for the rulers and for their ministers. It is easy to see Britain as resource-providing to the Electors, but also, due to its politics, a policy drag; although, in addition, George II (like his other Electors) could be cross about 'dilatory proceedings at Hanover' where there were fewer formal restrictions to his power.[41] The King's absence in Hanover led to delays for the ministry in London, and notably so in diplomatic and military matters and therefore during international crises, as in 1729 and 1755,[42] but also more generally.

As with other multi-state monarchies that lacked a combined government or legislature, the workings of the Anglo-Hanoverian polity depended on the joint ruler. In 1759, Newcastle noted that George II very much agreed with a letter written by the Duke and Holdernesse and, accordingly, wanted it used by the Hanoverian authorities:

> As proof of the King's approbation, His Majesty ordered My Lord Holdernesse to carry the letter to Mr Reich;[43] and to direct him to prepare a draft of a letter, from the King to Prince Ferdinand [of Brunswick-Wolfenbüttel], exactly agreeable to *that*.[44]

Ferdinand, who was commander of the British-funded Hanoverian Army of Observation, had direct access to George. The use of the military in Germany in wartime was contentious, something first seen in the Dettingen campaign.[45]

The *London Chronicle* of 7 May 1757 declaimed:

> The British government is neither a Monarchy, or the arbitrary government of one man, like that of France; nor an Aristocracy, or the government of the nobles, like that of Venice; nor a Democracy, or the government of the populace, like that of Holland... It is a mixed legislature.

The governmental system certainly worked, and there was no equivalent to the failure of the Swedish Age of Liberty (1719-72) or the Orangist overthrow of republican systems in Holland and Zeeland in 1747. Each demonstrated that the grounding of new constitutions in effective government was not inevitable. The methods of Prussia were not possible. Andrew Mitchell described Frederick the Great as 'a Prince, whose secret is known to no man; who executes before it is known that he has deliberated.'[46]

Instead, as kings and as Electors, roles that were very different, constitutionally and in terms of the threats they faced the Hanoverians had a more difficult task, one that involved ability and co-operation. Under the pressure of deteriorating international and domestic situations, Newcastle felt able to write to his confidant Hardwicke in 1755:

> I think both the King and my Lord Holdernesse very properly combine our home situation with the foreign one, and in order to support the one, His Majesty possibly might be brought to consent to whatever your Lordship and I should propose with regard to the other.[47]

It was instructive that in a moment of despair in 1782, when facing defeat in America and having to turn to the Opposition for the new ministry, George III could talk of abdicating and going to Hanover. His defence of Hanoverian interests became more pronounced in the 1780s, and the Foreign Secretary found himself obliged to defend it,[48] while British diplomats were heavily criticised over George's role[49] and there was concern among ministers about being uninformed. It was relevant that the King's knowledge of German was good and he spoke with German envoys in that language.[50]

Every week, those who attended Church would have heard of other kings, frequently those of the Israel of the Old Testament, and always of a divinely instituted order throughout time and space. The extent to which these arguments influenced views about Britain's monarchs is unclear, but links could be drawn. Thus, from 1797:

> It is impossible in these eventful days not to think of and dip into prophecies yet unfulfilled... One thing we are sure of, that the kingdoms of the world shall one day become the kingdoms of Christ; and I have often pleased myself with thinking, and still hope and trust, that the Church of England, partly through the blessing of God ... is and will be a distinguished instrument in the hands of Providence for the forwarding of that auspicious epoch. The language we speak and the religion we profess are planted in the Eastern and the Western world, and in the Southern Ocean.[51]

With his personal devotion, belief in the need for religion as a social guide, and appeal to integrity in politics, George III understood and responded to hopes that were beyond politics. In 1767, he emphasised integrity. His reputation in this respect was buttressed by his increasing identification with the Church of England and the frequent examples of praise for him by Anglican clergy:

> I am not less surprised than sorry that the Land Tax is to be reduced one shilling in the pound this year; those who have voted for it can have been guided only by the incitements that too frequently direct the conduct of politicians, the shadow of popularity (for the reality must consist alone in what is of real advantage to the country) and a desire of giving trouble; as the true interest of my People is the only object I wish to promote.[52]

The range of comparative contexts and contrasts for the Hanoverian Kings should not obscure the most important instances. These were twofold: past English monarchs and French contemporaries. The former were most significant under George I and II and became less so in the reigns of George III and George IV, although they were still cited.

As far as the French were concerned, the dominant figures were at either end of the period. Louis XIV (r. 1643-1715), who had dominated attention under the later Stuarts, continued to be much cited under George I and George II, in part because his great-grandson Louis XV was for many years a minor, and thereafter relatively insignificant, certainly as a threat. That role was played by Napoleon, who focused attention on a French monarchy of display and power, providing a contrast to George III and a rival of sorts to George IV, who lacked that power. Napoleon also presented a militaristic monarchy that was very different to the Hanoverian one, even for those rulers who had fought, George I and George II, and far more so for George III and George IV.

THE GEORGES AND POLITICAL DEVELOPMENT

> 'For my part I should be more glad to hear that he made a Progress in England, thinking that making himself popular in England, will be of more advantage than coming here.'
>
> John Clavering, Hanover, 1716,
> on hearing that George I was coming there.[1]

On 13 November 1755, in the House of Commons debate on the Address, William Pitt the Elder, never knowingly understated, claimed that 'the King owes a supreme service to his people' who had no such obligation to Hanover.[2] In January 1744, George, 2nd Earl of Halifax had told the House of Lords that 'a peasant of England has the same right to his cottage as the King to his palace.'[3]

The reigns of the Hanoverians were crucial to the long-term pattern of British political development. There was the bedding down of the 'Glorious Revolution' settlement including the successful defence against Jacobitism, with which the royal family was closely involved. In perhaps the most rapid constitutional changes in British history, this settlement meant the practice of limited government in the context of regular parliaments; a need for parliamentary-approved finances;

frequent elections; and scrutiny by the press. Adaptations in turn were attempted, and in part occurred, due to the challenges of the American and French revolutions; but also due to the governance of a more far-flung empire and, subsequently, the linking of monarchy to a more potent imperial nationalism. Wellington, the vanquisher of Napoleon, was imperious – but a servant of George IV. In contrast, there was no meritocratic monarchy based on the abilities of a new man, as seen with Washington and Napoleon.

Throughout, the monarch had great authority and considerable power, each of which depended on circumstances. This was notably so if the monarch behaved carefully and sought to mould policies and appointments by working well with the balance of parliamentary strength and ministerial influence. George I largely did so after turning to Walpole from 1720, George II after turning to Walpole promptly in 1727 and the Pelhams from 1744 and, more clearly, 1746, and George III after bringing first North and then Pitt the Younger into office. The willingness to do so was seen as important to royal authority, even if the kings may not have appreciated the point. In 1744, Horace Walpole wrote to his close friend Horace Mann:

> The King parted with great regret with Lord Cholmondeley;[4] and complains loudly of the force put upon him... It is not easy to say where power resides at present: it is plain that it resides not in the King: and yet he has enough to hinder anybody else from having it. His new governors have interest with him – scarce any converse with him.[5]

In 1746, William, 2nd Earl of Albemarle, then on campaign against the Jacobites in Scotland, wrote to Newcastle about his thwarting George II's attempt to bring back Carteret:

> Joy my Dear Lord Duke to you in particular, to the King my Master, and to all his servants and your friends, that you have

> by accepting again of your office restored him to his power and authority in his kingdoms and over his people, which I own I thought very precarious yesterday.[6]

A Lord of the Bedchamber to George II, first as Prince of Wales, from 1722 until 1751 when he became Groom of the Stole, a post he held until his death in 1754, Albemarle represented the close links between Crown and aristocracy through the nexus of Court, military and diplomatic service, in each of which he was significant.

Whatever the need to adapt in accepting ministerial appointments, George I, II and III remained important in government actions, especially foreign policy in a period in which central government was not responsible for health, education, social welfare and much of economic policy. Thus, in 1755, reflecting his quest for security for Hanover and perception of the state of Britain's alliances, George turned to his disliked nephew, Frederick II.[7] That the crucial negotiations occurred as a result of George's lengthy visit to Hanover that year underlined his significance. At the same time, Mirepoix, the French envoy, correctly reported that George did not care much about North America, but had no power to make concessions there in order to improve the situation for Hanover.[8] Despite the suggestion of critics, there was no equivalent to the French *secret du roi*, a large-scale and sustained secret diplomacy. Instead, rulers were 'pleased to enter into the several points of business depending' with foreign envoys, but with the knowledge of their ministers.[9]

The monarch was also able to control much preferment, especially in the army, the Church and the royal household, although having to take note of ministerial views, as in the resolution of the political crisis of 1746 when George II, with his characteristically blunt commentary, thought 'it is too indecent violence to rummage his Bedchamber.'[10]

Kings were trammelled by government methods. In 1758, Newcastle noted about money for Hanover: 'His Majesty wanted this money to be sent away in 24 hours. I told him this holiday time nobody was in town, no office, that caused very severe reflections.'[11] Baron von Görtz, the close advisor of Charles XII of Sweden, contrasted George I's attitudes as King and as Elector, albeit from a very hostile perspective, arguing that the liberties of Britain were inconvenient to a ruler brought up in Hanover with purely monarchical maxims.[12]

In the army, which defended state and dynasty from rebellion, George I and George II in particular sought to counter entrenched factionalism, amateurishness and the pursuit of the financial benefits of command. Many of the officers of the Minorca garrison, which fell rapidly to the French in 1756, were absent when the attack came. Thanks to hostility from the opposition and to governmental wishes to cut expenditure, little was spent on the army during the peacetime periods of the reigns of George I and George II, and morale among both officer and soldiers was not high. The rulers, however, promoted the principle of long service as the main way to advancement, and did their best to counter the purchase of commissions. George II sought to protect the army from ideas of reliance on a militia[13] and also used his formidable memory for names to good effect in overseeing the leading members of the officer class.

Although the desire of George I and George II to end corrupt financial practices and, in particular, officers' pecuniary perquisites, was only partially successful, the traditional character of proprietary soldiering at troop and company level was fundamentally changed, to the significant detriment of the incidental income of captains. Regimental entrepreneurship, however, largely escaped, and colonels maintained their private financial position until the reign of Victoria. Until the 1750s, regiments were known by the names of their colonels.

This was not the best basis for an effective response to the French army;[14] it was not a service nobility or élite comparable to that seen in Prussia, Russia and elsewhere. Indeed, the absence of such a development captured the nature of British governance. In so far as there was such a nobility, it was focused on an empire run by a parliamentary monarch in which the executive role of the monarch was limited. With its high participation rate in army officership, the Scottish aristocracy was the closest to a service nobility.

The central role of the monarch was much in evidence in crises. Prefiguring the roles of William IV during the Reform Act crisis of 1830-2 and of George V in the political crises of 1911 and 1931, George II was to the fore when Walpole proved unable to sustain his position in the House of Commons after the general election of 1741. Sir John Shelley, a defeated ministerial MP, told John, 1st Earl of Egmont, the following January, that he was 'apprehensive of a civil war'. Egmont replied: 'There could be no civil war where all the nation is on one side, as is the case at present. There might indeed be a revolt, but if His Majesty would throw Jonas (Jonah) into the sea all would be calm.'[15]

Egmont's use of a Biblical reference is instructive. In the event, breakdown was avoided when Walpole resigned. George's position was crucial, and he saved Walpole from some of the retribution aimed at him; but the King's hand was forced. So also for George in 1744, 1746 and 1757. As a result, the King had to take advice from ministers he disliked and/or did not respect, for example Pitt and Newcastle respectively. In 1759, Berkeley of Stratton recounted Newcastle trying to describe to George 'the plan of the country in those parts (North America) and their connexions and distances, about which he boggled, and hesitated, and blundered in such a manner, that I am confident he has not as yet a common knowledge of the map of it.'[16] Smollett was to poke fun in print at Newcastle's geographical ignorance of North America.

Yet, at the same time, monarchs could use the royal household as a way to obtain sound advice and develop and sustain links. Thus, having been First Lord of the Treasury in 1756-7, William, 4th Duke of Devonshire, a key member of the 'Old Corps' Whigs, was then made Lord Chamberlain and a member of the Inner

Cabinet, both positions he held until 1762 when he fell out with George III. Devonshire was recorded by the well-informed Sardinian envoy as being always consulted by George II on all the affairs of consequence.[17]

The British, their monarchy, politicians and public, had created a system that worked. This involved an uneasy interplay of royal intentions with pressure on the Crown, whether from parties or from factions in so far as the two can be differentiated. In practice, this involved applying, interpreting and reinterpreting often vague constitutional guidelines that sought to define the relationship of Crown and Parliament, such as the Act of Settlement of 1701. They provided scant guidance for most political eventualities and were dependent upon mutual goodwill, which ensured that diplomats endlessly evaluated the nature of relations between monarch and ministers.[18]

There was scant agreement on several central political issues, notably over the choice of ministers. Lord North told the House of Commons on 27 February 1782:

> The King had a right to admit and dismiss from his councils whomever he pleased; and he might, without assigning any cause, or without fixing any guilt upon the person, recall that confidence which he had been graciously pleased to bestow upon any one of his servants.[19]

These views were to be advanced anew by William, 2nd Earl of Shelburne, the first minister in 1782-3.[20] Meanwhile, in April 1743, Sir James Lowther had drawn attention to royal resistance to pressure:

> It has been talked of for some time there would be a good many changes in places at the rising of the parliament, but nothing has happened but filling vacancies in the army which could not be avoided. All other matters go on very heavily. Lord Carlisle's friends were giving out he was to be Lord Privy

> Seal but if Lord Gower is removed it is said the King will not give it to the other. To be sure there is great struggling for and teasing the King about places, but His Majesty is not fond of those that found such prodigious fault with others only to get into their places.[21]

The need to get government business through Parliament led to frequent complaints from British (and allied) diplomats that 'the business of Parliament will take up all the thoughts of our ministers at home,'[22] such that foreign policy was neglected. An emphasis on the need to manage Parliament could be advanced for tactical political reasons rather than as an objective assessment of the views of parliamentarians or the exigencies of parliamentary management.

The existence and role of independent MPs, particularly prominent in the reign of George III, showed the limited nature then of the party configuration in Parliament after the breakup of parties in the 1750s and early 1760s. Independents rarely took the initiative in matters of national politics, and they generally gave their support to the Crown and the ministers who enjoyed the confidence of the monarch. They were, however, willing to withdraw support over issues, and this represented an important, but unpredictable, constraint on government policy.[23] When ministerial defeats occurred in Parliament, it was not through the strength of the opposition, but the loss, on specific points, of the support of the influential and numerous independents.

Political and parliamentary confidence were not always measurable by objective criteria, not simply a matter of the size of majorities. This was especially the case in periods of crisis. The resort to the 'accusation' of parliamentary management in order to advance particular political goals was tactically valuable in political discussion as it was difficult to contradict. Parliament did need to be managed, and, for example, appointing William Pitt the Elder to office in 1746 and 1756 seemed likely to make this easier and could be explained accordingly. This, indeed, proved to be the case. George III and Bute accordingly needed Henry Fox in 1762 to help pass the Peace Preliminaries. He was made Leader of the House of Commons.

In 1744, George had to part with Carteret because of opposition by leading members of the ministry to what was presented as his excessive commitment to George's wishes as Elector of Hanover, a fair charge. The crisis led to speculation about the political system and consequent serious criticism of George's support for Carteret. *Old England*, a leading opposition London newspaper, emphasised the role of political pressure and, concerned that the King could protect a minister who did not enjoy Parliament's confidence, the paper pressed for a limitation of the royal prerogative in this respect.

In the event, in accordance with the characteristic nuances of the constitution and with the successful imprecision of the political system, the relationship between Crown, ministers, and Parliament resolved itself in 1744, and then repeatedly, in favour of those ministers able to lead Parliament. Given that he could not retire from office in the face of crisis as Newcastle did in 1756 and North in 1782, George II was possibly the most adept politician among his ministers and opposition, and certainly became highly experienced, although not of course in parliamentary or financial management. He was to be succeeded in this position by George III at least as far as experience was concerned, but never by George IV.

George II certainly understood the need to help the ministry. In June 1755, at a time of growing crisis, Holdernesse reported to Newcastle:

> The King entered much into conversation upon parliamentary and party matters and said you had promised to write me word at a proper time how *some people* stood affected to his measures, in short the King seems in that kind of temper at present that I am persuaded he would willingly give ear to any proposal you might now think proper to make.[24]

In response, in order to win support for subsidy treaties, Newcastle argued that George had to allow the ministers to seek 'the assistance of those who are necessary for us'.[25]

However, alongside instrumentalist accounts of the cohesion or at least flexibility of the system and the assessment of success and failure accordingly, it is also necessary to emphasise a significant cultural dynamic. Ministers felt personally involved in supporting the royal family. Thus, in 1753, Henry Pelham, the First Lord of the Treasury and a marked critic of peacetime subsidy treaties, told George that he needed four or five years to regulate the affairs of the nation, but that, if the royal honour demanded war, he would find the necessary resources.[26]

The theme of a system that worked was advanced from the outset, for the defence of the Revolution Settlement drew on ideas of its necessity. There was also a conflation of the traditional theme of Protestant monarchy with the mechanistic idea of a natural and necessary system that developed as a product of the 'New Science'. Newtonian physics was explicitly held out as a model in works such as Desaguliers' *The Newtonian System of the World, The Best Model of Government: An Allegorical Model* (1728). Such views persisted. On 9 August 1755, the first issue of the *Monitor* declared:

> By abusing the power and prerogative of the crown, and by creating a private and corrupt dependence upon ministers, by bribery, and other undue influences, the balance of power between the King and subject may soon be destroyed.

Confusing the argument, a common facet of discussion, the paper also announced that it was 'designed to emancipate the king from the shackles of an arbitrary administration'.

The 'Address to the Public' in 1791 at the beginning of the first volume of a new periodical devoted to reporting parliamentary debates, offered a summary of the established thesis of the constitution:

> ... that firmness, beauty, and magnificence of our excellent constitution, founded on the mutual consent of Prince and People; both moving, as it were, in one orb, reciprocally influencing, attracting and directing each other; whose united power may be compared to a machine for the determining the equality of weights; the sovereign and the representative body counterpoising each other, and the peers preserving the equilibrium.[27]

So, a self-righting system of balance and order. Such coordination was necessary to prevent disharmony, an ancient theme that drew on astronomical images, but also to prevent disintegration, a thesis given new strength by Sir Isaac Newton's emphasis on the atomic nature of matter: that God at the creation had formed matter in solid particles. Atoms were seen as possessing 'powers' of forces of attraction and repulsion, which were subject to mathematical analysis,[28] as an aspect of a more general necessity for what George III, writing of politics, referred to as rational.[29] This was true not only of the domestic sphere but also of 'the General System of Europe'.[30] The *Con-Test* in its first issue of 23 November 1756 declared: 'There is in all kingdoms, a real or permanent, and an accidental or immediate interest.' In practice, it was unclear how to differentiate them and that indeed was the stuff of politics.

The monarch in this respect was not a hidden or overt hand presiding over the domestic system, but rather part of it. At the same time, 'modelling' the monarch faced the problem seen with all models: was the role descriptive, as in this was what happened, or prescriptive, as in this was what ought to happen. The discussion of monarchy, particularly in the 1760s, continually revolved around that contrast, with the personality and capability of the king therefore a variable part of the equation. Thus, George III favoured 'keeping the constitution on its old footing ... [as agreeable] to the solid rules of policy, which have ever best suited the system of this country'.[31]

Personality emerges in any discussion, contemporary or subsequent, of individual monarchs. To some, this appears an 'anachronistic' or distorting aspect of history, one that ignores supposedly fundamental drives and structural forces. Yet, the latter emphasises how the system directs the individual, an approach that is questionable in itself, and inherently problematic when applied to the politics of a monarchical state. If the choices of Charles I, Charles II, James II, William III and Anne played, as they did, a crucial role in the period 1625-1714, then it is a little surprising to see the roles of later monarchs somehow downplayed.

Of course, there is a major role for Prime Ministers (also individuals), but their appointment, duration and removal owed much to the monarchs. Indeed, though some elections did usher in changes, notably that of 1741 leading to the fall of Walpole in February 1742, the system of parliamentary monarchy was rather one of ministries moderated by the Crown than by elections. A key factor in 1741 was the support for the opposition of Frederick, Prince of Wales.

The individual role cannot be readily fitted into a systemic account, either of monarchy or of its development. 'We are unhappily got into an age of conquering monarchs disgusted with their former boundaries,' observed William Sturrock, a travelling tutor, in 1743.[32] This was a reflection on the rulers, beginning with Frederick II of Prussia, who had attacked Austria, launching the War of the Austrian Succession.

The Georges were certainly ambitious for Hanover, but their ambition could be resisted by ministers; and more so with George II than his father. At the same time, the situation was more than a counterpoising of ambition and resistance, for the ministers responded to the needs of Hanoverian security while the rulers adapted to their circumstances, both as Electors and kings. Visits to Hanover created significant managerial and diplomatic problems for the British ministers (and practical issues of governance) as well as being a political issue in Britain. This was notably so in

1745 and 1755 when the King was abroad at a time of particularly serious and rapidly developing crises. As a consequence, the lack of any subsequent visits (other than a very brief one in 1821) was important to the success of governance.

While there was development in the British governmental system, there was no comparable one in an Anglo-Hanoverian polity, and British diplomats could express concern about being expected by the king to correspond with Hanoverian officials unbeknownst to their British superiors.[33] As a 'multiple monarchy,' Britain remained very much focused on the ruler. Furthermore, Britain's role in this monarchy lacked any real institutional or political development. This should not be seen as a failure by the Georges because there was no political traction for such a trajectory and it was not the pattern followed in other such unions such as Saxony-Poland or Hesse-Cassel and Sweden. Comparisons with those two unions are instructive as all three involved major problems for the German principality involved. In contrast, within the British Isles, there was convergence, first between England and Scotland and then with Ireland.

The comparable lack of political and governmental ownership for the Anglo-Hanoverian union was such that a major burden was placed on the capabilities, skill and popularity of individual monarchs. Moreover, this helped tarnish the political prospects for the dynasty, which made the public rejection of Hanoverianism by George III so significant. In this, George was following his father and, indeed, his grandfather, George II, when the latter had been in opposition from 1717; although not after he became King in 1727. The end of the Anglo-Hanoverian link in 1837, as female succession, in the person of Victoria, was not possible in Hanover, greatly helped to ease the political position of the British monarchy. Had that problem occurred earlier, then the consequences might have been significant for Britain as well as Hanover. Sophia, Mary and Anne could not have succeeded in Hanover, which could in 1714 have resulted in different monarchs in Britain (Sophia) and Hanover (George I).

One possibility that was not consistently followed, other than in the reactive sense of keeping out the Stuarts, was that of the monarchy as protector of Protestantism. This had both domestic and international dimensions, and was strongly pursued for a while by George I, notably in his alignments and policies in Germany, but also elsewhere.[34] Inconvenienced by the absence of a Hanoverian colleague,[35] Charles Whitworth, an experienced diplomat, told Stanhope that Britain was too forward in religious disputes in Germany,[36] which was a clear criticism of George I. Whitworth also criticised pressure to back Hanover in disputes with Prussia and pressed for Hanoverian moderation, fearing that the disputes would make it harder to cooperate with Prussia to contain Russian expansionism, notably intervention in Mecklenburg.[37]

Under George II, there were the same suggestions, but they tended to lack traction. In 1736, Cardinal Fleury, the leading French minister, spoke to the British envoy:

> He laid down as a principle that nothing but a strong Protestant league in Germany could hinder the Emperor from growing too powerful that it behoved the King of England and consequently the most powerful Protestant Prince in Europe to procure an union between the Protestant Princes to support one another against any ambitious views of the Emperor or anyone else, that it were to be wished that a hearty reconciliation could be made between His Majesty and the King of Prussia.[38]

In practice, British monarchs went along with ministers who focused foreign policy on alliance with Catholic powers: France in 1716-31, but usually Austria.

There was also the role of contingency in domestic affairs. This was made abundantly clear by the battle of Culloden in 1746, the most important event of the century. If the '45 revealed the vulnerability of the Hanoverian regime, its total failure showed the weakness of Jacobitism, especially the fragility of its support in England and its dependence on foreign assistance that never matched the success of William III's invasion in 1688. The suppression of the rebellion closed a long period of instability that went back beyond the overthrow of James II and VII in 1688-9 to the long-term factors that had contributed to that crisis. This was the Reformation crisis, one that included the English conquest of Ireland, the basis for domestic union between England and Scotland, greater power for the Westminster Parliament, and the rise of Puritanism.

The waning of Jacobitism and of the fears and anxieties to which it gave rise facilitated the dissolution of the Whig-Tory divide. Tory cohesion and identity was also affected by expectations about the future behaviour of the heir, first Frederick and then Prince George, by attempts to conciliate and comprehend opponents within ministerial ranks, and by eventual success in the Seven Years' War (1756-63).

Winning over Tories was taken much further after George III came to the throne in 1760 and sought to reign without restricting himself to reliance on only one political party. In the early 1760s, as a result, the Tories atomized, joining a variety of political groups including the government establishment in the Commons. Another important strand, cooperation in the localities between Whigs and Tories increased after 1746. In Scotland after Culloden, there was no alternative Jacobite or nationalist focus for loyalty, and, by the 1750s, there was a diminishing government emphasis on coercion. This unification of Britain helped the country in the Seven Years' War.

The decline of Jacobitism, both as a military threat and as a nostalgic cultural movement, also became part of the reconfiguration of British monarchy with the emphasis on Britain rather than Anglo-Hanoverianism. There was a parallel here with the sinologisation of the Manchu Dynasty after it conquered China in the 1640s and 1650s. The argument that George III (and George IV) were committed to Hanoverian concerns has been advanced from the 1970s as a counter to a 'British' presentation of Germany. However, this argument does not undermine the degree to which there was a shift in emphasis. In the peace negotiations of the early 1760s, George II's frequently reiterated ambitions for gains for Hanover, notably the neighbouring territories of Hildesheim and Osnabrück, were discarded by his grandson who wished to emphasise his British outlook. Thus, French and Spanish ideas of capturing Hanover to make George II more tractable no longer had much purchase.

The benign approach of depicting a system that worked has to address contingencies, but also the systemic issues affecting government. In the case of the first, in 1785, William Fraser, an Under Secretary in the Foreign Office, referred to

> ... these strange disjointed times. Where there is no ... system, but that of striving to ... overreach. Surely things must mend, and we shall again see a right understanding in those who ought to form a balance for the preservation of mankind, and not for the destruction of those they are born to protect and render happy, merely for the purpose of gratifying their own ambition. We may here say 'live' under a sovereign who really has no other wish but the laudable one of fulfilling the purposes for which he is placed at the head of a free people.[39]

As to systemic issues, there was an instructive instance in 1756. When Prussia sought a declaration of the consequences for its trade of the outbreak of war between Britain and France, its envoy was told that 'The King's authority did not reach to cases provided for by law,' so that a commercial treaty would be necessary. Prussia sent proposals which the ministry said had to be referred to the Board of Trade. Although George II was keen on speed, his Secretary of State sent instructions noting that 'from the forms of this government, the business is delayed.'[40] Such delay was not helpful in the fast-changing international crisis, and in

1785, George III pressed for 'speedy' ministerial deliberation.[41] In 1755, George II had been angered in the developing international crisis by the ministerial refusal to advance money to Hesse-Cassel to help secure prompt military assistance.[42] Similar points were made in other contexts, Thomas, 2nd Lord Grantham, the Foreign Secretary, complaining in 1783: 'I can only as a public man, wish, that our civil revolutions may not destroy all confidence from abroad in our councils.'[43]

The popularity of the monarch of course varied greatly depending on the observer. George III was delighted when he left London and received excellent receptions in southern England. For George II, there was a bleak response to his alleged Hanoverianism at Dettingen in 1743. Yet, his return to London was far better than anticipated, Horace Walpole observing:

> We were in great fears of his coming through the city after the treason that has been publishing for these two months: but it is incredible how well his reception was; beyond what it has ever been before... They almost carried him into the palace on their shoulders; and at night the whole town was illuminated... He looks much better than he has for these five years, and is in great spirits.[44]

This surge in popularity could also be found in the provinces, the *Newcastle Courant* recording the launching of a ship at Stockton called the *Dettingen* as well as printing the work of a local poet who proclaimed George and 'his conquering sword,' the Marlborough of 'this present age'.[45] a reference to John, the 1st Duke, victor of Blenheim (1704), another battle fought in Germany. modern writers I would argue tend not to focus on such responses but rather on signs of usually metropolitan discontent.

The Hanoverians did not respond to criticism or opposition by acting as Charles II and James II had done as recently as the 1680s, and as William IV of Orange, Gustavus III of

Sweden and William V of Orange did in 1747, 1772 and 1787 respectively. Instead, compromise repeatedly was adopted by, or forced on, kings. George III wrote on 7 March 1783 that he would never throw himself into the hands of a 'desperate faction',[46] on 2 April, after the formation of the Fox-North ministry

> ... finding on the coolest reflection that at an hour when the supplies are not yet found for the navy, army, and unfunded debt that bankruptcy must ensue if I did not sacrifice myself to the necessities of my people. I have therefore taken the bitter potion of appointing the seven ministers named by the Duke of Portland and Lord North to kiss hands, who are after that to form their plan of arrangements. I do not mean to grant a single peerage or other mark of favour, those cannot be called matters that regard the conduct of public affairs and if they fly out at that ... I cannot fail in such a case to meet with support.[47]

Yet, to critics, this approach by George was complacent, the Duchess of Manchester, having been to Court, writing to her husband that George's 'looks and manner strongly mark his dislike to all his present Court – he certainly is endeavouring to work a change as soon as he can... Lord Shelburne and the late Ministry are constantly with him.'[48]

Partly due to their adaptability, the monarchs represented continuity, and not only dynastic. This was especially true of George III, the youngest to the throne, whose court as Prince of Wales had also been politically influential. None of the other three succeeded young, and George I knew little of Britain before he did so. George IV's ability to learn from experience was greater than his sloth would suggest, but he was limited by his long years aligned with the opposition. George II was different, for, although like Frederick Prince of Wales he only came to Britain as an adult,

George was close to the political world throughout his period as Prince of Wales.

The significance of experience and the past more generally was enhanced by the characteristics of a society and political culture that sought to create a future but did so with greater engagement with the past than is generally the case today. This was not only particularly relevant for monarchical rule, after the abrupt discontinuity of 1688-9, but also for the aristocracy. So also for the contents of much politics, notably the concerns of foreign policy. Thus, with George II in Hanover in 1752, Newcastle, in seeking to advance the Imperial Election Scheme, revealed himself to Hardwicke – 'The dread of the politics of 1725 I have always had before me' – (referring to the Treaty of Hanover alliance with France and Prussia against the Spanish and Austria) soon after adding an admonition to remember 1742.[49] In 1742 Austria ceded territory to Prussia.

As with many instances of a supposed dichotomy between past and future, conservatism and modernisation, the period and indeed, more specifically, the British Enlightenments, involved both. The political system, which included the monarchy, arose from change, not only the 'Glorious Revolution' of 1688-9, but also the Revolution Settlement, the Act of Settlement of 1701, and the Union with Scotland. Subsequently, although the 'Old Corps' Whig ascendancy of the reigns of George I and II is not noted for change, there was in practice considerable change, not only the legislative burst of 1716-20, including the Septennial Act, but also subsequent developments, especially in fiscal administration and the governance of Scotland. Under George III, the reality and perception of change helped cause the American Revolution, but Britain also modernised to confront the French Revolutionary and Napoleonic Wars. The kings did not agree with all aspects, notably George III with Catholic Emancipation, but only George IV was really a persistent opponent of reform.

This variety again reflects differences between the monarchs, and their ability to adapt to and help mould the process of national development. This was attempted fitfully under George II, notably in celebrations of victory, but was seriously compromised, in his case and that of his father, by the Hanoverian commitment. Frederick represented a different direction. It was brought to fruition, eventually, by and under George III, thrown away by George IV, and revived by William IV.

POSTSCRIPTS TO THE PRESENT

Hail Western World! begin they better fate,
Hence let thy annals take a happier date...
George, feared in arms, beloved for gentle sway,
And Pitt, the vestal guard of freedom's ray;
Prompt to consummate heaven's supreme decree,
They give the mandate, and thy realms are free...
Thus, liberty, released by heroes' hands...
gives the new-known worlds a second birth...

Samuel Pullein, 'On the Taking of Louisburgh,'
Owen's Weekly Chronicle, 9 September 1758.

The situation in 1830 is of course very different from today. Yet, in practice, monarchy, in part as a testimony to its intrinsic importance, had modernised earlier than other aspects of the constitution, including the electoral system, the franchise, and the role of the aristocracy. Largely, as a result, monarchy in Britain has continued with far less pressure on its prerogatives than might have been anticipated, not least in a comparable perspective. Dynasties such as the Manchu (China), Mughal (India), Pahlavi (Iran), Romanov (Russia), Habsburg (Austria-Hungary) and Hohenzollerns (Germany) no longer rule, and a wide range of other states no longer have monarchies, from Brazil to Iraq, Egypt to Romania, Haiti to Greece, and many more. The British monarch is still head of state of other nations, notably Australia and Canada. Monarchies survive in Japan, Saudi Arabia, Oman, Qatar, Bahrain, Bhutan, Brunei, Cambodia, Eswatini, Jordan, Kuwait, Lesotho, Malaysia, Morocco, Thailand, Spain Denmark, Sweden, Belgium, Norway, and the Netherlands, and (very differently) the Papacy.

The reasons for this are varied. Contexts and contingencies were at play (as remains the case), and the character and abilities of individual monarchs were important in the response. Counterfactuals readily come to mind. What if Edward VIII, who had abdicated in 1936, had still been on the throne in 1940, when British forces were thrown from the Continent, would he have supported a deal with Hitler? Very probably so. How would the prospect for monarchy be different today if Harry, Duke of Sussex was the heir? This provides one way to look at the four Georges and, more generally, at the survival of monarchy and nation.

The succession was the major sticking point in a royal system, one hedged with predictions, anxieties and planning. The power of the Crown and the ability to direct patronage increased the concerns focused on the succession, but so also did the history of a resulting political disorder or conflict. What did not occur can be highly instructive. In 1727, 'James III and VIII' saw an opportunity when George I died. He left Italy for Lorraine, en route he hoped to a Channel port. However, despite mention of a possible invasion of South-West England, there was no Jacobite groundswell or even conspiracy in Britain. In fact, 1727 proved only the second 'easy' succession since that of Charles I in 1625; the other was Anne's in 1702: returning in 1660, Charles II had to wait until the Interregnum regime was overthrown and William III had to invade and intrigue, while James II and George I soon faced rebellions, even if both were overcome.

In 1727, reports of Jacobite support, of the difficulties facing the British government, and of better relations between France and Spain, all proved baseless. Rather, French pressure obliged the Pretender to leave Lorraine. The outcome showed the significance of international relations for the position of the British monarch. Consider the contrast between the conspiracies against James II in 1685 and 1688-9, the latter successful with the leadership of William III. There was also the contrast between 1688-9 and the failure of the 1715 Jacobite rising.

The peaceful accession of George II in 1727 was to be the first of a sequence of untroubled successions, including the Abdication Crisis of 1936; although the last, like the Regency Crisis of 1788-9, highlighted the possibility of less happy outcomes. That by 1830 the Hanoverian dynasty had not had to leave London showed the value as well as prestige of adding Britain to Hanover.

For Hanover itself, repeated threats of attack, variously from Russia, Prussia, and France, had culminated with French conquest in 1757 (pushed out the following year), and French seizure followed Prussian conquest in the 1800s. As Prussia itself demonstrated, overrun by the French in 1806 and under Napoleon's sway until 1813 but by 1866-71 dominant in Germany, conquest did not mean failure in the longer term; but the difficulties for the Hanoverians would have been far greater had they not also had Britain. Conversely, had Britain been defeated, then their situation would have been far bleaker, Hanover would have been more clearly vulnerable to attack.

The successful integration of a new dynasty and the creation of the Anglo-Hanoverian polity contrasted with the failure of many political initiatives under the Stuarts and the Interregnum, although legislation of 1701-7 provided the basis for the Hanoverian Settlement and for parliamentary union between England and Scotland. Under the four Georges, it proved possible to manage change in many other aspects of Britain, including the established churches, the distinctive natures of Ireland and Scotland, and the peerage. Not all the attempts to manage change worked. Thus, the Peerage Bill of 1719, which would have brought the aristocracy under the control of George I and his ministry but only by limiting the potential for new creations by future rulers and ministries, was stopped by political opposition. In contrast, however, under George III there was a massive expansion of the peerage, from 181 on 1 January 1760 to 267 on 1 January 1800. This expansion brought more influence for the Crown as head of a differentiated social hierarchy,[1] but that was criticised by some for destroying continuity of social position.[2] To some extent this expansion was due to the major expansion of the armed forces, as senior military and naval figures were rewarded with peerages. In fact, most of the peerage creations had previous peerage connections.[3]

There was also continuity in a monarchy that was politically engaged, in the sense of the appointment of ministries, but not governmentally so. There were suggestions of the opposite. Thus, in 1727, Hill Mussenden had reported from London:

> All that can be gathered for the present is that whatever side be uppermost, they will not have the same authority, that the last ministry had, since the King seems resolved to enter into all manner of affairs himself, and it is even said that he pretends to sit in person at the Treasury, the War Office, and the Admiralty Office.[4]

Neither George II nor any of the other Hanoverian kings actually did this. Instead, much initiative was left to the ministers and notably so when the King was in Hanover, as in 1720: 'His Majesty finding no likelihood of any disturbance abroad left it to the Lords Justices whether squadron which was fitting out should be laid up or not.'[5]

Continuity of a different type was offered by the ability of the British élite to present expansionism as justified and in line with the British constitution. The Crown spread its imperial sway across the seas of the world, such that the Congress of Vienna confirmed its control of Heligoland, the Ionian Islands and Malta. Due to its constitution, Britain and its monarchy was seen as different to the European model, not least by the British.

The same settlement brought royal status and considerable territorial expansion that made the monarch ruler of the fourth largest state in Germany after Austria, Prussia and Bavaria. However, when he was still lucid, George III had argued that his stance as Elector was defensive[6] and as King had praised the avoidance of alliances that might lead to war[7] and opposed aggrandisement.[8]

The consideration of continuity under the four Georges underlines the significance of the monarchs who followed them. Two in particular were in the shadow of the four Georges: William IV (r. 1830-7) and Victoria (r. 1837-1901), the first son of George III and brother of George IV, the second his granddaughter and niece. In many respects, William had similarities with George IV, not least in decided political commitments and in a willingness to bend to circumstances, in George's case over Catholic emancipation and in William's over Parliamentary reform. William had more political success than his elder brother and was able to win popularity as George did not. In specifics, William's stance could be problematic to the cause of reform, but the general impression was of a 'People's King,' which was enhanced by the popularity over the army of the navy with which he had served.

Although initially her accession was very popular, Victoria was not popularised in the same way, and her particular political positions could also be problematic. Yet, helped by skilful politicians, she was able to manage with (not manage) a constitutional change toward a more democratic political culture and one in which the Crown's obligation to accept unwelcome ministries and policies was readily apparent. Victoria became a national icon notably after she emerged from the seclusion of her widowhood.

Victoria's reign was an important preparation for the royal politics of the twentieth century, which were far from solely ceremonial. Monarchs could play a central role in political crises, notably that by which, with the help of George V, the Conservative-dominated National Government in 1931 (with a Labour Prime Minister, MacDonald, much admired by George V) replaced a Labour one that seemed unable to cope with the fiscal crisis. Monarchs also had the astuteness to accept the partial dismantling of the context within which the Crown had seemed naturally defined: notably the place of the aristocracy, the role of the House of Lords, and the new implications of the existence of the Empire.

From that perspective, there is a direct continuation between the Hanoverians and the contemporary monarchy. Indeed, by bringing the 'Glorious Revolution' to the fore, the Hanoverians established the modern monarchy.

An understated way in which they did so was in ending the succession dispute caused by the 'Glorious Revolution' and subsequent Jacobite claim and avoiding any subsequent such dispute. This contrasted with many other ruling lines. In France, the lack of any child to Louis XV prior to 1729 led to a focus on the problematic claim of his uncle, Philip V of Spain. As a result, in 1726, one Lorraine diplomat responded to Louis' ill-health by fearing very major trouble across all of Europe,[9] and that was before his smallpox attack in 1728. Spanish and Austrian branches of the Habsburg family ran out of sons, in 1700 and 1740 respectively, as did the Wittelsbachs of Bavaria, and the Romanovs in Russia faced repeated problems with the succession during the century. Helped by the British practice of accepting female rulers, the Hanoverians were spared this, and that looked toward the future situation.

So also with the commitment of monarchy to an orderly public philanthropy and to a Protestantism in which there was no equivocation toward Catholicism. Both were to be significant to modern British monarchy and each was seen with the Hanoverians. The Crown was important to the public affirmation and fixing of projects, as with George III supporting the foundation of the Royal Academy in 1768, and with the establishment of the National Gallery under George IV in 1824. George gave the necessary support to a project that was already in the public debate, as outlined, for example, by John Gwynn in his *An Essay on Design: Including Proposals for Erecting a Public Academy ... for Educating the British Youth in Drawing and the Several Acts Depending Thereon* (1749). This utilitarianism that was seen as meritorious, an approach that helped in an anglicisation of culture and symbolism. Alongside the cosmopolitanism of the period, there was a neo-imperial, modern pride in the country, an emphasis on national culture. Commentators claimed Rome's mantle of civilisation and asserted a British superiority.[10]

It was no coincidence that 'God Save the King' and 'Rule Britannia' both emerged in mid-century, the first, annexed for George II in 1745, became an indication of loyalty and a popular song. Whig confidence had broadened into the cultural moulding of the notion and reality of a united and powerful country, one in which the Crown played a useful role, especially once it could be separated from Hanoverianism. This was not only the case for the monarchs but also for Handel, celebrated from 1784 in commemorations that were supported by George III and linked to the Church of England with the emphasis on cathedral festivals of music. This was a world away from the cultural preferences of Charles II and James II.[11]

The concept of grandeur was focused more on the monarchy and less on the individual monarch. George IV might not appear to fit very clearly into this, but his reclusive later years ensured a continuation of the pattern. Significantly, there was no great public enthusiasm for statues and monuments to the Hanoverian monarchs.[12]

There was also a move away from *levées*, with Courts becoming less important public occasions. George I was by temperament private, a choice supported by his circumstances, notably language issues. George II became more private after the death of Queen Caroline in 1736, while if George III revived Drawing Room days and instituted *levées*, these, in turn, became less frequent and open than earlier in the reign.

George IV built splendidly, but there was a relative caution on the part of his predecessors. There was no replacement to

Whitehall Palace, and no symbolic equivalent to Versailles.[13] The kings as Electors did have their palaces in Hanover, notably the Leineschloss in the capital (part of which was rebuilt after a fire in 1741) and Herrenhausen near the city. Göhrdre, the major hunting lodge, effectively a palace, was demolished in 1829.[14] In Britain, they were more modest in their building, and, prior to George IV, avoided a conspicuous consumption that could arouse sustained criticism. The most palatial building of the eighteenth century was Wentworth Woodhouse, which was rebuilt by Thomas, 1st Marquess of Rockingham and greatly extended by Charles, the 2nd Marquess, an opponent of George III. For rulers, it was important to avoid as much as to lead, include, offer, and follow. Indeed, avoidance could be the most significant politically.

Thanks to triumph in the Seven Years' and later Napoleonic wars, George became defined by military success. *The Reign of George VI*, an anonymous work of 1763, dealt with the future, the early twentieth century. George VI, an ideal monarch, comes to the throne at a time of major difficulties, notably wars, but victories bring peace, prosperity, growth and territorial gains, including France and Mexico. Nine years earlier, the visiting Louis, Count of Gisors, an observant French aristocrat (who was to be mortally wounded at the battle of Krefeld in 1758, a Hanoverian-Prussian victory), was told by Joshua Vanneck, a prominent Dutch-born merchant who was politically well-connected in London, that the Hanoverians were very popular. Significantly, Vanneck said that this was because they did not try to change the constitution.[15] That was a central part of the Whig account, one that was to be amplified under George III as opposition politicians pushed to the fore the idea that any political commitment by the monarch was inappropriate, indeed unconstitutional, Sir Gilbert Eliot wrote in 1789: 'The King always expected to be of no party, and it is an unconstitutional thing that he should even express openly either favour or disfavour on account of any vote in Parliament.'[16] This was certainly not George III's view. He combined a presentation of general benignity with a political commitment, writing in 1766 to Henry Seymour Conway, Secretary of State for the Northern Department:

> The debate of yesterday has ended very advantageously for Administration; the division on the motion for adjournment will undoubtedly show Mr Grenville[17] that he is not of the consequence he figures to himself. I [am] so sanguine with regard to the affair of the East India Company that I trust Tuesday will convince the World that whilst Administration has no object but the pursuing what may be of solid advantage to my People; that it is not in the power of any men to prevent it... I have no one desire but what tends to the happiness of my people.[18]

Conway's political career was ended by his unsuccessful Rockinghamite opposition to George's policies, although he was able to accrue military promotions.

George was helped by Napoleon to make the 'happiness' of the people appear focused on the monarchy. Thus, James Gillray's caricature *Pacific Overtures* (1806), had George defy French threats: 'We are not in the habit of giving up either ships, or commerce or colonies – merely because little Boney is in a pet to have them!!!'

The warship in the background was *The Royal Sovereign* and George linked national interests with a resolve that spoke to a hope for posterity. As the symbol of the nation and the head of the state, he had helped craft an effective support in the long struggle with France, a composition in which he was also valuable to others across society. Monarchy was not welcome to all, and many queried aspects of George's real or alleged beliefs. Yet, a century after its accession, the dynasty did more than survive; it triumphed in part because of its spiritual and ideological as well as pragmatic and utilitarian value to so many.

SELECTED FURTHER READING

All works published in London unless otherwise stated.

Beattie, J., *The English Court in the Reign of George I* (Cambridge, 1967).

Birke, A.M. and K. Kluxen (eds), *England und Hannover/England and Hanover* (Munich, 1986).

Black, J.M., *The Hanoverians. The History of a Dynasty* (2004).

Black, J.M., *George II: Puppet of the Politicians?* (Exeter, 2007).

Black, J.M., *George III. America's Last King* (New Haven, Conn., 2008).

Black, J.M., *George III. Madness and Majesty* (2020).

Blanning, T.C.W., *George I: The Lucky King* (2019).

Brooke, J. (ed.), Horace Walpole, *Memoirs of King George II* (New Haven, Conn., 1985).

Colley, L.J., *Britons: Forging the Nation 1707-1837* (New Haven, Conn., 2nd edn, 2005).

Davies, N., *George II: Not Just a British Monarch* (2021).

Ditchfield, G.M., *George III: An Essay in Monarchy* (2002).

Eagles, R., *Champion of English Freedom: The Life of John Wilkes, MP and Lord Mayor of London* (Stroud, 2024)

Harding, N., *Hanover and the British Empire, 1700-1837* (Woodbridge, 2006).

Hatton, R.M., *George I: Elector and King* (New Haven, Conn., 1988).

Hay, W., *Lord Liverpool: A Political Life* (Woodbridge, 2018).

Orr, C.C. (ed.), *Queenship in Britain 1660-1837* (Manchester, 2002).

Parissien, S., *George IV: The Grand Entertainment* (2001).

Roberts, A., *The Last King of America* (2021).

Simms, B. And T. Riotte (eds), *The Hanoverian Dimension in British History, 1714-1837* (Cambridge, 2007).

Smith, E.A., *George IV* (New Haven, Conn., 1999).
Smith, H., *Georgian Monarchy: Politics and Culture, 1714-1760* (Cambridge, 2006).
Smith, R. and J. Moore (eds), *The Monarchy* (1998).
Tillyard, S., *George IV: King in Waiting* (2019).
Thompson, A., *George II: King and Elector* (New Haven, Conn., 2011).

ENDNOTES

Preface

1. Townshend to Stephen Poyntz, envoy in Stockholm, 20 July 1725, BL. Add. 48981 f. 103.
2. Charles-François d'Iberville, French envoy, to Louis XIV, 16 Oct. 1714, AE. CP. Ang. 259 f. 89.
3. Eg William, Lord Harrington, Secretary of State for the Northern Department, to Horatio Walpole, envoy in The Hague, 7 Aug. 1735, NA. SP. 84/345 f. 172.
4. Cadogan to Dashwood, 5 Dec. 1719, Bodl. MS. D.D. Dashwood (Bucks) B7/1/1a-b.
5. Daniel Dering to John, Lord Perceval, 23 June 1715, BL. Add. 47000 f. 13.
6. Newcastle to Horace Walpole, 23 May 1726, BL. Add. 32746 f. 139; Josias Cederhielm, Swedish envoy in Paris, to Count Henning von Bassewitz, Holstein minister, 24 May 1726, Paris, Bibliothèque de la Sorbonne, Fonds de Richelieu 31 f. 53.
7. Count of Cambis to Jean-Jacques Amelot, Foreign Minister, 11 Dec. 1738, AE. CP. Ang. 399 f. 309.
8. René, Marquis of Argenson to Louis, Marquis de Valory, envoy in Berlin, 16 Ap. 1746, NA. SP. 78/331. For parliamentary claims of Carteret's influence, Philip to Joseph Yorke, 17 Ap. 1746, BL. Add. 35363 f. 120.
9. Robethon, report from London to George's brother, Ernst August, from 1715 Prince-Bishop of Osnabrück, 9 Nov. 1714, Osnabrück, Staatsarchiv, Repertorium 100, Abschmitt 1, no. 196 f. 13.
10. Haslang to Preysing, 7 Jan. 1757, Munich, Bayr. Ges. London 233.
11. Bussy to Rouillé, 29 July 1755, AE. CP. Brunswic-Hanovre 52 f. 18-20.

12. Eg Count Viry, Sardinian envoy, to Charles Emmanuel III, 25 Aug. 1755, AST. LM. Ing. 59.
13. Vergennes to Jean-Balthazar d'Adhémar, 3 Jan. 1784, AE. CP. Ang. 547 f. 14.
14. Newcastle to Hardwicke, 15 Oct. 1759, BL. Add. 32897 f. 90.
15. Account of discussion on 3 Mar. 1783, Bedford, Bedfordshire Record Office, Lucas papers, L29/596. A reference to William Pitt the Younger.
16. Newcastle to Pelham, 14 June 1752, BL. Add. 35412 f. 132.
17. Holdernesse to Newcastle, 29 June 1755, BL. Add. 32856 f. 380.
18. Amelot to Bussy, envoy in London, 23 Feb. 1743, NA. SP. 107/55.
19. Richard Rigby to Sir Charles Hanbury Williams, 10 Ap., cf Duke of Bedfored to Hanbury Williams, 8 June 1756, Farmington, Hanbury Williams papers vol. 64 f. 136, 193; Horace Walpole to Townshend, 23 Nov. 1716, BL. Blakeney papers, vol. 18.
20. Townshend to Mr Hermann, agent at Copenhagen, 7 May, Townshend to Cyril Wych, envoy at Hamburg, 7 May 1728, NA. SP. 75/51 f. 65, 82/45 f. 194-6.
21. Harrington to Walter Titley, 10 July 1733, NA. SP. 75/62 f. 19-20.
22. Robert, 4th Earl of Holdernesse to Sir Charles Hanbury Williams, 11 Ap., 24 July 1755, Newport, Public Library, Hanbury Williams papers; see also BL. Add. 32996 f. 79.
23. George had reigned in Hanover from 1698 so saw himself as a ruler from then.
24. Stone to Newcastle, 16 Feb. 1745, BL. Add. 32704 f. 72-3.
25. That George should not go to Hanover due to the international crisis.
26. Hardwicke.
27. Kennicott to Thomas Bray, undated [1754], Exeter College, Oxford.

1 'Church, and King, and the Royal Family': An Era of Change

1. He was to spectate not participate.
2. M. Glover, *A Very Slippery Fellow* (Oxford, 1978), p. 150.
3. Holdernesse to Andrew Mitchell, envoy in Berlin, 9 Dec. 1759, NA. SP. 90/74.
4. Anon. account, BL. Add. 32704 f. 75.
5. Wallace to Mitchell, 20 Aug. 1756, BL. Add. 6823 f. 13.
6. Anon., *An Answer to a Pamphlet, called, 'A Second Letter to the People'* (London, 1755), p. 32.
7. Clavering to Lady Cowper, 15 Dec. 1716, Hertford CRO. D/EP F196 f. 42.
8. Fife to Mrs Rose, 25 Mar. 1783, A. and H. Taylor (eds), *Lord Fife and his Factor* (London, 1925), p. 156.
9. Newcastle to Lady Catherine Pelham, 26 Sept. 1755, Captain Gordon to Sir Robert Murray Keith, envoy in Vienna, 3 May 1785, BL. Add. 32859 f. 220, 35534 f. 131.

10. Robethon, George's Secretary, to Stair, 25 Oct. 1717, NAS. GD. 135/141/12.
11. Lascaris, Sardinian envoy, to Sardinian Foreign Minister, 6 July 1752, AST. LM. Ing. 57.
12. Diede, report, 14, 17 Ap. 1772, Copenhagen, England 1953.
13. *Mist's Weekly Journal*, 21, 28 Aug. 1725.
14. James Craggs and James Stanhope, 3 Nov. 1719, NA. SP. 44/269A.
15. Sunderland to Mylord, 12 Nov. 1719, Maidstone, Kent Archive Office U1590/0146.
16. Hoadly to Mrs William Clayton, 23 Aug. 1716, Beinecke, Osborn Shelves, fc 110 2 f. 22.
17. Hill Mussenden to his brother Carteret Mussenden, 17 June 1727, Ipswich, East Suffolk CRO. HA 403/1/10.
18. Holdernesse to Onslow Burrish, 14 July 1755, NA. SP. 81/105.
19. Petkum, Holstein envoy, to Baron Gortz, 25 Dec. 1716, BL. Add. 61572 f. 94.
20. Gibson to Nicolson, 18 Dec. 1716, Bod. MS. Add. A. 269, p. 67.
21. Yorke to --, 22 Dec. 1716, BL. Add. 35584 f. 164.
22. Count Watzdorf, Saxon envoy, to Augustus II of Saxony-Poland, 5 Feb. 1732, Dresden, vol. 2676 f. 45.
23. Charles, 8th Lord Carteret to Hugh, 3rd Earl of Londoun, 10 Nov. 1716, HL. LO. 7956.
24. De Loss, Saxon envoy, to Augustus III, 1 Dec. 1733, Dresden, vol. 638, I, f. 212-15.
25. Newcastle to Horatio Walpole, 4 July 1735, NA. SP. 84/344 f. 246.
26. Lady to Lord Bristol, 26 July 1735, *Letter Book of John Hervey, 1st Earl of Bristol* (3 vols, Wells, 1894), III, 132.
27. Bayntun Rolt diary, 25 Nov. 1754, Bristol, University Library.
28. Lasowski report to François, Duke of Rochefoucauld-Liancourt, 1784, London, University of London archives, MS. 138 f. 177-82.
29. Anonymous, *A Letter from the Right Honourable Charles James Fox, to the Worthy and Independent Electors of the City and Liberty of Westminster* (London, 1793), pp. 23-4.
30. Le Coq, Saxon envoy, reports of 14, 18 Sept. 1725, Dresden, vol. 2673 f. 73, 75.
31. Re a commission from the Queen of Prussia, Charles Whitworth, envoy in Berlin, to Sir Luke Schaub, 25 Oct. 1719, New York, Public Library, Hardwicke papers vol. 46.
32. Willem Bentinck to William IV of Orange, 22 Aug. 1747, T. Bussemaker (ed.), *Archives ou Correspondance Inédite de la Maison d'Orange-Nassau* (4th series, I, Leyden, 1908), p. 5.
33. Newcastle to Sandwich, 31 July 1747, BL. Add. 32809 f. 121.

34. Mirepoix to Rouillé, 16 Jan. 1755, AE. CP. Ang. 438 f. 29.
35. Allen to Newcastle, 9 Aug. 1732, PRO. SP. 92/34.
36. Joseph Yorke to Duke of Cumberland, 22 Mar. 1749, RA. Cumb. P. 43/144.
37. Richmond to Newcastle, 18 Dec. 1748, BL. Add. 32717.
38. Bedford to Keene, 2 Mar. 1749, NA. SP. 94/135.
39. Bedford to Villettes, 9 Mar. 1749, NA. SP. 92/58; Newcastle to Pelham, 7 June 1740, NeC. 102; Weymouth to Walpole, 8 Nov. 1768, NA. SP. 78/276.
40. D.B. Horn, 'The Diplomatic Experience of Secretaries of State, 1660-1832', *History*, 41 (1956), pp. 88-99.
41. Newcastle to Pelham, 7 Aug. 1748, RA. Cumb. P. 38/72.
42. Newcastle to Pelham, 23 July 1748, NeC643.
43. Hardwicke to William, 3rd Duke of Devonshire, 17 Mar. 1754, Chatsworth.
44. Perron to Charles Emmanuel III, 9 Jan. 1755, AST. LM. Ing. 59.
45. Andrew Stone to Pelham, 26 June 1748, NeC. 596. On his political qualities, Alt to William of Hesse Cassel, 13 Feb. 1748, Marburg 249; R. Lodge, 'The Mission of Henry Legge to Berlin, 1748', *Transactions of the Royal Historical Society*, 4th ser. 14 (1932), pp. 1-38; P. Kulisheck, 'The Favourite Child of the Whigs: The Life and Career of Henry Bilson Legge, 1708-1764' (PhD, Minnesota, 1996), pp. 61-127; George to Pitt, 11 Dec. 1787, CUL. Add. 6958.
46. Townshend to William Finch, 21 Jan. William Finch to Earl of Nottingham, 12 Feb. 1724, Leicester, CRO. DG/7/4952.
47. Fox to Hanbury Williams, 10 May 1748, Farmington, Hanbury Williams 52; Newcastle to Pelham, 13 Sept. 1750, BL. Add. 35411.
48. Sir James Harris to Keith, 24 Dec. 1783, BL. Add. 35530 f. 277.
49. Horatio Walpole to Trevor, 5 Dec. 1740, Aylesbury, Buckinghamshire CRO, Trevor papers, vol. 24.
50. Newcastle to Hardwicke, 6 Sept. 1751, BL. Add. 35412 f. 3.
51. Holdernesse to Mithcell, 7 Dec. 1756, NA. SP. 90/67.
52. Newcastle to Holdernesse, 2 Ap. 1751, NA. SP. 84/457; Holdernesse to Hanbury Williams, 17 June 1755, Newport, Public Library, Hanbury Williams papers.
53. William Fraser to Keith, 17 Aug. 1784, BL. Add. 35532 f. 203.
54. John Russell (ed.), *Correspondence of John, Fourth Duke of Bedford* (London, 1843), II, 51.
55. HMC *Polwarth*, V, 272.
56. Ossorio to Charles Emmanuel III, 23 Feb. 1748, AST. LM. Ing. 54.
57. Rouillé to Aubeterre, envoy in Vienna, 17 July 1755, AE. CP. Autriche 254 f. 225.

58. Noël to Lebrun, acting foreign minister, 10 Sept. 1792, AE. CP. Ang. 582 f. 109.
59. Walpole to Horace Mann, 5 May 1747, *Walpole-Mann corresp.* III, 397.
60. Newcastle to Hardwicke, 24 Oct. 1754, BL. Add. 32737 f. 191.
61. Newcastle to Hardwicke, 10 Nov. 1744, BL. Add. 35408 f. 88-9.
62. Newcastle to Sandwich, 4 Aug. 1747, BL. Add. 32809 f. 134.
63. Chesterfield to Gower, 15 Aug. 1747, NA. PRO. 30/29/1/11 f. 309.
64. Newcastle to Sandwich, 19 May 1747, BL. Add. 32808 f. 236; Ossorio to Charles Emmanuel III, 26 May 1747, AST. LM. Ing. 53
65. Newcastle to Harrington, 4 June, 19 July 1745. NA. SP. 43/37.
66. Alexander Straton to Keith, 25 Mar. 1783, BL. Add. 35528 f. 133.
67. Mirepoix to Rouillé, 23 Jan. 1755, AE. CP. Ang. 438 f. 44.

2 *The Inheritance of Monarchy*

1. Barrillon, French envoy in London, 30 Oct, 29 Dec. 1687, AE. CP. Ang. 162 f. 241, 362-3.
2. Yorke to --, 26 Mar. 1732, NA. SP. 36/20 f. 144.
3. J.P. Kenyon, *Revolution Principles. The Politics of Party, 1689-1720* (Cambridge, 1977).
4. R. Browning, *Political and Constitutional Ideas of the Court Whigs* (Baton Rouge, La, 1982).
5. J. Toland, *The Art of Reasoning* (London, 1714), p. v; Anon., *The Second Part of the Dissusasive from Jacobitism ... To Which is Added, King William the III. His last speech to the Parliament* (London, 1714).
6. *Old England*, 1 Aug. 1752.
7. George I to Charles VI, 2 Dec. 1719, New York, Public Library, Hardwicke papers, vol. 54.
8. Churchill College, Cambridge, Erle-Drax Mss. 2/12.
9. Hort to – 1 Feb. 1723, NA. SP. 35/41 f. 137.
10. Yorke to his brother Philip, 14 Dec. 1753, BL. Add. 35363 f. 341.
11. Frederick II to Klinggraeffen, envoy in London, 4 Feb. 1749, *Polit. Corr.* VI, 362.
12. Joseph Yorke to his father, to Hardwicke, 22 Dec. 1752, BL. Add. 35356 f. 107.
13. H. Snyder, 'David Jones, Augustan Historian and Pioneer English Annalist,' *Huntington Library Quarterly*, 44 (1980), pp. 11-26.
14. Anon., *Reasons Against the Succession of the House of Hanover* (London, 1713), a pamphlet satirising reasons given.
15. George Ridpath to Hans Caspar von Bothmer, Hanoverian envoy in London, 17 Aug. 1713, HL. HM. 44710.

16. Marlborough to Robethon, secretary to George I, 8, 22 July 1713, HL. HM. 44710 f. 63, 79.
17. Ridpath to Bothmer, 24 Oct. 1713, HL. HM. 44710 f. 263.
18. Kreienberg, Hanoverian agent in London, to Robethon, 14 July 1713, HL. HM. 44710 f. 58.
19. Verse on South Sea Company, 1720, Alnwick Castle, Northumberland papers, letters vol. 114.
20. N. Aston, 'Burke and the Conspiratorial Origins of the French Revolution: Some Anglo-French Resemblances,' in *Conspiracies and Conspiracy Theory in Early Modern Europe* (Aldershot, 2004), pp. 213-33.
21. John Graeme to John, Earl of Inverness, Jacobite Secretary of State, 13 July 1726, Windsor, RA. Stuart P. 95/82.
22. G. Eland (ed.), *Shardeloes Papers* (London, 1974), p. 50.
23. W. Gibson, 'Changes in Dissenting perceptions of the Hanoverian Succession, 1714 to *c.* 1765,' in N. Aston and B. Bankhurst (eds), *Negotiating Toleration. Dissent and the Hanoverian Succession, 1714-1760* (Oxford, 2019), pp. 53-75.
24. Bussy, French envoy, to Amelot, French Foreign Minister, 4 Mar. 1743, BL. Add. 32803 f. 111.
25. S. Brewer (ed.), *The Early Letters of Bishop Richard Hurd, 1739-1762* (Woodbridge, 1995).

3 George I

1. Perceval to Charles Dering, 30 July 1716, BL. Add. 47028 f. 160-1.
2. L. Colley, 'Apotheosis of George III,' *Past and Present*, 102 (1984), p. 95.
3. AE. CP. Ang. 259 f. 212-13.
4. Referring to Tory views, Iberville to Louis XIV, 12 Nov. 1714, AE. CP. Ang. 259 f. 283.
5. Marlborough to Robethon, 22 July, Marlborough to Bothmer, 13 Aug. 1713, HL. HM. 44710 f. 80, 137.
6. Iberville, French envoy, to Torcy, French Foreign Minister, 13 July 1714, AE. CP. Ang. 265 f. 33.
7. T.C.W. Blanning, *George I: The Lucky King* (London, 2019).
8. Torcy to Cardinal Annibale Albani, 23 Aug., Torcy to Filippo Gualtieri, 25 Aug., Louis XIV to Cardinal de la Tremoille, 27 Aug. 1714, AE. CP. Rome 538 f. 219, 228-9, 245.
9. Iberville to Louis XIV, 29 Sept., 3 Oct. 1714, AE. CP. Ang. 259 f. 8, 13.
10. Sophia to Bothmer, 24 Feb. 1711, R. Doebner (ed.), *Briefe der königin Sophie Charlotte von Preussen und der kurfürsten Sophie von Hannover an honoversche Diplomaten* (Leipzig, 1905), p. 298.

11. Iberville to Torcy, 11 Sept., Iberville to Louis XIV, 3 Oct. 1714, AE. CP. Ang. 265 f. 43, 259 f. 10-11.
12. C. Roberts, 'Party and Patronage in Later Stuart England', in S. Baxter (ed.), *England's Rise to Greatness*, p. 205.
13. Ralph Palmer to Ralph Verney, 30 Oct. 1714, Lady Verney (ed.), *Verney Letters of the Eighteenth Century*, II (London, 1930), p. 19.
14. George I to Stair, 14 Jan. 1715, NA. SP. 78/160 f. 3; Newsletter from London, 15 Jan. 1715, Osnabrück, staatsarchiv, 196 f. 42.
15. Robethon to Stair, 16 Ap. 1716, NAS, GD 135/141/7.
16. Edmund Gibson to Nicolson, 27 Nov. 1714, Bodl. MS. Add. A. 269, pp. 36-7.
17. Iberville to Torcy, 25 Dec. 1714, AE. CP. Ang. 260 f. 279.
18. Iberville to Torcy, 25 Dec. 1714, AE. CP. Ang. 360 f. 28.
19. London newsletter, 11 Jan. 1715, Osnabrück f. 40.
20. AE. CP. Ang. 259 f. 39.
21. BL. Add. 32686 f. 152, 175.
22. BL. Add. 32686 fol. 269.
23. Iberville to Louis XIV, 16 Oct. 1714, AE. CP. Ang. 259 f. 81. See also, R. Eagles, https://thehistoryofparliament.wordpress.com/2019/06/06/ich-bin-in-meinem-herzen-englisch-could-george-i-speak-english/.
24. Gibson to Nicolson, Bod. Ms. Add. A. 269, p. 52.
25. *Three Speeches against Continuing the Army* (London, 1718), p. 7.
26. Destouches, French envoy, to Dubois, French Foreign Minister, 26, 31 Jan., 9 Mar., 27 Ap., 4 May 1719, AE. CP. Ang. 322 f. 130-1, 154, 323 f. 35, 266, 324 f. 33-4.
27. HHStA, England, Varia, 7.
28. Chammorel to Dubois, 19 June 1719, AE. CP. Ang. 324 f. 128.
29. Iberville to Louis XIV, 10, 22 Oct. 1714, AE. CP. Ang. 259 f. 49, 152.
30. Cadogan to Whitworth, 18 Mar. 1718, BL. Add. 37367 f. 251.
31. J. Black, 'Parliament and Foreign Policy in the Age of Walpole: the case of the Hessians', in J. Black (ed.), *Knights Errant and True Englishmen: British Foreign Policy, 1660-1800* (Edinburgh, 1989), pp. 41-54.
32. Iberville to Torcy, 8 Nov. 1714, AE. CP. Ang. 259 f. 256.
33. Townshend to Walpole, 15 Nov. (ns), 10 Dec. (ns) 1723, NA. SP. 43/5 f. 253, 337.
34. Mademoiselle Schulenburg to Cowper, 25 Oct. 1717, Hertford CRO. D/EP. F.56 f. 64. Cf. *A True Translation of Baron Bothmar's Letter to Monsieur Schutz* (London, 1717).
35. Horatio Walpole to Malton, 10 Oct. 1738, Sheffield Archives, Wentworth Woodhouse Mss. M3.
36. Townshend to Walpole, 2 Oct. 1723, NA. SP. 43/5 f. 103.

37. Anon., probably Sir David Dalrymple, to Stair, 18 Ap. 1718, NAS. GD. 135/147 no. 17.
38. Diemar, Hesse Cassel envoy, to Landgrave of Hesse Cassel, 20 June 1727, Marburg, 4f England 195.
39. BL. Add. 32686 f. 193.
40. NA. SP. 43/4 f. 150, 292; Bod. MS. A. 269 pp. 99-100; C. Realey, *The Early Opposition to Sir Robert Walpole* (Philadelphia, 1931).
41. Townshend to Walpole, 2 Oct. 1723, NA. 43/5 f. 98; NA. SP. 43/5 f. 111.
42. HL. Lo. 7628, 7667, 7664, 7608.
43. H.T. Dickinson, *Bolingbroke* (1970), p. 219.
44. R. Hatton, *George I* (London, 1978).
45. Robethon to Stair, 24 Aug. 1716, NAS. GD. 135/141/7.
46. Bevern to Elector Palatine, 21 Sept. 1725, Munich, Kasten blau 13/4.
47. Stanhope to Townshend, 8 Sept. 1716, BL. Blakeney papers, vol. 18.
48. Dubois to Iberville, 15 Sept. 1716, AE. CP. Brunswick-Hanovre sup. 2 f. 509.
49. Craggs to William Stanhope, 16 Nov. 1719, NA. SP. 104/31.
50. Stair to Stanhope, 5 Feb. 1715 [for 1716], NAS. GD. 135/137 no. 41.
51. Anon., manuscript pamphlet *An Address to the Peers of England* (undated, c. 1716), University of London, MS. London 93 f. 9.
52. Stanhope to Paul Methuen, Secretary of State for the Southern Department, 16 Oct. 1716, NA. SP. 43/1 f. 101.
53. Townshend to Edward Finch, envoy in Stockholm, 10 Dec. 1728, NA. SP. 95/51 f. 22.
54. Iberville to Torcy, 1 Nov. 1714, AE. CP. Ang. 259 f. 213.
55. Fairfax to Lord Burlington, 10 Oct. -, BL. Althorp papers, B5.
56. Anon. [probably Sir David Dalrymple] to Stair, 18 Ap. 1718, NAS. GD. 135/147 no. 17.
57. Petkum, Holstein envoy, to Baron Görtz, 25 Sept. 1716, NA. SP. 107/1B f. 93-4.
58. Wesley, *History*, IV, 109-11.
59. James Craggs, Secretary of State, to John, 2nd Earl of Stair, envoy in Paris, 9, 12, 16, 30 Mar. 1719, NA. SP. 104/30.
60. For example, Robert Daniel, envoy in Brussels to George Tilson, Under Secretary, 13 Aug. 1727, NA. SP. 77/74 f. 223.
61. Townshend to Stanhope, 13, 17 July, 25 Aug., 1716, NA. SP. 44/268, pp. 4, 9, 38-40.
62. James, Duke of Liria to his father, James, Mashal-Duke of Berwick, 3 Jan. (ns) 1718, C. Petrie, *The Marshal Duke of Berwick* (London, 1953), p. 72.
63. Louis XIV to Iberville, 15 Nov., Iberville to Torcy, 25 Dec. 1714, AE. CP. Ang. 259 fol. 252, 260 f. 256, 283.

64. Charles, 8th Lord Cathcart to Hugh, 3rd Earl of Loudoun, 6 Oct. 1716, HL. LO 7963.
65. Sunderland to Townshend, 26 Oct. 1716, BL. Blakeney papers, vol. 18.
66. Stanhope to Townshend, 6 Nov. 1716, BL. Blakeney Papers, vol. 18.
67. Cathcart to Hugh, 3rd Earl of Loudoun, 4 Dec. 1716, HL. LO. 7955.
68. *Treasury Warrants*, 11 Dec. 1716.
69. Schulenburg to Görtz, 19 Nov. 1717, Darmstadt, F23 fol. 125.
70. Pentenrriedter, Austrian envoy in London, to Königsegg, 14 Dec. 1717, HHStA, GK42 fol. 29.
71. BL. Add. 47028 fol. 223.
72. Craggs to Stair, 28 Ap. 1718, NAS. GD. 135/141/13B.
73. C. Petrie, *The Marshal Duke of Berwick: The Picture of an Age* (London, 1953), p 72.
74. Perceval to Charles Dering, 24 Dec. 1717, BL. Add. 47028 f. 216.
75. Sunderland to Newcastle, 1 Oct. 1717, BL. Add. 32686 fol. 108.
76. Anon. [probably Sir David Dalrymple] to Stair, 18 Ap. 1718, NAS. GD. 135/147 no. 17.
77. Bonet to Frederick William, 14, 25, 28 Jan. (ns) 1718, Berlin, vol. 41.
78. James, 1st Duke of Chandos to Simon, 1st Viscount Harcourt, 25 Jan., Charles, 8th Lord Cathcart to Hugh, 3rd Earl of Loudoun, 25 Jan. 1718, HL. ST57 vol. 15, p. 92, LO. 7953.
79. *Original Weekly Journal*, 18 Jan. 1718.
80. Cathcart to Loudoun, 8 Mar. 1718, HL. LO. 7927.
81. Schulenburg to Görtz, 30 Nov. 1717, 4, 26 Mar. 1718, Darmstadt, F23 fols 132, 194, 203; Bonet to Frederick William, 15 Mar. (ns) 1718, Berlin, vol. 41.
82. *St James's Post*, 8 Jan., *Original Weekly Journal*, 11 Jan., *Post Boy*, 11 Jan. 1718.
83. Craggs to Stair, 28 Ap. 1719, NA. SP. 104/30.
84. See also *Protester*, 14 July 1753.
85. Hattorf to Whitworth, 29 Dec. 1719, Whitworth to Tilson, 9, 13 Jan. 1720, NA. SP. 90/11.
86. *Diary of Mary, Countess Cowper* (London, 1864), pp. 134, 158, 163-4, 168.
87. C.S.S. Cowper (ed.), *The Diary of Mary, Countess Cowper* (London, 1864), pp. 134, 152, 157-8, 164, 168; J.H. Plumb, *Sir Robert Walpole: The Making of a Statesman* (London, 1956), pp. 208-85.
88. Stanhope to Newcastle, 27 Oct. 1719, BL. Add. 32686 f. 156.
89. Newcastle to --, 29 Nov. 1719, BL. Add.32686 f. 88. See also Sunderland to Mylord, 12 Nov. 1719, Maidstone, Kent Archives Office, Stanhope papers U1590/0146.

90. Craggs to Schaub, 30 June 1719, Mahon, *History of England* (3rd ed., London, 1853), II, lxxix.
91. Chammorel to Dubois, 9 Mar. 1719, AE. CP. Ang. 323 f. 30.
92. Hugh Thomas to the Jacobite Court, 15 May 1719, RA Stuart P. 43/93.
93. Anon, Memorandum concerning stock transactions by Directors, 1720, Beinecke, Osborn Papers, Townshend Box 1 has each receiving £10,000 and the nieces of the latter another £10,000.
94. von Schele to Görtz, 19 July, Görtz to Sunderland, 20 Aug. 1720, Darmstadt F23 151/30/28.
95. Eg. Chammorel to Morville, 11 June 1725, AE. CP. Ang. 351 f. 172.
96. Broglie to Morville, 2 June 1727, AE. CP. Ang. 359 f. 180.
97. L'inventaire reports, 3, 13 June 1720, AN. AM. B7 279; Broglie report, 20 July 1724, AE. CP. Ang. 348 f. 129.
98. Le Coq, Saxon envoy, report 14 Sept. 1724, Dresden, 2672, f. 14.
99. Townshend to Walpole, 25 Oct. 1723, NA. SP. 43/5 f. 175.
100. James Craggs to Stair, 27 Oct., 27 Nov. 1718, NA. SP. 104/30.
101. Newcastle to Thomas Robinson, 12 Jan. 1727, BL. Add. 32749 f. 34.
102. Craggs to Stair, 4 May 1719, NA. SP. 104/30.
103. Craggs to Stair, 9 Mar. 1719, NA. SP. 104/30.
104. William Finch to Townshend, 9 May 1727, NA. SP. 84/293 f. 339.
105. Horatio Walpole to Newcastle, 9 May 1727, BL. Add. 32750 f. 230.
106. Tilson to Delafaye, 23 Nov. 1725, NA. SP. 43/8 f. 76.
107. Stanhope to Sunderland, 3 Aug. 1719, BL. Add. 61513 f. 141.
108. Townshend to Sutton, 5 May 1727, NA. SP. 81/122.
109. Arundell to Earl of Burlington, 14 Ap. 1726, BL. Althorp Mss. B3.
110. Graeme, Jacobite envoy in Vienna, to Hay, Jacobite Secretary of State, 13 Oct. 1725, RA. Stuart P. 86/142.
111. Townshend to Newcastle, 24 Aug. 1725, NA. SP. 43/6 f. 359-61.
112. Giuseppe Riva, Modenese envoy, to Konrad, Count Starhemberg, Austrian diplomat, 5 Mar. 1726, Canberra, National Archives of Australia, 9/4/12; James Hamilton, Jacobite agent, to Thomas, 1st Marquess of Wharton, 18 Feb. 1726, RA., Stuart Papers, 90/128.
113. Broglie to Morville, 13 May 1726, Canberra, MS 1458/9/1/5.
114. Walpole to Newcastle, 20 Aug. 1725, NA. SP. 35/57 f. 250.
115. Walpole to Newcastle, 21 Aug. 1725, NA. SP. 35/57, f. 255.
116. Robinson to Newcastle, 4 Feb. 1727, BL. Add. 32749 f. 75.
117. Le Coq, dispatch, 22 July 1727, Dresden, 2676 f. 126-7.
118. Cooke to Sir William Fownes, former member of Irish Parliament, 24 June 1727, Dublin, National Library of Ireland, MS. 8802/2.

4 George II

1. Seidelin was Danish. J. Hansen, 'The Coronation of George II,' [Oxford and Cambridge Club], *Club News*, 145 (Summer 2023), p. 17.
2. BL. Add. 32996 f. 81-2.
3. AE. CP. Ang. 394 f. 22.
4. *Cobbett* XIII, 564-5.
5. Dodington to --, 14 Oct. 1743, Exeter, Devon CRO. 64/12/29/1/153.
6. Newcastle to Waldegrave, 20 June 1727, Chewton. The Cardinal, Fleury, was French first minister.
7. Iberville to Louis XIV, 8 Oct. 1714, AE. CP. Ang. 259 f. 39.
8. Watzdorf to Augustus II, 12 Feb. 1732, Dresden, 2676 III f. 53.
9. Newcastle to Hardwicke, 5 July 1752, BL. Add. 35412 f. 164.
10. Delafaye to Stephen Poyntz, 14 Jan. 1729, BL. Althorp papers, vol. E3.
11. P. Woodfine, 'Horace Walpole and British Relations with Spain, 1738', *Camden Miscellany*, 32 (London, 1994), pp. 277-311.
12. Horatio Walpole to Weston, 3 July 1739, Farmington, Lewis Walpole papers, Weston papers, vol. 12.
13. Horatio Walpole to Henry Pelham, 3 Sept. 1747, NUL. NeC 489.
14. Ossorio to Charles Emmanuel III, 17 Oct. 1747, AST. LM. Ing. 53.
15. Anon. to Duncan Forbes, the Lord President, 13 Sept. 1744, *More Culloden Papers* III, 232.
16. R. Browning, *The Duke of Newcastle* (New Haven, Conn., 1975).
17. Newcastle to Hardwicke, 14 Oct. 1739, BL. Add. 35406 fol. 167.
18. Newcastle to Sandwich, 7 Ap. 1747, BL. Add. 32808 f. 23.
19. Newcastle to Holdernesse, 11 July 1755, BL. Add. 32857 f. 54.
20. *Original Weekly Journal*, 18 Jan. 1718.
21. Holdernesse to Newcastle, 29 Dec. 1756, BL. Add. 32869 f. 422.
22. Waldegrave to Newcastle, 6 July 1740, NA. SP.
23. Delafaye to Essex, 24 July 1733, BL. Add. 27732 fol. 206.
24. Sarah Churchill to John, Earl of Stair, 15 July 1737, BL. M/687.
25. Newcastle to William, 3rd Duke of Devonshire, 26 Nov. 1737, Chatsworth, Devonshire papers.
26. Ryder diary, 16 Feb. 1739, Sandon, Harrowby Papers.
27. BL. Add. 33052 f. 266.
28. John to Richard Tucker, 10 Ap. 1746, Bod. MS. Don c. 108 f. 21.
29. Utterodt and Flemming, Saxon envoys, to Brühl, Saxon Foreign Minister, 25 Jan. 1743, NA. SP. 107/55.
30. Edward Harley, diary, Dec. 1744, Cambridge, University Library, Harley Diary, f. 88.
31. Ryder Diary, Sandon, 21 R. 130.

32. *York Courant*, 29 Jan. 1745.
33. Harrington to Robert Trevor, envoy at The Hague, 26 Ap. 1737, NA. SP. 84/365 f. 36.
34. Walpole to Trevor, 22 Mar. 1737, Aylesbury, Buckinghamshire RO, Trevor papers.
35. Newcastle to Albemarle, 18 Oct. 1752, NA. SP. 781245 f. 160.
36. Joseph Yorke to Hardwicke, 22 Dec. 1752, BL. Add. 35356 f. 107.
37. Harrington to Titley, 20, 27 July 1733, NA. SP. 75/62 f. 30, 39; De Loss to Augustus III, 6, 9, 20 Oct., 6, 10, 13, 27 Nov. 1733, 15 Jan. 1734, Dresden 638, I, f. 73, 76, 78, 82, 85, 96, 117, 127, 175, 200, 638, II, f. 40.
38. De Loss to Augustus III, 23 Oct. 1733, Dresden 638, f. 103.
39. Chesterfield to Sandwich, 14 Ap. 1747, BL. Add. 32808 f. 71.
40. *Old England*, 12 Nov. 1752.
41. For attribution see *London Chronicle*, 11 Ap. 1769.
42. *A Sixth Letter to the People of England, on the Progress of National Ruin; in which it is shown that the present grandeur of France, and Calamities of this nation, are owing to the influence of Hanover on the Councils of England* (London, 1757), frontispage.
43. Viry to Charles Emmanuel III, 18 July, 15 Aug., 22 Sept. 1758, AST. LM. Ing. 63.
44. *Owen's Weekly Chronicle*, 8 July 1758.
45. Eg. General Diemar, Hesse-Cassel envoy, to Baron de Stain, 29 Oct. 1734, Marburg, 4f Eng. 203.
46. Anon. memorandum, 7 Dec. 1744, AE. MD. Ang. 8 f. 269.
47. Lady Isabella Finch to Lord Malton, 22 Feb. 1737, Sheffield, Archives, Wentworth Woodhouse papers.
48. Iberville to Louis XIV, 3 Oct. 1714, AE. CP. Ang. 259 f. 11.
49. Diemar to Eugene, 20 Ap., 4 May 1734, HHStA. GK. 85a f. 487, 497; Count Philip Kinsky, Austrian envoy in London, to Eugene, 20 Ap. 1734, GK. 94(b) f. 244.
50. John Maule to Andrew Fletcher, 24 Ap. 1746, NLS. MS. 16630 f. 124.
51. Alt to Landgrave of Hesse Cassel, 14 July 1747, Marburg 4f London 245.
52. Tweeddale, Secretary of State for Scotland, to William Forrester, 2 Oct. 1745, NLS. MS. 7078 f. 154; Chesterfield to Cumberland, 20 Oct., Newcastle to Cumberland, 23 Oct. 1747, RA. Cumberland Papers, 229/87, 113; Newcastle to Sandwich, 20 Oct. 1747, BL. Add. 32810 f. 166.
53. Richard Potenger, Under Secretary, to Charles Hanbury Williams, 17 June 1755, Newport, Public Library, Hanbury Williams papers.
54. Newcastle to Holdernesse, 10 June 1752, NA. SP. 36/118 f. 343, William Murray to Rockingham, 21 July 1752, Sheffield, Archives, Wentworth Wodehouse papers R1-15.

55. R. Potenger to Hanbury Williams, 17 June 1755, Newport, Public Library, Hanbury Williams papers.
56. Ryder Diary, 2 Dec. 1753, Sandon, Ryder diary.
57. Viry to Charles Emmanuel III, 8 Sept. 1755, AST. LM. Ing. 59.
58. AE. CP. Ang. 395 f. 52; Alt, Hessian envoy, to Heim, 2 July 1754, Marburg 4f London 255.
59. Charles, 8th Lord Cathcart to Hugh, 3rd Earl of Loudoun, 6 Oct. 1716, HL. LO. 7963; report to Prince-Bishop, 18 Dec. 1716, Osnabrück 196 f. 549.
60. Harrington to Dunant, agent in Vienna, 29 Nov. 1737, NA. SP. 80/128.
61. Perron to Charles Emmanuel III, 15 Nov. 1753, AST. LM. Ing. 57.
62. Minutes of ministerial meeting, 17 Ap., Holdernesse to Joseph Yorke, 22 Ap. 1755, BL. Eg. 3446 f. 103-5.
63. G. Black to Edward Weston, 29 Oct. 1759, Farmington, Lewis Walpole Library, Weston papers vol. 4.
64. Haslang to Preysing, 13 July 1759, Munich, London 235.
65. Lady to Lord Anson, 4, 11 July 1758, Stafford, Staffordshire CRO. D 1615/P(S)/1/2/7, 9.
66. Viry to Charles Emmanuel, 22 Aug. 1760, AST. LM. Ing. 65.
67. Robinson to Newcastle, 5 Ap. 1755, BL. Add. 32854 f. 55.
68. Holdernesse to Anson, 3 Aug. 1755, BL. Add. 15956 f. 61.
69. Viry to Charles Emmanuel, 4 June 1756, AST. LM. Ing. 60.
70. Bedford to Anson, 16 May 1747, BL. Add. 15955 f. 139.
71. Ossorio to Charles Emmanuel, 7 July 1747, AST. LM. Ing. 53.
72. Newcastle to Holdernesse, 26 July 1752, NA. SP. 36/119.
73. BL. Add. 32856 f. 380.
74. AE. CP. Ang. 438 f. 15.
75. Holdernesse to Mitchell, 28 May 1756, NA. SP. 90/65.
76. Elizabeth, Countess of Waldegrave, Gower's daughter, to her brother, Viscount Trentham, 16 Oct. 1756, NA. PRO. 30/29/1/17 f. 962.
77. Edward Harley, diary, -- Feb 1746, Cambridge, University Library, f. 101.
78. Iberville to Torcy, 25 Dec., 8 Nov. 1714, AE. CP. Ang. 282, 259 f. 259.
79. *Diary of Mary, Countess Cowper* (London, 1864), p. 134.
80. Peterborough to Howard, no date, BL. Add. 22625 f. 96.
81. W. Michael, *Das Zeitalter Walpoles* (Berlin, 1937), p. 603.
82. Ryder diary, 30 Jan. 1745, Sandon.
83. AE. CP. Ang. 395 f. 20.
84. Pelham to Waldegrave, 10 July 1737, Chewton.
85. AE. CP. Ang. 395 f. 110.
86. Ignaz Johann Wasner, Austrian envoy in London, to Chancellor Sinzendorf of Austria, 15 Mar. 1737, NA. SP. 107/21.

87. Reporting letters from London, Lagau, French agent in Hamburg, to Minister of Marine, 17 July 1747, AN. Am. B7 360.
88. Henry Pelham to George Lyttleton, 11 July 1747, Sotheby's *Catalogue of the Lyttleton Papers* (12 Dec. 1978).
89. Newcastle to Earl Gower, 18 July 1747, NA. PRO. 30/29/1/11 f. 303.
90. AE. CP. Ang. 397, f. 379.
91. Walpole to Devonshire, 4 Dec. 1737, Chatsworth.
92. N. Aston, 'The View from St James's Palace in 1759: A Court Perspective on the Annus Mirabilis,' in F. de Bruyn and S. Regan (eds), *The Culture of the Seven Years' War* (Toronto, 2014), pp. 191-212.
93. N. Aston, 'The Court of George II: Lord Berkeley of Stratton's Perspective,' *Court Historian*, 13 (2008), p. 182-3.
94. Henry Fox to Devonshire, 5 Feb. 1756, Chatsworth, papers of 3rd Duke.
95. Newcastle to Pelham, 9 Nov. 1748, BL. Add. 35401 f. 74-5.
96. Lincolnshire Archives, Berkeley Diaries, BQ 2/1/24.
97. Mirepoix, French envoy, to Puysieulx, French Foreign Minister, 18 Aug. Mirepoix, 'Portrait de la Cour d' Angleterre,' Nov. 1751, AE. CP. Ang. 432 f. 129, MD. Ang. 51 f. 158-62.
98. Anon. memorandum on state of British government, 31 Jan. 1754, AE. M. Ang. 51 f. 200; Mirepoix to Rouillé, 6 May 1755, AE. CP. Ang. 439 f. 11; Rigby to Earl Gower, 16 Oct. 1755, NA. PRO. 30/29/1/14.
99. Ossorio, Sardinian envoy, to Charles Emmanuel, 17 Jan., 10 Oct. 1747, AST. LM. Ing. 53.
100. Sandwich to Newcastle, 20 July 1747, BL. Add. 32809 f. 40.
101. *Ibid.*
102. Perron to Charles Emmanuel, 25 Jan. 1753, AST. LM. Ing. 57.
103. Ossorio to Charles Emmanuel, 18 Aug. 1747, AST. LM. Ing. 53.
104. Philip to Joseph Yorke, 24 July 1747, BL. Add. 35363 f. 179.
105. Horatio Walpole to Pelham, 12 Aug. 1747, NUL. NeC 487.
106. Ryder to Newcastle, 16 Oct. 1749, NA. SP. 36/111 f. 115.
107. Flemming, Saxon envoy, to Brühl, Saxon minister, 26 Ap. 1743, NA. SP. 107/57.
108. Colloredo to Chernuishev, Russian envoy in London, 12 Nov. 1753, NA. SP. 100/53.
109. Ilchester (ed.), *Letters to Henry Fox*, p. 100.
110. Perron to Charles Emmanuel, 2 May 1754, AST. LM. Ing. 58.
111. Perron to Charles Emmanuel, 17 July 1754, AST. LM. Ing. 58.
112. Perron to Charles Emmanuel, 14 Mar. 1754, AST. LM. Ing. 58; Diary entry for 19 Mar. 1754, G.W. Pilcher, *The Reverend Samuel Davies Abroad* (Urbana, Ill., 1967), p. 84.
113. Bonnac to St Contest, 22 Mar. 1754, AN. KK 1400, p. 193.

114. Bonnac to Rouillé, 9 May 1755, AE. CP. Hollande 488 f. 249.
115. Perron to Charles Emmanuel III, 21 Nov. 1754, AST. LM. Ing. 58.
116. Robinson to Keene, 12 Dec. 1754, Leeds, Archive Office, Vyner papers no. 11863.
117. Fox to Devonshire, 11 Dec. 1755, Chatsworth.
118. Viry to Charles Emmanuel III, 24 Sept. 1756, AST. LM. Ing. 60.
119. Newcastle to Hardwicke, 11 Oct. 1756, BL. Add. 35416 f. 89.
120. Andrew Mitchell, envoy in Prussia, to Holdernesse, 17 Nov. 1756, NA. SP. 90/67.
121. Viry to Charles Emmanuel III, 30 July 1756, AST. LM. Ing. 60.
122. Newcastle to [J. Yorke], 28 Oct. 1760, BL. Add. 32913 f. 399.
123. Carteret to his daughter, Lady Sophia Carteret, 30 Oct. 1760, Bod. Ms. Lyell. empt. 35.
124. Newcastle to Holdernesse, 11 July 1755, BL. Add. 32857 f. 53.
125. J. Wright to Mitchell, 7 Nov. 1760, BL. Add. 6823 f. 105.
126. A. Hartshorne (ed.), *Memoirs of a Royal Chaplain* (London, 1905), p. 314.
127. Richard Blacow to Thomas Bray, 26 Mar. 1755, Exeter College, Oxford, Bray papers.
128. Robinson to Newcastle, 22 Sept. 1754, BL. Add. 32736 f. 563.
129. Mirepoix to Rouillé, 25 Ap. 1755, AE. CP. Ang. 438 f. 444.
130. Iberville to Torcy, 25 Dec. 1714, AE. CP. Ang. 260 f. 283.
131. Holdernesse to Yorke, 20 Aug. 1756, BL. Eg. 3447 f. 294.
132. Essex to his father-in-law, Hanbury Williams, 8 June 1756, Lady Essex to her father, undated, Farmington, Hanbury Williams papers vol. 71.
133. Zamboni, Hesse-Darmstadt agent, to Landgrave of Hesse-Darmstadt, 15 Nov. 1746, Darmstadt, Staatsarchiv, E1 M10/6; Alt Hesse-Cassel envoy, to Landgrave of Hesse-Cassel, 18 Nov. 1746, Marburg 4f England 241.
134. Henry Fox to William, 4th Duke of Devonshire, 27 Mar. 1756, Chatsworth; Eg Viry to Charles Emmanuel III, 13, 27 June 1758, AST. LM. Ing. 63; Hardenberg, Hesse-Cassel envoy, report of 21 Nov. 1758, Marburg 4f England 257.
135. Perron to Charles Emmanuel III, 13 Dec. 1753, AST. LM. Ing. 57.
136. Lady to Lord Anson, 19 June 1758, Stafford, Staffordshire CRO. D 1615/P(S)/1/2/4.
137. Carteret to Lady Sophia Carteret, 17 Sept. 1759, Bod. Ms. Lyell empt 35 f. 33.
138. Newcastle to Hardwicke, 1 Sept., 15 Oct. 1759, BL. Add. 35418 f. 246, 35419 f. 9.
139. Preysing to Eyck, 19 Jan. 1760, Munich, Paris 19.

140. Gerlach Adolf von Münchhausen, head of the Hanoverian administration, to Robert Keith, 14 Ap. 1758, Hanover, Niedersächisisches Hauptstaatsarchiv, Hann. Des. 91 von Münchhausen I Nr. 45a f.1.
141. Elizabeth to Edward Montagu, 18 Jan. 1760, HL. MO. 2380.

5 Interlude: Frederick I

1. Zamboni, Saxon agent (and for other rulers), to Count Ernst von Vanteuffel, Saxon minister, 27 June 1727, Bodl. MS. Rawlinson 120 f. 9.
2. Hervey to Henry Fox, 30 Aug., Hervey to Count Algarotti, 17 Sept. 1737, Earl of Ilchester (ed.), *Lord Hervey and His Friends, 1726-38* (London, 1950), p. 268.
3. AE. CP. Ang. 397 f. 209, 212, 224, 287-8, 299; Walpole to William, 3rd Duke of Devonshire, 22 Oct. 1737, Chatsworth.
4. C. Gerrard, *The Patriot Opposition to Walpole: Politics, Poetry, and National Myth, 1725-1742* (Oxford, 1994).
5. *York Courant*, 20 Feb. 1739.
6. Bussy to Amelot, 30 Nov. 1742, AE. CP. Ang. 416 f. 60; Horace Walpole to Mann, 24 Dec. 1744, *Walpole-Mann corresp.* II, 551.
7. Hardwicke to Pelham, 11 Nov. 1744, Nottingham UL. NeC 116.
8. Alt to Landgrave of Hesse-Cassel, 28 Feb. 1747, Marburg, 4f London 245.
9. Horace Walpole to Mann, 27 Jan. 1747, *Walpole-Mann corresp.* III, 360.
10. John to Richard Tucker, 19, 26 Feb. 1747, Bod. Ms. Don. c.109 f. 151, 160.
11. John, 4th Earl of Sandwich, envoy in The Hague, to Newcastle, 27 Jan. 1747, BL. Add. 32807 f. 25-6; Ossorio to Gorzegna, Sardinian Foreign Minister, 10 Feb. 1747, AST. LM. Ing. 53; Newcastle to Cumberland, 11 Mar. 1747, BL. Add. 32714 f. 326.
12. Horace Walpole to Mann, 5 June 1747, *Walpole-Mann corresp.* III, 412.
13. Newcastle to Cumberland, 17 May 1747, RA. Cumberland Papers 20/415; Philip to Joseph Yorke, 18 June 1747, BL. Add. 35363 f. 170; Thomas Orby Hunter to Henry Pelham, 20 June 1747, Beinecke, Osborn Shelves, Pelham Box; Frederick Frankland MP to Thomas Robinson, Leeds, Archive Office, Newby Hall papers 2832 no. 17; Ossorio to Charles Emmanuel III, 16 June 1747, AST. LM. Ing. 53.
14. Cole to Brockman, 27 June 1747, BL. Add. 42591 f. 33.
15. Philip to Joseph Yorke, 27 Sept. 1747, BL. Add. 24177 f. 187.
16. Ossorio to Charles Emmanuel III, 1 Dec. 1747, AST. LM. Ing. 53.
17. Frederick II to Andrié, Prussian envoy in London, 13 Dec. 1746, *Polit. Corr.* V, 265.
18. Perron to Charles Emmanual III, 6 Feb., 12 Mar. 1750, AST. LM. Ing. 56; re that June, Newman (ed.), 'Leicester House Politics,' *Royal Historical Society*, p. 176.

19. Wasenberg to Gyllenborg, 23 Jan. 1742, NA. SP. 107/52.
20. Mirepoix to Puysieulx, 3 Jan. 1750, AE. CP. Ang. 428 f. 7; Mirepoix, 'Portrait de la Cour d'Ang', MD. Ang. 51 f. 160; Koch to Kaunitz, 17 Ap. 1751, H. Schlitter (ed.), *Correspondance secrete entre le comte A.W. Kaunitz-Rietberg, ambassadeur imperial à Paris et baron Ignaz de Koch, secretaire de l'Imperatrice Marie Therese, 1750-1752* (Vienna, 1899), p. 97.
21. Ossorio to Gorsegna, 19 Dec. 1747, AST. LM. Ing. 53.
22. John to Richard Tucker, 12 Mar. 1747, Bod. Ms. Don. c.109 f. 177.
23. Heunisch, Austrian agent, to Count Coblentz HHStA GC. 305.
24. Cobbett, *Parliamentary History* XIV, 158-9.
25. Lady Anson to Thomas Anson, 28 June 1749, Stafford, Staffordshire CRO. D615/P(S)/1/3/8.
26. A.N. Newman (ed.), 'Leicester House Politics, 1750-60,' *Royal Historical Society, Camden Miscellany*, 23 (1969), pp. 193-5.
27. Bayntum Rolt diary, 7 Ap. 1751, Bristol, University Library, Bayntum Rolt diary.
28. For a Whig magnifico welcoming his election, Marquess of Rockingham to Stapylton, 13 July 1747, Sheffield, Archives, Wentworth Woodhouse papers.
29. G. Glickman, 'Parliament, the Tories and Frederick, Prince of Wales,' *Parliamentary History*, 30 (2011), pp. 120-41.
30. A. Wilson, 'Conflict, Consensus and Charity: Politics and the Provincial Voluntary Hospitals in the Eighteenth Century,' *English Historical Review*, 111 (1996), pp. 599-619.
31. Anon. to Trelawny, 14 July 1751, Washington, Library of Congress, Vernon-Wager Papers, reel 93.
32. P. de Rapin-Thoyras, *History of England*, trans. Nicholas Tindal, vol. 1, 2nd ed (London, 1732), dedication.
33. *Harcourt*, 46-50.
34. For example, *Commons Debate on Regency Bill*, 16 May 1751, p. 1036.
35. Heunisch, Austrian agent, to Johann, Count von Cobenzl, 28 Ap. 1747, HHStA GK. 305.
36. Newcastle to Sandwich, 22 Dec. 1747, BL. Add. 32810 f. 388.
37. London report in *Cirencester Flying Post*, 12 Sept. 1743.
38. *Old England*, 18 July 1747.
39. Holdernesse to Joseph Yorke, 20 July 1756, BL. Eg. 3447 f. 258.
40. C. Gerretson and P. Geyl (eds), *Briefwisseling en Aanteekeningen van Willem Bentinck* (Utrecht, 1934), p. 241.
41. Newcastle to Bentinck, 24 Nov. 1747, BL. Add. 32810 f. 297 cf. Ossorio to Charles Emmanuel, 1 Dec. 1747, AST. LM. Ing. 53.

42. Newcastle to Sandwich, 4 Dec. 1747, BL. Add. 32810 f. 307.
43. Chesterfield, Secretary of State, to Cumberland, 24 Feb. 1747, RA. Cumberland Papers 20/282; Newcastle, 'Considerations for His Majesty's Servants,' in Newcastle to Cumberland, 17 Mar. 1747, RA. Cumberland Papers 20/416.
44. Hardwicke to Cumberland, 16 Ap. 1747, RA. Cumberland Papers 21/261.
45. Richard Blacow to Thomas Bray, 26 Mar. 1755, Exeter College, Oxford, Bray papers.
46. Charles Cathcart to Earl of Loudoun, 11 Oct. 1755, HL. LO. 7083.
47. Eg. Cumberland to Sandwich, 29 Dec., Memorandum submitted to Cumberland, 31 Dec. 1747 and revisions, Newcastle to Cumberland, 25 Feb. 1748, RA. CP. 30/335, 30/346-8, 32/113; Newcastle to Sandwich, 17 Nov. 1747, BL. Add. 32810 f. 286; Ossorio to Charles Emmanuel, 2 Feb. 1748, AST. LM. Ing. 54; Henry Legge to Anson, 11 Feb. 1748, BL. Add. 15956 f. 201.
48. Ossorio to Gorsegna, 12 Dec. 1747, AST. LM. Ing. 53.
49. Eg. BL. Add. 32996 f. 149, 160.
50. Perron to Charles Emmanuel, 14 Aug. 1755, AST. LM. Ing. 59.
51. Newcastle to Halifax, 1 Jan. 1756, BL. Add. 32862 f. 1.
52. Alt to William VIII, Regent of Hesse-Cassel, 12 Jan. 1748, Marburg, 4f England, 241; Frederick II to Chambrier, envoy in Paris, and also to Princess Royal of Sweden, 25 Jan. 1749, *Polit. Corr.* VI, 351, 372.
53. Sohlenthal, Danish envoy, to Schulin, Danish Foreign Minister, 1 Feb. 1743, NA. SP. 107/55.
54. Watzdorf to Augustus II, 6 May 1732, Dresden 2676 III f. 133; Newcastle to Hardwicke, 17 Sept. 1758, BL. Add. 35428 f. 24. Re a Brunswick marriage for George III, Newcastle to Gerlach Adolf von Münchhausen, 25 July 1755, BL. Eg. 3481 f. 132 and Bussy to Rouillé, 29 July 1755, AE. CP. Brunswic-Hanovre 52 f. 29.
55. Viry to Charles Emmanuel, 27 Sept. 1758, AST. LM. Ing. 63.
56. Cumberland to Henry Fox, 23 Sept. 1757, Earl of Ilchester (ed.), *Letters of Henry Fox* (London, 1915), p. 120.
57. The Convention, 9 Sept. 1757, Paris, Bibliothèque de la Sorbonne, Fonds Richelieu 58, f. 96-9.
58. Sackville to Robert Wilmot, 8 Sept. 1757, Derby, Library, Catton Collection WH 3454.
59. Cumberland to Holdernesse, 15 Sept. 1757, BL. Eg. 3442 f. 252.
60. Newcastle to Hardwicke, 19 Sept. 1757, BL. Add. 35417 f. 73.
61. Newcastle to Hardwicke, 8 Oct. 1757, BL. Add. 35417 f. 92.
62. George to Frederick, 20 Sept. 1757, BL. Eg. 3425 f. 86.

63. Bernis to Ogier, French envoy in Denmark, 18 Oct. 1757, AE. CP. Denmark 136 f. 80.
64. Cumberland to Fox, 23 Sept. 1757, Ilchester (ed.), *Letters to Henry Fox*, pp. 120-1.
65. Newcastle to Sandwich, 28 Ap. 1747, BL. Add. 32808 f. 136.
66. Heads for an answer for the King to the Princess Royal's Letter, BL. Add. 32879 f. 248; Bonnac, French envoy in The Hague, to St Contest, French Foreign Minister, 8 Nov. 1753, Paris, Archives Nationales, KK 1400, p. 337.
67. Horatio Walpole to Henry Pelham, 3 Aug. 1747, NUL. NeC 486.
68. Holdernesse to Joseph Yorke, envoy in The Hague, 1 Nov. 1754, NA. SP. 84/467; Perron to Charles Emmanuel III, 14 Nov. 1754, AST. LM. Ing. 58.

6 *George III, A Monarch in Contention*

1. Sinclair to Lord Hawkesbury, 2 July, 26 Nov. 1787, BL. Add. 38222 f. 90, 152.
2. Lascaris, Sardinian envoy, to Charles Emmanuel III, 23, 30 Nov., 7 Dec. 1752, AST. LM. Ing. 57.
3. Baron Rosencrantz, Danish envoy, to Frederick V of Denmark, 27 Feb. 1753, Manchester, John Ryland Library, Eng. Mss. 669 no. 3.
4. Count Preysing, Bavarian foreign minister, to Eyck, Bavarian envoy in Paris, 19 Nov. 1760, Munich, Paris 19.
5. Yorke, *Hardwicke*, II, 392.
6. J. Harris and M. Snodin (eds), *Sir William Chambers: Architect to George III* (London, 1996).
7. Anon, 'The Advantages of Cultivating Peace,' Feb. 1760, *Royal Magazine*, II, 81.
8. Hanbury Williams to Henry Fox, 17 June 1751, BL. Add. 5193 fol. 52.
9. Perron to Charles Emmanuel III, 17 July 1754, AST LM. Ing. 58.
10. Anon., *Letter to the Whigs* (London, 1762), p. 15.
11. R.R. Sedgwick (ed.), *Letters from George III to Lord Bute 1756-1766* (London, 1939), pp. 28-9, 78-9, 177.
12. Haslang report, 11 June 1769, Munich, London 247.
13. Haslang to Baron Beckers, Palatine Foreign Minister, 17 July 1772, Munich, London 250.
14. George, draft, BL. Add. 32684 fol. 121.
15. Rockingham to Sir George Saville, 30 Oct. 1760, Bod. Ms. Eng. Lett. c. 144 fol. 284.
16. Viry to Charles Emmanuel III, 21 Nov. 1760, AST. LM. Ing. 65.
17. Elizabeth to Edward Montagu, 20 Nov. 1760, HL. MO. 2404.
18. Newcastle to Mitchell, 8 Sept. 1760, BL. Add. 6832 fol. 51.

19. Haslang to Baron Wachtendonck, Palatine foreign minister, 10, 31 Mar. 1761, Munich, London, 238.
20. P. Langford, 'Politics and Manners from Sir Robert Walpole to Sir Robert Peel,' *Proceedings of the British Academy*, 94 (1996), pp. 103-25.
21. Frederik Hannecken, Danish Legation Secretary, report, 3 Jan. 1772, Copenhagen, England 1953.
22. J. Boswell, *Life of Johnson* (Oxford, 1980), p. 157.
23. George to Gloucester, 9 Nov. 1771, RA. GEO/15938.
24. RA. GEO/Add. 32.
25. George to William, Lord Grenville, Foreign Secretary, November 24, 1799, BL. Add., 58861 fol. 64.
26. Hannecken, 11, 18, 25 June 1771, Copenhagen, vol. 1952.
27. BL. Add. 37833.
28. George to North, 13 Oct. 1778, RA. GEO/3094.
29. George to North, 12 Nov. 1778, RA. GEO/3114.
30. Dreyer, report, 29 Mar. 1782, Copenhagen, England 1965.
31. Rayneval, 18 Sept. 1782, AE. CP. Ang. 538 f. 203.
32. Dreyer, report, 11 Mar. 1783, Copenhagen, England, 1966.
33. Pitt to George, 25 Mar. 1783, NA. PRO. 30/8/101 f. 1.
34. George to Pitt, 23 Dec. 1783, NA. PRO. 30/8/103 f. 14.
35. Buckinghamshire to Sir Charles Hotham, 12 July 1783, Hull, University Library, DDHo/4/22.
36. Duke of Leeds, Political Memoranda, undated, BL. Add. 27918 f. 119.
37. John Adams to John Jay, Secretary of State, 2 June 1785, C.F. Adams (ed.), *The Works of John Adams* (10 vols, Boston, Massachusetts, 1853), VIII, 255-7.
38. P.L. Ford (ed.), *The Autobiography of Thomas Jefferson 1743-1790* (New York, 1914), p. 94; C.R. Ritcheson, 'The Fragile Memory: Thomas Jefferson at the Court of George III', *Eighteenth-Century Life*, 6, pts 2-3 (1981), pp. 1-16.
39. George to Carmarthen, 28 Dec. 1783, BL. Add. 27914 f. 1.
40. Gottlob Schönborn, Danish Chargé des affaires, reports, 28 Nov., 9 Dec. 1788, Copenhagen, vol. 1971.
41. Beinecke to Nathanael Wraxall, 5 Feb. 1789, Beinecke, Osborn Files, Dorset.

7 *George III, Father of the Nation*

1. Herbert to Sir Robert Murray Keith, 22 Sept. 1779, BL. Add. 35517 f. 170.
2. Boringdon became 1st Earl of Morley in 1815.
3. George to Carmarthen, 6 July 1784, BL. Add. 27914 f. 3.
4. George to Grenville, 25 June 1791, Bod. Bland Burges papers vol. 52 f. 117.

5. Gower to William, Lord Grenville, 1 July 1791, BL. Add. 59021 f. 1.
6. Frederick Jarlsberg, Danish envoy, report, 23 Nov. 1792, Copenhagen, vol. 1975.
7. Jarlsberg, report, 16, 23 Nov. 1792, Copenhagen, vol. 1975.
8. S. Horsley, *Sermons*, ed. H. Horsley (London, 1816), III, 293-321.
9. George to Henry Dundas, 21 Ap. 1797, BL. Add. 40100 f. 190.
10. George to George, 2nd Earl Spencer, 1st Lord of the Admiralty, 9 May 1797, BL. Add. 75805.
11. George to Spencer, 12 July 1800, BL. Add. 75839.
12. George to Spencer, 17 Mar. 1795, BL. Add. 75779.
13. Memorandum by George of 30 Nov., enclosed with George to William Grenville, Foreign Secretary, 1 Dec. 1794, BL. Add. 58858 f. 113.
14. Malmesbury (ed.), *The Works of James Harris* (2 vols, London, 1801) I, vi; L. Colley, 'The Apotheosis of George III: Loyalty, Royalty and the British Nation,' *Past and Present*, 102 (Feb. 1984), pp. 94-129.
15. Lansdowne to Keith, 23 Sept. 1785, BL. Add. 35535 f. 162.
16. F. Prochaska, *Royal Bounty. The Making of a Welfare Monarchy* (New Haven, Conn., 1995).
17. Wraxall, 'Anecdotes of My Own Time: Private, Beinecke, Osborn MSS c. 26.
18. George to Yorke, 18 Oct. 1810, BL. Add. 45035 f. 7.

8 George IV

1. Robert Wharton to Thomas Brand, 4 July 1783, Durham, University Library, Wharton papers; *Public Advertiser*, 18 Feb. 1792.
2. Christof Dreyer, Danish envoy, reports 4 July, 5 Aug. 1783, Copenhagen, vol. 1966.
3. A. Leslie, *Mrs Fitzherbert* (London, 1960).
4. Ewart to Robert Murray Keith, 1 Feb. 1787, BL. Add. 35538 f. 5.
5. *The Martial Face: the Military Portrait in Britain, 1760-1800* (Catalogue of exhibition at Brown University, 1991), p. 87.
6. E.A. Smith, *A Queen on Trial: The Affair of Queen Caroline* (Stroud, 1993).
7. F. Fraser, *The Unruly Queen: The Life of Queen Caroline* (London, 1996).
8. Sidmouth to Liverpool, 11, 27 Aug. 1821, Exeter, 152M/C 1821/OR 37, 72.
9. Sidmouth to Liverpool, 29 Aug. 1821, Exeter, 152M/C 1821/OR 73.
10. Robert, 2nd Marquess of Londonderry to Sidmouth, 24 Oct. 1821, Exeter, 152 M/C 1821/OR 90.
11. G. Finley, *Turner and George the Fourth in Edinburgh 1822* (London, 1981); J. Prebble, *The King's Jaunt: George IV in Scotland* (London, 1989).
12. *Maggs Catalogue*, 1345, no. 88.

13. Sir Matthew John Tierney, Physician in Ordinary to George.
14. Liverpool to Addington, 28 July 1820, Exeter, 152M/C 1820/OR 44.
15. Exeter 152M/C 1821/OR 71.
16. W. King, *Political and Literary Anecdotes of his Own Times* edited by P.B. Duncan (London, 1818), p. 41; Peter Lord King, *The Life of John Locke* (2 vols, London, 1830 edn), I, iii-iv.
17. Wellington to Knighton, 29 May 1827, draft, Southampton, University Library, Wellington Papers. Knighton's papers were destroyed by his widow.
18. 'My dear boy…' in some accounts.

9 British Monarchs and the Others

1. George speaking to Count Haslang, Bavarian envoy, Haslang to Charles VII, 26 Mar. 1743, Munich, London, 208.
2. *Mist's Weekly Journal*, 23 Mar. 1728.
3. Henley's Oratory, 8 Ap. 1744, BL. Add. 33052 f. 277.
4. Yorke to Cumberland, 1 Mar. 1749, RA. Cumberland Papers 43/122.
5. Bristol to Pitt, 14 Jan. 1760, NA. SP. 90/161.
6. Reporting Joseph Yorke, Lady to Lord Anson, 26 May [1758], Stafford, Staffordshire CRO. D 615/P(S)/1/1/57.
7. Perron to Charles Emmanuel III, 25 Jan. 1753, AST. LM. Ing. 57.
8. T. Keymer, *Politics of the Pillory: English Literature and Seditious Libel, 1660-1820* (Oxford, 2019); Iberville to Ministry of Marine, 26 Mar. 1715, AN. AM. AE. B[I] 760.
9. Joseph to Philip Yorke, 24 Dec. 1754, BL. Add. 35364 f. 25, re France.
10. Cathcart to Hugh, 3rd Earl Loudoun, 2 Jan. 1718, HL. LO. 7898.
11. Pelham to Newcastle, 23 Sept. 1733, BL. Add. 32688 f. 423.
12. *Monitor*, 9 Sept. 1758.
13. R.J. Smith, *The Gothic Bequest. Medieval Institutions in British Thought, 1688-1863* (Cambridge, 1987).
14. Anon., *Apology for a Late Resignation* (London, 1747), p 8.
15. BL. Althorp MSS E13. See already, the *Craftsman* 6 Ap. 1728.
16. Anon., *A Speech Without Doors, Addressed to the National Creditors* (London, 1737), pp. 1-2.
17. Delafaye to Stanhope, 6 Nov. 1719, NA. SP. 43/63.
18. Harcourt to George Venables Vernon, 1 Nov. 1747, *Harcourt* III, 37.
19. G. Ditchfield, *The Letters of Theophilus Lindsey* (Woodbridge, 2007), I, 39, 55.
20. Robinson to Robert Keith, envoy in Vienna, 1 Aug. 1755, BL. Add. 35480 f. 36.

21. Rouillé, French Foreign Minister, to Mirepoix, 3 Ap., Mirepoix to Rouillé, 10 Ap. 1755, AE. CP. Ang. 438 f. 349, 389.
22. Rouillé to Bonnac, envoy in The Hague, 17 Mar. 1756, AN. KK. 1402, p. 257.
23. Anonymous, *A Letter to the King of xxx* (London, 1756): 5.
24. Mitchell to Keith, 14 June 1759, BL. Add. 35482 f. 205.
25. E. Corp, *The Stuarts in Italy, 1719-1766: A Royal Court in Permanent Exile* (Cambridge, 2011).
26. Pelham to Henry Fox, 27 Sept. 1743, Earl of Ilchester (ed.), *Letters to Henry Fox* (London, 1915), p. 3.
27. Keene to Newcastle, 24 Mar. 1734, NA. SP. 94/119.
28. Newcastle to Pelham, 26 July 1752, BL. Add. 35412 f. 209.
29. Newcastle to Hardwicke, 26 July 1752, BL. Add. 35412 f. 184. For an explanation, reply, 7 Aug., f. 250.
30. *Polit. Corr.*, II, 424.
31. Haslang to Baron Preysing, Bavarian Foreign Minister, 7 Jan., and to Baron Wachtendonck, Palatine Foreign Minister, 11 Jan. 1757, Munich, Bayr. Ges. London 233.
32. George to Frederick, 7 Jan. 1757, *Polit. Corr.* XIV, p. 251.
33. Holdernesse to Mitchell, 8 Feb. 1757, BL. Add. 6832 f. 112.
34. Richard Blacow to Thomas Bray, 7 Mar. 1755, undated but mid-March 1755, Exeter College, Oxford, Bray papers; Lady Harcourt to son, Lord Nuneham, 15 Mar. 1755, *Harcourt Papers*, III, 69.
35. Perron to Charles Emmanuel III, 20 Mar., 17 Ap. 1755, AST. LM. Ing. 59.
36. Emperor Charles VII to Haslang, 18 Aug. 1743, Munich, London, 208.
37. Holdernesse to Mitchell, 12 Ap. 1757, NA. SP. 90/68.
38. Holdernesse to Mitchell, 29 Ap. 1757, NA. SP. 90/68.
39. Diemar to Landgrave of Hesse-Cassel, 22 Ap. 1732, Marburg, 4f England 202.
40. HMC. *Egmont*, I, 321.
41. Holdernesse to Cumberland, 6 May 1757, BL. Eg. 3442 f. 56.
42. Elizabeth, Lady Anson to Marchioness Grey, 27 June 1755, Bedford, Bedfordshire CRO. L30/9/3/44.
43. Andreas von der Reiche, Secretary with George for the affairs of Hanover.
44. Newcastle to Hardwicke, 30 June 1759, BL. Add. 35418 f. 188.
45. 2nd Duke of Richmond to Newcastle, 23 Sept., 13 Oct. 1743 BL. Add. 32701 f. 133, 143.
46. Mitchell to Holdernesse, 17 May 1757, NA. SP. 90/69.
47. Newcastle to Hardwicke, 6 July 1755, BL. Add. 35415 f. 3-4.
48. Minute of conversation with Johann Friedrich, Count Kageneck, Austrian envoy, 26 May 1785, NA. FO. 7/10.

49. Eg Alleyne Fitzherbert, envoy at St Petersburg, to Keith, 2 Aug., 8 Dec. 1785, BL. Add. 35535 f. 31, 35535 f. 293.
50. Diede, 17 Ap. 1772 Hannecken, 13 Sept. 1776, Copenhagen, England, 1953, 1957.
51. Ralph Churton to Sir Roger Newdigate, 22 Nov. 1797, Warwick, Warwickshire CRO. CR 136 B 1561.
52. George to General Conway, 27 Feb. 1767, BL. Eg. 982 f. 28. For popularity as an 'empty shadow,' cf. 16 Feb. 1768, f. 36.

10 The Georges and Political Development

1. Clavering to Lady Cowper, 28 Ap. 1716, Hertford, CRO. D/EP F196 f. 24.
2. Gilbert Elliot to his father, Lord Minto, 15 Nov. 1755, NLS. MS. 11001 f. 15; Walpole, *Memoirs of George II*, II, 69-72; Farmington, Hanbury Williams papers, 63 f. 22.
3. *Cobbett* XIII, 591.
4. George, 3rd Earl of Cholmondeley, son-in-law of Robert Walpole, Lord Privy Seal, 1743-4.
5. Walpole to Mann, 24 Dec. 1744, *Walpole-Mann corresp* II, 552.
6. Albemarle to Newcastle, 17 Feb. 1746, BL. Add. 32706 f. 159.
7. U. Dann, *Hanover and Great Britain 1740-1760* (Leicester, 1991).
8. AE. CP. Ang. 439 f. 169.
9. Holdernesse to Joseph Yorke, 12 Ap. 1758, NA. SP. 90/71, re Prussian envoy.
10. Henry to Stephen Fox, 13 Feb. 1746, BL. Add. 51417 f. 213.
11. Newcastle to Hardwicke, 3 Jan. 1758, BL. Add. 35417 f. 171.
12. Görtz to Gyllenborg, Swedish envoy in London, 29 Dec. 1716, NA. SP. 107/1B f. 326.
13. Viry to Charles Emmanuel III, 25 May 1756, AST. LM. Ing. 60.
14. A. Guy, *Oeconomy and Discipline: Officership and Administration in the British Army, 1714-63* (Manchester, 1985).
15. HMC. *Egmont* III, 240.
16. Aston, 'Court of George II,' p. 191.
17. Viry to Charles Emmanuel III, 20 Feb. 1759, AST. LM. Ing. 64.
18. Haslang to Preysing, 19 Sept. 1758, Munich, London 234.
19. *The Parliamentary Register*, 6 (1782), p. 324.
20. Cobbett, XXIII, p. 191.
21. Lowther to his agent, John Spedding, 21 Ap. 1743, Carlisle, Cumbria CRO. D/Lons/W.
22. Harris to Keith, 8 Feb. 1785, BL. Add. 35533 f. 213.
23. Pitt to Charles, 4th Duke of Rutland, Lord Lieutenant of Ireland, 21 May 1785, Earl Stanhope (ed.), *Miscellanies* (London, 1863), pp. 2-3.

24. Holdernesse to Newcastle, 29 June 1755, BL. Add. 32856 f. 380.
25. Newcastle to Holdernesse, 11 July 1755, BL. Add. 32857 f. 53-4.
26. Perron to Charles Emmanuel, 19 July 1753, AST. LM. Ing. 57.
27. *Senator*, I (1791), p. iii.
28. A. Thackray, *Atoms and Powers: An Essay on Newtonian Matter-Theory and the Development of Chemistry* (Cambridge, Mass., 1970).
29. George to Pitt, 6 May 1785, Manchester, John Rylands Library, Eng. Mss. 912 no. 28.
30. Carmarthen to Ewart, 14 May 1785, NA. SP. 64/7.
31. George to Leeds, 1 Dec. 1789, BL. Add. 27914 f. 25.
32. Sturrock to Lady Hertford, 25 Mar. 1743, Alnwick Castle, Northumberland papers, vol. 113 p. 218.
33. Horatio to Robert Walpole, 10 July 1734, Cambridge, Cholmondeley Houghton correspondence, no. 2259.
34. Eg. Robethon to Stair, 16 Ap. 1716, NAS. GD. 135/141/7, Whitworth to Stanhope, 23 Mar. 1720, NA. SP. 90/12; Whitworth to George I, 9 Jan., to Stanhope, 23 Mar. 1720, NA. SP. 90/11-12; A.C. Thompson, *Britain, Hanover and the Protestant Interest, 1688-1756* (Woodbridge, 2000).
35. Whitworth to Tilson, 24 May 1721, NA. SP. 90/14.
36. Whitworth to Tilson, 27 Dec. 1721, NA. SP. 90/15. See also Whitworth to Townshend, 18 Mar., 11 Nov. 1721, 90/13, 15.
37. Whitworth to Tilson, 27 May, 24 Aug., 2, 11 Nov., 2 Dec. 1721, NA. SP. 90/14, 15; Whitworth to Bothmer, 25 Mar., 6 Dec. 1721, NA. SP. 90/13, BL. Add. 37387 f. 23.
38. Waldegrave to Sir Robert Walpole, 23 Oct. 1736, Chewton.
39. Fraser to Keith, 7 June 1785, BL. Add. 35534 f. 208.
40. Holdernesse to Mitchell, 11 May 1756, NA. SP. 90/65.
41. George III to Carmarthen, 12 Nov. 1785, BL. Add. 27914 f. 11.
42. Alt report, 1 Oct. 1755, Marburg 4f England 258.
43. Grantham to Keith, 22 Feb. 1783, BL. Add. 35528 f. 22. See also Alexander Straton to Keith, 25 Feb. 1783, BL. Add. 35528 f. 39.
44. Horace Walpole to Horace Mann, 17 Nov. 1743, W.S. Lewis (ed.), *Horace Walpole-Mann Corresp*, II (London, 1955), p. 340.
45. *Newcastle Courant* 13 Aug., 3 Sept. 1743.
46. George to Edward, Lord Thurlow, 7 Mar. 1783, *Bonham Books*, 15 Ap. 1989, lot no. 147. On Thurlow, still, recently, with much information on the thoughts and actions of figures close to George, B. Gilding, *The Great Pillar: The Political Career of Lord Thurlow, 1741-1806* (Oxford, 2023).
47. George to --, 2 Ap. 1783, Bod. Ms. Eng. Lett c. 144 f. 77.

48. Elizabeth, Duchess to George, 4th Duke of Manchester, 27 May 1783, Huntingdon, Huntingdonshire CRO. DDH 2/B/6.
49. Newcastle to Hardwicke, 14 June, 5 July 1752, BL. Add. 35412 f. 121, 164.

11 Postscripts to the Present

1. J. Naylor, *The British Aristocracy and the Peerage Bill of 1719* (London, 1968); J. Cannon, *Aristocratic Century: The Peerage of Eighteenth-Century England* (Cambridge, 1984), p. 15.
2. Anon., *Reflections on the Late Augmentations of the English Peerage* (London, 1798), eg. pp. 10, 15-16, 29.
3. Cannon, *Aristocratic Century*, pp. 24-6.
4. Hill Mussenden to Carteret Mussenden, 20 June 1727, Ipswich, East Suffolk CRO HA 403/1/10.
5. Delafaye to Newcastle, 26 July 1720, BL. Add. 62686 f. 101.
6. George to Pitt, 7 Aug. 1785, Manchester, John Rylands Library, Eng. Mss. 912.
7. George to Carmarthen, 4 Oct. 1785, BL. Add. 27914 f. 9.
8. George to Carmarthen, 30 Jan. 1786, BL. Add. 27914 f. 15.
9. Ambrosio Andriani, Resident in Madrid, to Secretary of Duke Leopold of Lorraine, 12 Aug. 1726, Nancy, Archives du Meurthe-et-Moselle, 3F 202 no. 272.
10. H. Hoock, *The King's Artists. The Royal Academy of Arts and the Politics of British Culture, 1760-1840* (Oxford, 2005) and *Empires of the Imagination: Politics, War, and the Arts in the British World, 1750-1850* (London, 2010).
11. W. Weber, *The Rise of Musical Classics in Eighteenth-Century England: A Study in Canon, Ritual and Ideology* (Oxford, 1992).
12. N. Smith, *The Royal Image and the English People* (Aldershot, 2001).
13. R.O. Bucholz, 'Going to Court in 1700: a visitor's guide,' and W. Burchard, 'St James's Palace: George II's and Queen Caroline's Principal London Residence,' *Court Historian*, 5 (2000), pp. 213-14, 16 (2011), pp. 183-2003.
14. For plans to both, see P. Barber and T. Harper, *Magnificent Maps: Power, Propaganda and Art* (London, 2010).
15. Gisors, Journal of Visit to England, 7 Feb. 1754, AE. MD. Ang. 1 f. 28.
16. Eliot to wife, 9 Ap. 1789, I, 300.
17. George Grenville, an opposition leader.
18. George to Conway, 6 Dec. 1766, BL. Eg. 982 f. 26.

INDEX

Act of Settlement 52, 59, 62, 91, 229, 241
Act of Union 32
Adams, John 164
Addington, Henry, Viscount Sidmouth 179
Adelaide, Queen 191
Albemarle, William, 2nd Earl of 217, 225-6
Alfred, Masque 129, 213
Amelia, Princess, daughter of George III 58, 119, 129, 184-5
An Introduction to Old English History 39
Anne, Princess of Orange, daughter of George II 40, 47, 123, 129, 140
Anne, Queen 13, 20, 25, 43-4, 47, 49-52, 62-66, 79, 86-9, 134, 152, 234, 235, 244
Argyll, John, 2nd Duke of 40, 76-7, 108, 113
Auerstädt, Battle of 193
Austen, Jane 204
Australia 183, 244
Austria 9, 68, 77, 90-91, 106, 108, 118, 120, 150, 174, 176, 217, 219, 234, 236, 241, 247

Bedford, John, 4th Duke of, First Lord of the Admiralty 15, 25, 30, 111, 117, 133, 138, 179
Benedict XIV, Pope 217
Berlin 27-9, 82, 112
Blenheim, Battle of 239
Bolingbroke, Henry, Viscount 70, 134-5
Bonaparte, Napoleon/Napoleonic 14, 22, 174, 177-179, 186, 193, 195-196, 201, 204, 208, 223, 225, 245, 251
Boyne, Battle of the 41, 43
Brighton 199, 201
Brunswick, Prince Ferdinand of, Duke Ferdinand of Brunswick-Wolfenbüttel 107
Brunswick-Wolfenbüttel, Prince Louis of, Captain-General of the Netherlands 61, 137, 221
Buckingham House 50, 201-202

Bute, John, 3rd Earl of 9, 51, 99, 144-145, 149, 188, 205
Byng, Admiral John 111

Cadogan, William, 1st Earl of 8, 68, 71, 76-7, 81, 85
Calvinism 46
Canning, PM George 205
Carlton House 191, 200-201
Carmarthen, Francis, Marquis of 165, 196
Caroline of Ansbach 58, 78, 113, 115
Caroline of Brunswick 25, 195
Carteret, Lord John, later Earl Granville 9, 28, 32, 65, 67-68, 70-71, 85, 99-100, 104-105, 114, 116-117, 120, 124, 130, 133, 154, 178, 213, 225, 231
Cathcart, Charles, 8th Lord 78, 211
Catholic Emancipation 144, 175, 179, 187, 194, 197, 205, 241, 247
Catholic Relief Act 1829 205
Centinel 36
Charles I 37-39, 52, 127, 157-158, 172, 234, 244
Charles II 20, 36-39, 52, 56, 134, 234, 239, 244, 249
Charles III of Spain 209
Charles VI, Emperor 52, 58
Charles XII of Sweden 73, 159, 227
Charlotte of Mecklenburg-Strelitz, Queen 28, 173, 185-6, 203
Charlotte, Princess, daughter of George IV 191, 193, 201
Chesterfield, Philip, 4th Earl of 28, 33, 102, 111, 113, 180
Clement XIII, Pope 218
Cologne 24
Common Sense 125, 214
Concise History of England 62, 75
Congress of Vienna 246
Con-Test, the 149, 233
Convention of the Estates 44
Copenhagen 12, 16
Craftsman Extraordinary, the 211
Cromwell, Oliver 37-9, 134, 158
Cruickshank, George 198
Culloden, Battle of 58, 96, 108, 131, 137, 216, 236-237
Cumberland, Ernest, Duke of, son of George III, later King of Hanover 182, 205
Cumberland, Henry, Duke of 158
Cumberland, William, Duke of 28, 40, 61, 96, 101, 136, 147, 216

Daily Courant 47
Dashwood, Sir Francis 8
Denmark 12, 23, 43, 52, 159, 244
Devonshire, William, 4th Duke of 90, 179, 228-9
Diemar, General Ernst 10, 87, 108
Dorset, John, 3rd Duke of 29-30, 115, 130, 167
Dettingen, Battle of 108-9, 221, 239
Dublin 175, 177, 196-197, 199, 202-203

East India Bill 163
Ecclesiastical History to the Eighteenth Century 122
Edinburgh 17, 51, 199
Edward VII 47, 127, 189, 200
Edward, Duke of Kent, George IV's brother
Elibank Plot 216, 218
Elizabeth I 49, 123, 134, 212

Elizabeth, Lady Conyngham 197, 199-200, 207
Erle, General Thomas 54-5
Eugene, Prince 23, 57, 77
Exclusion Crisis 1679-81

Fife, James, 2nd Earl of 22
Fitzherbert, Maria Anne 190-191
Fog's Journal 48
Fox, Charles James 149, 163, 167
Fox, Elizabeth 191
Fox, Henry, 1st Baron Holland 30, 112, 121
Fox-North ministry 153, 164, 240
France 9, 19-20, 23, 27, 29, 33-4, 40-41, 50-51, 56, 60, 68, 74, 77, 90-91, 97, 107-108, 110-111, 117-118, 22, 124, 138-141, 144, 148, 154-155,160-161, 166, 169, 172, 174-179, 182-183, 194, 196, 202, 208-210, 212-213, 215, 217-218, 220-221, 236, 238, 241, 244-245, 248, 250-251
Frederick II 29, 56, 76, 101, 106, 118,120, 139-140, 159, 210, 219, 226, 234
Frederick, Duke of York, son of George III 109, 154, 181, 186, 189
Frederick, Lord North, First Lord of the Treasury 155, 161, 186, 229, 240
French Revolution 42, 146, 169, 171, 175, 179

George V 127, 228, 247
Germany 9, 77, 107, 139-140, 170, 195, 219, 221, 236, 239, 243, 245, 247
Gillray, James 172, 251
Glorious First of June, the Fourth Battle of Ushant 173
'Glorious Revolution' 33, 43, 47-8, 51, 145, 158, 205-206, 224, 241, 248
Grafton, Augustus, 3rd Duke of 115, 149
Grantham, Thomas, 2nd Lord 11, 28, 239
Granville, George, 2nd Earl Gower, Ambassador in Paris 32, 112, 116-117, 120, 130, 133
Gustavus III of Sweden 159, 239

Halifax, George, 2nd Earl of 138, 224
Hamilton, musical 143, 146
Hampton Court 46, 50, 78, 81
Handel, George Frideric 22, 78, 89-90, 108-9, 249
Hanover 7, 10-11, 17, 20, 22-23, 25, 30-31, 33, 41, 48, 52-3, 56, 60-61, 63-4, 66, 69, 73-4, 76-8, 81-2, 84-6, 89-92, 95-6, 99-100, 105-107, 109-111, 113-114, 116, 118-121, 124-125, 132, 137, 140-141, 147, 150-154, 167, 170, 176, 185, 193, 196-199, 206, 209, 217-220, 222, 224, 226-227, 231, 234-236, 238, 241, 245-246, 250
Hardwicke, Lord Chancellor Philip 43, 148, 152, 241
Haslang, Count Joseph 10, 151, 154, 219
'Henry IX' 42, 158, 182
Herschel, William 22

Hertford, Isabella, Marchioness of 191, 194, 199
History of England 135, 137
Hogarth, William 211
Holdernesse, Robert, 4th Earl of 11, 19, 28, 111-112, 220-222, 231
Holy Roman Empire 20, 53, 219
Howard, Henrietta 113, 115

Imperial Election Scheme 97, 117, 241
India 163, 177, 215, 243, 251
Ireland 9, 19-20, 32, 41, 43, 75, 85, 122, 144-5, 170, 174-175, 180, 196-7, 205, 215, 218, 235, 237, 245
Italy 110, 244

Jacobites/Jacobitism 89, 31-2, 40-41, 43, 48, 53, 57-55, 57-66, 73-5, 79, 83-4, 90, 94-6, 116, 123, 133, 146-7, 160, 162, 175, 206, 210, 215-218, 215, 237, 244-5, 248
James II 38-39, 42, 44, 52, 75, 80, 92, 96, 102, 140, 158, 234, 237, 239, 244-5
'James III' 19, 40, 42, 57, 64, 75, 158, 216-217, 244
James VI of Scotland and I of England 39, 47, 51-2, 60, 134, 206
Jenkinson, Robert, 2nd Earl of Liverpool 177, 194-5, 201, 204-5
Johnson, Samuel 143, 156, 158, 212
Jülich-Berg succession dispute 9

Kennicott, Benjamin 14
Keppel, Augustus, 1st Viscount 162
King's College London 204
Knighton, Sir William, Keeper of the Privy Purse 203, 206
Kopenhagischer Post-Reuter 12

Lawrence, Sir Thomas 193
Letters on a Regicide Peace 175
Life of John Locke 206
Locke, John 48, 206
London Chronicle, the 211, 221
Londonderry, Robert, 2nd Marquess of, formerly Viscount Castlereagh 198
London Packet, the 203
Louis XIV 23, 40-41, 43, 50, 52, 64, 75, 142, 223
Louis XV 28, 102, 141, 208-209, 216, 223, 248
Louis XVI 38, 159-160, 171, 192
Louis XVIII 179, 189
Ludwig, Johann, CiC of the Hanoverian army 62, 64, 114

Maitland, Second Lieutenant Frederick, later Rear-Admiral 174
Malmesbury, James, 1st Earl of 15, 176
Marlborough, John, 1st Duke of 8, 57, 63, 68, 76, 95, 108, 239
Marlborough, Sarah Churchill, Duchess of 50, 103
Mary II 43, 140
Mary of Modena 40
Mary, Queen of Scots 45
Minden, Battle of 110
Ministry of all the Talents 153
Minorca 21, 111, 227
Mitchell, Andrew 112, 217, 221
Monitor, the 74, 212, 217, 220, 232
Monmouth, James, Duke of 81

Monthly Repository 207
Munich 17

Nader Shah Afshar 214
Namur 43
Napoleon III 177
Napoleonic wars 140, 182, 241, 250
Nash, John 201-202
National Gallery 202, 248
Nero the Second 210
Newcastle Courant 239
Newcastle, Thomas, Duke of 9-14, 21, 25, 30, 32-4, 65-70, 79-80, 82, 85, 92, 95, 97, 99-105, 109-111, 114, 116-125, 131-3, 138-9, 147, 151-4, 161, 212, 218-232 passim, 239, 241
North America 21, 35, 74, 122, 226, 228
North Briton, the 211-212

'Old Corps Whigs' 35, 48, 105, 131, 134, 149, 152-3, 155, 209, 228, 24
Old England 7, 137, 212, 231
Osnabrück 79, 96, 125, 139, 154, 238
Oudenaarde, Battle of 107-108
Owen's Weekly Chronicle 243, 265

Paris 9, 16, 28-30, 42, 85, 165, 167, 171, 174-175, 210, 216-217
Peerage Bill 1719 8, 245
Pelham, First Lord of the Treasury Henry 11, 104, 116, 212, 232
Perceval, PM Spencer 60, 79-80, 185, 194
'Peterloo' massacre 195
Pigot, Captain Hugh 173
Pitt the Elder, William 149, 163, 176, 179, 224, 228, 230
Pitt the Younger, William 22, 144-179 passim, 204, 225
Plato Redivius 39
Poland 20, 30, 64
Portland, William, 3rd Duke of 22, 25, 163, 240
Portugal 20, 179
Presbyterianism 58
Prussia 9, 13, 23, 28, 34, 59, 64, 76, 90-91, 105-106, 118, 120, 132, 153, 159, 174, 176, 192, 210, 219, 221, 227, 234, 236, 238, 241, 245, 247
Public Advertiser 155

Quatre Bras, Battle of 193

Remembrancer, the 55, 132
Reflections on the French Revolution 175
Regency Act 1811 185, 194
Richmond, Charles, 3rd Duke of 27, 92, 96, 139
Robinson, Mary 190
Robinson, Thomas, Secretary of State 11, 28, 119
Rochford, William, 4th Earl of 27-29
Rockingham, Charles, 2nd Marquess of 126, 149, 152-153, 163, 250
Rockinghamite Whigs 126, 163, 251
Rococo 22, 129, 214
Romanovs 178, 243
Royal Academy 22, 89-90, 157, 193, 248
Royal George, yacht 198
Royal Marriages Act 1772 190
Royal Society for Literature 203

Russia 72, 75, 91, 119-120, 159, 166, 178-179, 227, 243, 245, 248
Ryder, Dudley, Attorney General 103, 110, 118

Sacheverell, Henry 51
St George's Chapel 186
St James's Weekly Journal 216
St Petersburg 12
Salamanca, Battle of 185, 193
Saxe-Gotha, Princess Augusta of 127, 186
Saxony 59, 62, 64, 120, 154, 235
Scotland 8, 17, 19, 39, 44, 51, 57, 73, 75, 80, 96, 116, 125, 170, 196, 198, 206, 215, 225, 235, 237, 241, 245
Scottish Episcopalian Church 44
Scott, Mary, Dowager Countess of Deloraine 113
Sedgemoor, Battle of 39
Shelburne, William, 2nd Earl of, 1st Marquess of Lansdowne 11, 105, 163, 178, 229, 240
Shrewsbury, 1st Duke of 8-9
Sophia Dorothea of Celle 25, 63, 91, 195
Sophia of Hanover, daughter of Elizabeth Stuart 53
Sophia of the Palatinate, mother of George I 62, 64
Spain 20, 28, 50, 53, 61, 72, 74, 90, 106, 128, 144-145, 148, 160-161, 209-210, 212-213, 244, 248
Stockholm 28-9
Stone, Sub-Governor Andrew 13, 147
South Sea Company 57, 70, 84
Stuart, Charles Edward, Bonnie Prince Charlie 42, 96, 196, 216-217
Stuart, Elizabeth, daughter of James VI and I 52-3
Stuart, James Francis Edward 42
Suffolk, Henrietta, Countess of 123
Sunderland, Charles, 3rd Earl of 23, 68, 70-71, 77-78, 80-82
Sweden 7, 20, 29, 49, 61, 73-74, 143, 159, 208, 227, 235, 244

Test Act, the 39
The Hague 23, 30
The Madness of King George 143
The Newtonian System of the World, The Best Model of Government: An Allegorical Model 232
The Reign of George VI 250
The Times 195, 198, 207
Thirty Years' War (1618-48) 52, 61
Thurlow, Edward, 1st Lord, Lord Chancellor 177-178
Townshend, Charles, 2nd Viscount Townshend 7, 24, 28, 66, 70-71, 76, 85, 98, 220
Turkey 54, 214-215

Vergennes, Charles, Count of 10
Victoria, Queen 44, 148, 180, 191, 227, 235, 247
Vienna 17, 28, 57, 90, 92, 220, 246
Villiers, Frances, Countess of Jersey 190
von der Schulenburg, Melusine 63, 69, 115
von Hinüber, Carl Heinrich 151
von Wallmoden, Amalie Sophie Marianne, Countess of Yarmouth 26, 113

Waldegrave, James, 2nd Earl 15-16, 102, 148
Wallace, James, Under Secretary 21
Walpole, Horace, later 4th Earl of Orford 13, 32, 99, 101, 136, 225, 239
Walpole, Horatio, later 1st Lord Walpole 9, 30, 71-2, 99, 106, 140-141
Walpole, Sir Robert, later 1st Earl of Orford 51-2, 55, 67-72, 82-3, 85, 90-92, 96-9 101-106, 113-115, 128-130, 146, 155, 178, 194, 205-6, 210-211, 225, 228, 234
War of American Independence 140, 155, 171, 175, 182
War of the Austrian Succession 109, 234
War of the Polish Succession 103, 108
War of the Spanish Succession 49, 76, 98, 108
Washington, George 22, 38, 225
Waterloo, Battle of 18, 185, 193
Weekly Journal or British Gazetteer 55
Weekly Miscellany 12
Weekly Register 48
Wellington, Duke of 18, 193, 205-206, 225
Weymouth 164, 170, 203
Whig split of 1717-20 65, 68
William I of Prussia 23, 64, 76
William I of the Netherlands 197
William III 13, 40, 42-43, 47-48, 60-61, 65, 75, 79, 134, 138, 234, 237, 244-245
William IV 13, 43, 47, 140, 148, 162, 182, 189, 191, 228, 239, 242, 247
William IV, Prince of Orange, 47, 140, 239
William V of Orange 179
Willis, Dr Francis 167-8, 185

Yorke, Joseph, MP 24, 43, 56, 184, 209
York, Frederick, Duke of, son of George III 109, 135, 137-8, 154, 170, 181, 186, 206